Sanybel Light

An Historical Autobiography

by

Charles LeBuff

**AMBER
PUBLISHING**
Sanibel, FL
1998

Printed in the United States of America.

Published by:

Amber Publishing
Post Office Box 493
Sanibel, FL 33957–0493

First Printing, January 1998

Library of Congress Catalog Card Number: 96–95126

ISBN 0–9625013–1–X

To Jean, Leslie, and Chuck — all islanders true — with love.

CONTENTS

The Cover   *vii*

Acknowledgments   *xi*

Preface   *xiii*

Map   *xv*

1	Everyone's Story Has a Beginning	1
2	To Get There, You Take a Ferryboat	5
3	A Turtle Person To Be	11
4	Looking Toward the Future	19
5	Return to Sanible	27
6	Sanibel Island Light Station	39
7	Drinking Water — Heaven-Sent	55
8	"Ding"	69
9	Skeeter Heaven	79
10	Turtle Times	89
11	The Sanctuary Island	107
12	A Fitting Memorial	115
13	Donna	127

Photograph Section   145

14	Caretta	159
15	On a Scale From One to Ten	177
16	The 'Gator War	187
17	A New Father — Founding, That Is	203
18	The Unholy Trinity	217
19	Perils in Paradise	237
20	Lighthouse Life	247
21	Everyone's Story Has an Ending	281

THE COVER

Sanibel Island Light Station, 1898

"Shall I use a color photograph for the book's cover? Should the picture be from the '50s, the '60s, or from the current decade?" I asked myself as I planned this book's design.

I enjoy trying to be artistically creative, so was determined to be entirely responsible for both the content and design of this book. So I answered myself, "I'll paint a rendition of the Sanibel Island Light Station for the cover." You, the reader, can be the judge and make an evaluation as to just how accurate, or successful, my efforts turned out to be. For accuracy, I relied on old photographs from the period, reviewed early *Light Lists* published by the Lighthouse Board, and recalled oral information provided to me by men who, prior to 1920, were assistant light keepers at the station.

From the outset of the planning stage, I wanted the cover illustration for this book to be different. Different, because of its artistic perspective alone, wouldn't meet what I envisioned the cover to contain. I wanted the Sanibel Island Light Station to appear as few living people have seen it, although the station continued to look very much as I have depicted it in my painting until 1923, when major remodeling occurred. In 1944, the light station's appearance was further altered when a major hurricane damaged the facility.

I insisted the subject of my painting should look as it did soon after the station had been constructed and activated, and when the Sanibel Lighthouse was the most prominent architecture on about

400 miles of Florida's pristine island-studded coastline. There was no structure higher, and definitely none more important, along Florida's Gulf coast between Tampa Bay and the Dry Tortugas.

The closest light station to Sanibel Island, when the Sanibel Light was first lit in 1884, was the 87-foot-tall Egmont Key Lighthouse. A light station had originally been constructed on this barrier island, which is located at the entrance to Tampa Bay, in 1848. However, within ten years, severe erosion had undermined the foundation of the first lighthouse. The original light structure was replaced with another tower, at its present location, in 1858.

In 1890, a light station was constructed a few miles north of Sanibel and Captiva Islands on Gasparilla Island, on the north shore of Boca Grande, at the entrance to Charlotte Harbor. The focal plane of the Charlotte Harbor Lighthouse's lantern is 44 feet above sea level.

South of Sanibel, the closest light station is located across open water in the Dry Tortugas. The 157-foot-tall Loggerhead Key Lighthouse, which marks the deep-water entrance into the Gulf of Mexico, was also erected in 1858.

My illustration depicts the light station from a vantage point at Sanibel's easternmost projection, looking westward from the Point Ybel beach, with the light tower, Lighthouse Quarters 2 (my former residence), and the oil house all visible. The light tower and dwellings were part of the original light station, and each are still standing for your close inspection and comparison. Quarters 1 is not visible from this perspective. The present oil house was not constructed until 1894.

Other than roseate spoonbills, alligators in the J. N. "Ding" Darling National Wildlife Refuge, and island sunsets, the Sanibel Lighthouse is probably the most photographed object on either Sanibel or Captiva Islands. The light station is also one of the most painted landmarks in southwest Florida.

My family and I lived in the dwelling, which is represented in my painting, for a little under 22 years. It is that residency, Sanibel life, the island's unique natural history in general, and my interaction with Sanibel's diverse ecology that I have drawn on for much of what is contained between the covers of this book.

I'd like to call your attention to the following elements in my light station rendering that are no longer consistent with the modern appearance of the station or depicted by contemporary artists.

1. No Australian pines are in my painting. They did not exist in southwest Florida in 1898.

2. It is daytime, so the beige-colored lantern curtains have been hung by the attending light keeper to protect the delicate prisms of the Fresnel lens from damaging sunlight radiation. Curtains are no longer needed to safeguard the simpler, modern, fully-automated lens.

3. The iron work around the lantern and watch room is black, not brown as it is in modern times. The tower's color functions as a distinctive daymark.

4. The small windows in the light tower's stairway tube have white wooden frames and glass panes.

5. The exterior metal frames and handholds around the storm panes of the lantern are white.

6. The roof of the oil house is covered with heavy corrugated sheet iron. The oil house is depicted a little to the left of its actual position — a little artistic license to fit it into the illustration.

7. The siding on the quarter's exterior walls is exposed painted wood, not a covering of asbestos shingles.

8. The roof shingles on Quarters 2 are asbestos, not asphalt or fiberglass.

9. Gutters and downspouts are in place on the building.

10. The downspouts lead to a large circular cypress cistern which rests above an elevated brick foundation.

11. The quarter's privy closet and waste chute, a standard of living prior to indoor plumbing, can be seen to the left of the cistern.

12. A stairway leads from the quarter's porch to the landing at the light tower's entrance door.

13. Staircases lead down to ground level from both sides of the quarters.

14. The wrought-iron pilings which support the dwelling are brown like most of the light tower, not white.

15. A low fence, made from two-inch pipe and supported on stout decorative cypress posts, runs along the perimeter of the compound.

16. The grounds are immaculate. All ground-cover vegetation has been removed, and bare natural shell dominates the earth's surface within the 150- x 190-foot rectangular compound of the light station. Ground cover was not permitted to grow there — to reduce the threat to the station's improvements should wildfire ever occur near the compound. Low vegetation and palm trees occupied the area outside the fence. However, due to design constraints, I omitted all plants in my painting.

ACKNOWLEDGMENTS

Writing this book has been an enjoyable and satisfying pastime. As I put each paragraph to paper, I would either cringe or be highly entertained by the mental flashbacks my writing aroused.

Since most of the subject matter contained in the following pages is based on personal experiences, it is not easy to recall each person who shared the events I describe or contributed to the quality of my island life in some way. I offer thanks to my more recent acquaintances and friends and all the old-timers I can remember — all who have helped make living on Sanibel Island so special.

My discussion on the early 20th-Century history of the Sanibel Island Light Station was gleaned from frequent, one-on-one, interesting, and often rambling conversations with three former assistant light keepers. These were Broward Keene, Clarence Rutland, and Webb "Pappy" Shanahan. Unfortunately, all are deceased. For an intermediate historical overview, prior to the commencement of my independent knowledge on the subject which started just after the beginning of the second half of the century, I'm indebted to Bob and Mae England. When a member of the U. S. Coast Guard, Bob served as the last full-time resident Coast Guard light keeper at the station. This was close to the time the first half of the 1900s was coming to an end.

The popular published work of long-time islander Elinore Dormer, *The Sea Shell Islands*, has been an invaluable source. Her writing helped me put some early island history into perspective with the historical tidbits I have included. When Ellie was working on the manuscript of her first edition, we often ventured into the field together. We located remnants of long-lost home-steads in the J. N. "Ding" Darling National Wildlife Refuge, and we once visited the mangrove forest of eastern Pine Island. We were searching for a mysterious and elusive stone artifact said to have been engraved at the direction of none other than Juan Ponce de Leon to document his purported legendary landing on that neighboring island.

Jim Dunlap and Tom Taylor of the Ponce de Leon Inlet Lighthouse Preservation Association, Ponce Inlet, Florida, were helpful in providing information on third-order Fresnel lenses. They also helped me identify some U. S. Lighthouse Establishment artifacts in my personal collection.

Joanna Hulsman of Sanibel graciously provided her profession-al editorial support and design assistance. I appreciate her many suggestions which improved my book.

As always, special thanks go to my wife, Jean, for putting up with this cranky writer. I wasn't much fun to be around for the two years it took me to do the writing and artwork for this book.

PREFACE

You might wonder how this book came to be. Well, I had just completed conducting a special lecture to a group of visiting travel agents who were on a tour of Sanibel and Captiva Islands sponsored by the Lee County Tourist Development Council. They were put in touch with me through Dick Noon, Parks and Recreation Director for the City of Sanibel, because they wanted an authoritative presentation on the Sanibel Lighthouse. I had spent about 45 minutes out on the Point Ybel beach sharing my knowledge of Sanibel Island, and in particular its lighthouse, with this motivated group. They had been the kind of audience I like to deal with.

After I had concluded the program, I was informally responding to questions from individuals in the group when a very sexy young lady gracefully walked up to me and coyly told me she was a travel agent from Alabama. She was the epitome of a true southern belle, with delightful charismatic feminine charm, and her words were laced with that special accent of someone from the deep south. She commented, "Mr. LeBuff, that was an excellent presentation; you're such a wonderful and knowledgeable speaker; thank you so much. I learned more about lighthouses and ya'll's life here on Sanibel Island from your program than from any of the reading materials that were recommended to me. You should write a book and share your knowledge with others!"

Her suggestion, that I write a book, stuck with me. For years, I had been sharing my knowledge of Sanibel's natural values, lighthouse history, and real-life island experiences with new and old residents and visitors who accompanied me on my original Sanibel beach walk or attended my special island-life seminars. Several months later, I decided to tackle writing this book which I have based, for the most part, on my life and adventures on Sanibel Island. It's an "historical autobiography," if you will.

xiii

There have been several excellent books, written from an historical perspective, about Sanibel and Captiva Islands. More recently, exquisite pictorial books have appeared, as have works of fiction that use these islands as a backdrop for the writers' tales. No doubt other books will follow this one, but I doubt any will impart the essence of the wide spectrum of genuine island life that my family and I have experienced here. Many of the published historically-oriented authors, whose works chronicled the earliest times, were part of our local history too. However, they did not live or make some of the history as I did.

In the late 1950s, as I started a prestigious and long-time Federal career in the field of wildlife conservation, I was presented with a small notepad — known as a "field diary" — and was instructed to record my daily activities faithfully. I was a good employee and did just that. My diaries, virtually hundreds of them, have been invaluable tools with which I could reach back in time and vividly recall the very essence of my life, experiences, and work on Sanibel Island.

For example, in 1959, soon after my arrival the previous year to become a permanent resident of Sanibel Island, I was assigned duties which included providing logistical and physical assistance to the two-man U. S. Coast Guard team stationed in downtown Fort Myers. This team was responsible for the operation and maintenance of the Sanibel Lighthouse. Because of that role, I am the last Federally-employed civilian resident of the Sanibel Island Light Station to serve as a light keeper.

Much of the information included in this book is published for the first time and would likely have been lost to posterity had that beautiful, charming, intelligent, and anonymous young lady from Alabama not suggested that I write this book.

In the following pages, I hope you will become involved in my unique life, its dangers and the pleasures I have experienced and shared with my family, on this sandbar that once was a real island.

Enjoy!

Charles R. LeBuff, Jr.
Sanibel Island, Florida
January 1998

Map   *xv*

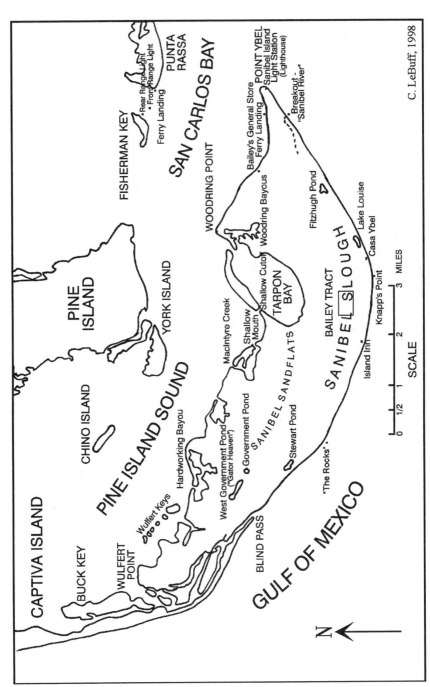

C. LeBuff, 1998

Sanibel Island, 1958

1

EVERYONE'S STORY
HAS A BEGINNING

I came into this world at 10:20 in the morning on Wednesday, March 25, 1936, at Lawrence Memorial Hospital in Medford, Massachusetts. Like most human babies, I entered Earth's atmosphere kicking and screaming, but I was also in a rush. I had people to meet, places to see, things to do, my life to live, and I had a career plan!

My parents were Charles R. and Ruth V. (Mick) LeBuff, both natives of Massachusetts. I was their first child. My father was the youngest of three sons from a marriage between the sign-painting son of a French sea captain and the daughter of Maine Yankee blue-bloods. My mother's heritage was also of mixed nationalities: Her father was of German descent and was one of nine children born to a farmer/miner in West Virginia. My maternal grandfather had migrated to Massachusetts because of economic hardships. There he met my Prince Edward Island, Canada-born grandmother, the daughter of store keepers. They produced three children; my mother was the eldest.

By profession, my father was a master stairbuilder. He was known throughout the New England construction industry for his ability to design and build some of the region's most exquisite circular and elliptical staircases. He was also a unique individual. For example, during his long 87-year life, he never drove a motor vehicle. In 1952, due to health problems, he and my mother decided to sell out and leave Massachusetts. Our family did not own an automobile; we had always relied on public transportation. So when the house was sold, my folks bought a 1951 Ford Country Squire station wagon — that is, after my mother had taken professional driving lessons for two weeks and obtained her driver's license.

My parents decided to move to Florida, instead of Arizona or south Georgia, both of which were under consideration because of a young man named Don Carroll. Don was a few years older than I, and as a teenager, he had worked for my father during a few summer school vacations at the shop in Chelsea, Massachusetts. He had left home at an early age, joined the Army, and later married and settled in Bonita Springs, Florida. There he managed the Everglades Wonder Gardens wildlife attraction. Between Chelsea and the Army, he worked for the famous rattlesnake specialist Ross Allen at his Silver Springs Reptile Institute. In early June of 1952, Don traveled north on vacation to see his family and came to our residence in Medford for a visit.

He told us stories of the Fort Myers/Naples area and his snake and wild-hog hunting exploits. It was on that basis that my parents chose to move to Bonita Springs.

Probably in an attempt to frighten me, I recall my father asking him, "Aren't you afraid to handle dangerous snakes?" Don replied, "Hell no, I'll get bitten someday, but it won't kill me."

I'll never forget those words. In November 1956, at the age of 28 and while employed as an education officer with the Florida Game and Fresh Water Fish Commission, he was lecturing to a group of school children in Perry, Florida. During his presentation, Don received his first and last bite by a venomous snake. He was struck once, solidly behind the left knee just above his new knee-high snake-proof boots, by a recently caught and nervous $4^1/_2$-foot eastern diamondback rattlesnake.

During his lecture, the snake had attempted to move off a low stage into the audience. Fearing for the safety of the children, Don tried to stop the rattler by stepping on it. In an unusual move, the snake suddenly swung around and both fangs penetrated the back of Don's unprotected leg. Despite valiant medical efforts to save his life, my friend Don died in a Tallahassee hospital 22 hours later.

For some obscure reason, as a very small child, I developed an interest in wildlife biology, particularly reptiles. In the Summer of 1950, at age 14, I wrote a short paper on the reproductive habits of the smooth green snake, commonly called the grass snake in New England. I submitted this for publication to the editor of *Herpetologica*, the scientific journal of the Herpetologist's League. I was surprised and excited when I learned it had been accepted and would be published.

After the paper appeared in the journal in late 1951, I received an invitation to speak on the subject before a joint meeting of the Herpetologist's League and the American Society of Ichthyologists and Herpetologists, which was scheduled to be held in Texas that year. My father wrote back and informed the person that I was only 15 and that our family would soon be moving. He informed him that I was honored, but it would be impossible for me to attend. This paper has been cited in the scientific literature as recently as 1992.

Just after Thanksgiving 1952, my parents loaded up their excited children: my brothers Laban and Laurence, my sister Natalie, our dog "Pal," my six-foot-long pet, an eastern indigo snake named "Beauty," and I. It was Florida or bust!

I was absolutely elated to be leaving Massachusetts. Books and magazines I had read, movie documentaries I had seen, and the recent stories we had been told by Don Carroll were conjuring up visions of a wilderness (the Everglades) full of wildlife. I pictured a new and happy life for me and the whole family. Since the subject of moving was first discussed among us and the decision was made to go for it, I have fervently believed through the years that this was the best decision my parents ever made. I think my siblings will agree.

On November 29th, we arrived in Bonita Springs. Our new lives were about to begin!

2

TO GET THERE,
YOU TAKE A FERRYBOAT

There it was again — and again — a flash of light that got my attention. It was near the horizon and off to the north-north-west. No other lights, save stars, illuminated the darkening sky and beach that night in mid-December 1952. Pitch blackness had caught up with me and new friend, Don McKeown, as we walked north toward Big Hickory Pass. We were heading back to his car after our small-scale commercial shelling expedition on Bonita Beach.

I asked, "Don, what's that flashing light out there?"

He replied, "The Sanible light."

"Sanible." I had first heard the word a few weeks before when I enrolled as a junior at Fort Myers High School. I learned that two students lived on a place called Sanible Island. Their names were Jim Pickens and Ralph Woodring; both were in my English class. The light continued to intrigue me and I asked more about it.

Don related, "Sanible's an island off Punta Rassa. The only way to get there is by ferryboat, or maybe [you can] fly into a grass airstrip they have over there somewhere, unless of course you've got your own boat. When I was younger, Mama would take us there to find shells. Shells are thick over there, and that's what makes Sanible famous."

He continued, "There's a lighthouse at this end of the island, and that's the only light we can see because Sanible's not built up very much, sort of like here at Bonita. This beach runs roughly north and south, but Sanible runs sort of east and west. Mama told me that's one reason shelling is so good there, because of the way Sanible's positioned."

A few days later at school, it was announced that the Sanible bus was late ... again! Subconsciously, I connected with the message and thought "Sanible, Sanible, that's a neat name, really sort of romantic sounding. It has a special rhythmic ring to it whenever I hear the word spoken, or just think about it for that matter."

I decided then, I just had to go there and see the place. So, during the 1952 Christmas school vacation, Don and I climbed into his 1939 Buick sedan and left Bonita Springs early for the trip to the settlement of Punta Rassa. Arriving at the ferry landing at about 8:00 A.M., Don maneuvered us across a short ramp and onto the deck of an old wooden ferry named *Islander*. Along with drivers and passengers from seven other cars, we shared the cost of the one-way $2.00 toll ($1.00 for the car and 50 cents for each of us).

The pitching boat headed across windswept San Carlos Bay bound for Sanible Island. The 20-minute, nearly three-mile trip provided a panorama of Sanible. We could scan along the shore of the island from the lighthouse to the east to what I later learned was Woodring Point to the west. The landscape was lush and green, and there were no more than a half dozen buildings visible in the vista ahead of us as we approached the ferry landing on the distant shore. I was hooked on Sanible already.

As we left the ferry off-ramp, I noticed a weathered sign to our right. Shallow router-carved letters announced to all who passed: Entering Sanibel National Wildlife Refuge. Glancing at the sign again for an instant, I thought to myself, "S-a-n-i-b-e-l. Hmm, someone must have misspelled it. That's not the way everyone pronounces it."

Don drove straight ahead, and the road led to a small park on the Gulf side of the island. This was known as Kinzie Park, named by the owners of the ferry line. The Kinzie family owned a wide strip of land from San Carlos Bay to the Gulf. From their park, we walked eastward in the direction of the lighthouse. Along the way, each of us collected nearly half a bucket of beautiful sea shells, many of which were still alive. These had been cast up on the beach by the recent, and still raging, northwest winds from the slow passage of a severe cold front. Don could identify many more of the shells than I could because his mother was a long-time shell collector. In fact, she worked at the Shell Factory in downtown Bonita Springs and our Sanible shells would later be sold there (for resale) for a modest amount.

Suddenly, above the Australian pine trees, which lined the highest part of the beach, the Sanible Lighthouse loomed. This lighthouse was nothing like what I expected. It was skeleton-like, different from any lighthouse I had ever seen before. It was nothing like the enclosed brick lighthouses of New England and Canada's Maritime Provinces, which I was more familiar with.

The light tower was centered between two white clapboard-sided buildings which were raised off the beach several feet on pilings. The very rusted metal pilings seemed to be made out of the same material as the lighthouse tower. The area was unfenced, so Don and I walked under and around the buildings, lighthouse, and two water tank towers which were nearly centered between the buildings. A large metal water tank, positioned horizontally on a concrete foundation, was located to the north of the high tank towers. Still further north, on the opposite side of the lighthouse, was a small brick building. About 75 feet north of the easternmost large elevated building stood a small cottage-like structure. Still further east was an old tower of some kind, which was leaning toward the water to the east. This structure, which I assumed had been some kind of observation tower in its youth, was about 30 feet tall.

Leaving the immediate lighthouse grounds, we walked toward the bay side and discovered, and followed, a concrete walkway which ran between two rows of low Australian pines interspersed with small coconut palms. These trees looked as though they were at one time part of a formal landscaping scheme and the pines might have been maintained, maybe pruned into a hedge of some kind. The concrete ended near a rusted boat railway which led from the submerged bay bottom to a boathouse just to the east of the walkway. The walkway continued on, terminating at the base of a T-shaped pier that extended out into the bay about 150 feet. The pier had a roofed section across it, and on each side of the walkway under the roof were openings which appeared to have been used as boat slips. We walked out onto the pier and joined a couple of fisherman, each of whom had substantial strings of large sheepsheads. The waters under and around the pier, over a 100-foot radius, were black with gyrating and jumping mullet — Don told me they were probably spawning. Despite the numbers we saw, and despite our liking of fried and smoked mullet which Don had introduced me to only days earlier, we couldn't have gigged or netted any of them had we been so equipped. It was closed season, and the taking of mullet was prohibited at this time of year.

We walked back to the lighthouse and followed the road behind the beach back to Kinzie Park. Again in the car, we headed west. At the first real intersection, Don made a right turn northward toward the bay. We soon arrived at Bailey's General Store, which he had visited before, and watched as the mailboat unloaded a few touring passengers and bags of mail. Then we went into Bailey's to look around and buy a soft drink.

Once our curiosity and thirst were satisfied, we headed off to do some more exploring. Don turned westward along the bay on a road that in those days led to Woodring Point. Eventually we came to a dead end at a two-story house on the extreme point, turned around, and retraced our tracks back to the main road. Heading west, we drove through the wild lands of Sanible along Captiva Road. Despite the posted 65-mph speed limit, the highway was in poor shape. We proceeded with caution.

Later we turned off this road and headed in the general direction of the Gulf of Mexico. A network of curving, undulating, sandy roads led us to Blind Pass, a tidal opening which separated Sanible from its sister island, Captiva. We shelled for a few hours on this beautiful unspoiled section of coast, filled our buckets with a variety of live beach-stranded shells, then headed home. It would be six years before I walked on Sanible again.

In late November 1952, my family took up permanent Florida residence in Bonita Springs in southern Lee County. In June 1953, I completed the 11th grade at Fort Myers High School. At the same time, my parents bought a new home in Naples, and at summer's end I entered Naples High School.

My interests in a variety of subjects continued. Up north, I had been advancing toward a career in commercial art, but I also had developed a keen interest in the field of herpetology, the study of amphibians and reptiles. I liked turtles in particular.

My first real employment was with Don Carroll at the Everglades Wonder Gardens, then a well-manicured botanical and wildlife attraction in downtown Bonita Springs on the bank of the Imperial River. This was a very popular tourist attraction, which specialized in the educational exhibition of native Florida wildlife.

Two middle-aged brothers, Bill and Lester Piper, owned the business. Lester supervised day-to-day operations, and over several years, I absorbed a considerable amount of common sense and knowledge of wildlife from this eccentric man. It was because of Lester Piper that I acquired a deep-rooted environmental ethic that accompanied me into the future, guiding my life.

In the beginning, my work hours at Piper's were not regulated, just afternoons and weekends when I was needed — that is, if they could find me. I was usually canoeing the river or roaming through a cypress head looking for alligators, yellow rat snakes, or some bird or other critter I hadn't seen in the wild yet.

After the family moved to Naples, I had no car of my own to travel back and forth to Bonita Springs. So I began working in the architectural woodworking field with my father, picked up some part-time jobs lettering signs, or did some other aspect of freelance art work.

3

A TURTLE PERSON TO BE

After a few weeks at Naples High School, and after getting my courage up, I managed to introduce myself to an attractive young lady named Jean Williams, at the time a 10th grader. She was the third daughter and middle child of Duke and Louise Williams, and she lived on Marco Island. Her father came to Florida from southwest Georgia at an early age, and his family settled in Taylor County, Florida, for a time. By 1918, Duke's family resettled in Lee County, at Iona, where he spent his teen years. Later, as an adult, he returned to Perry, in Taylor County, to live with and help an older widowed sister.

During this period, Duke met Louise Clark, a fourth-generation Floridian. They were married a few years later when Louise joined Duke after he returned to Lee County, after his parents and younger siblings had relocated to Bonita Springs. In Bonita Springs, the first three Williams girls were born. Jean was delivered by her father because the doctor did not arrive from Fort Myers in time. Later, another daughter and finally a son were born at a birthing center and a hospital in Fort Myers, respectively.

Duke Williams was a commercial fisherman. To better accommodate the demands of this livelihood, the Williams family relocated to Marco Island in 1941. Although I began dating Jean in late 1954, her father's reputation of being mean-tempered intimidated me, and I didn't meet him one-on-one until 1957. I then found him to be one of the wittiest people I ever had the privilege of knowing. Throughout his long life, his memory remained clear. Especially while partaking of a few sizeable swallows of moonshine, or his favorite Canadian whiskey, and hand-rolling a Prince Albert cigarette or three, he enjoyed telling stories of his childhood in southwest Florida. He talked of hard times and good times and how, as a teenager, he had worked at the Punta Rassa cattle docks loading cattle headed for Key West, Cuba, and other West Indian countries.

In 1954, the Williams family left Marco Island and returned to Bonita Springs, where Jean entered the Lee County school system. By then I was in better shape transportation-wise — my parents had bought me my first car, a well-used 1942 Ford convertible. Night after night, I burned up the two lanes of U. S. Highway 41 between Naples and Bonita to be with Jean. It all ended in January 1956 when Jean decided to move to Massachusetts, of all places, to live with her older sister, Floy, who had met and married Ed Phillips and left home for the north country.

I buckled down to my studies at Naples High School and was part of the 31-member graduating class of 1954. In May, our senior class trip took us to Havana, Cuba. I became attached to that beautiful country and visited it again before Señor Castro came to power.

My studies proved fruitful. Prior to graduation, I learned I had been awarded a full scholarship to the School of Forestry at the University of Florida. But a quirk of fate, based on erroneous information about my draft eligibility which was given to my mother by an incompetent clerk at the regional Fort Myers Draft Board, would later force me to decline the scholarship. I did not resent the decision, because I had learned that most positions available in the forestry field in Florida were at the county level and were grossly under-compensated.

In retrospect, I have always convinced myself that this was a wise career choice. Although I would later take many college-level courses, I would never receive a degree. Instead I would lead a lifestyle of my own design and according to my plan — something I would have been unable to do at the level of personal satisfaction that I have been fortunate enough to enjoy if I had the piece of paper. Financially, I was already better off, since I was now working full-time at the Everglades Wonder Gardens and moonlighting in my own sign-painting business or subcontracting in my spare time to local signmakers in Bonita Springs and Naples.

In June 1954, something else happened that changed my life forever. A huge beach party was underway on Vanderbilt Beach north of Naples. I bet that every teenager from Naples was there, enjoying a bonfire and the *esprit de corps* at the end of another school year.

Someone in the crowd yelled, "There's a loggerhead over here. She's getting ready to nest!"

Everyone gathered around the sea turtle. Many of us watched in awe while others plotted to use her as fresh meat for their family's table. I had seen my first loggerhead turtle the summer before on Bonita Beach, but I was still fascinated nonetheless. After she nested and covered her eggs, the turtle slowly turned around and started toward the water. Suddenly, someone from the group stepped forward and in one quick, fluid movement flipped the turtle upside down.

The next thing I knew, some other kid pulled out a good-sized pocket knife and announced, "I'm going to slit her throat and take the flippers home!"

I pushed through the crowd to stand beside the flailing turtle and announced, "I'm not going to stand here and let that happen. Let's let her go!"

Next came a shouting match, and the guy with the knife yelled in my face, "You're nothing but a goddamned Yankee and you ought to go back to where you came from before I kick your ass!"

I was beginning to get a little intimidated! I reacted and said, "The-hell-you-say! I've probably got more southern in my heart than you have in your blood!"

Suddenly out of nowhere, my guardian angel appeared. He seemed older and wiser as he stepped out of the darkness into the ring of people standing around the turtle. He announced to everyone that he agreed with me and some of the others standing around who wanted to spare the loggerhead, and the turtle was going to return to the Gulf safely. He reached down and righted the turtle, who was throwing sand in every direction.

"Whew," I said to myself, relieved. "I'm sure glad he arrived when he did and came to my rescue and saved my butt — mine *and* the turtle's!"

I watched in amazement as my comrade in arms stepped into the turtle's pathway, took a small flashlight from his pocket, and shined its beam on the ground a few feet in front of the 300-pound giant. Almost magically, the loggerhead followed his light to the water's edge, then paused briefly. Before moving ahead into the dark surf, I believe she looked up at me with tearful eyes and said, "Thanks, Charles." I never found out who my guardian angel was.

For the rest of that summer, I spent many nights out on the beaches near Naples. Sometimes I walked, other times I rode in cut-down Model A Fords or old jeeps with my brother Laban or friend Jimmie Jones. I decided that sea turtles were for me; however, I wasn't completely dedicated yet. The beaches were patrolled at night by officers of the State Board of Conservation who were the authorities responsible for protecting sea turtles while they were on the beach. It seems that some of my former classmates felt it was their responsibility to make the officers work for a living. Driving on the beach was not illegal — It was often the only way that fishermen could get to some of the more remote passes or that turtle poachers could do their thing. Loggerhead turtles were harvested on those beaches despite law-enforcement efforts, but it was seldom wanton waste. Some families did, or at least claimed to, depend on turtle meat for subsistence. Every one of them with whom I ever discussed this told me they were convinced they were actually conserving the species, because they took turtles in accordance with long-approved custom — They always waited to kill a turtle until *after* it had nested.

Written information on sea turtles was limited in 1954. Archie Carr had published his classic work *Handbook of Turtles* in 1952, and I had purchased a copy in 1953 with the proceeds of a lettering and graphics job that I had been commissioned to do on an early version of a motor home.

To better understand loggerhead turtles, and to fill in some of the missing elements of information for my own level of curiosity, I began to mark their nests. I mapped nest sites, opened and examined nests to make egg counts, and monitored nest success by again opening nests where hatchlings had emerged. When beach residents learned what I was doing, I began to receive telephone calls from interested parties who informed me of where a loggerhead had laid eggs, or when a nest had been depredated by raccoons or had successfully hatched. It was about this time that I made a commitment to myself — I decided that sea turtles were going to play an important role in my life.

In 1956, the Bureau of Commercial Fisheries, then part of the U. S. Fish and Wildlife Service, Department of the Interior, opened a field station in one of the old military buildings at Naples Airport. The unit was charged with investigating the red tide that periodically plagued the lower Florida Gulf coast. A major red tide outbreak caused fish kills of unbelievable proportions, resulting in the outer beaches and tidal mangrove areas to be literally covered with dead fish. A 48-foot research vessel, the *Kingfish*, was assigned to the laboratory and was docked at Crayton Cove in Naples. Late in 1956, I learned the Government planned to fill several vacancies at the laboratory.

The organism that caused red tide was known. During a severe red tide in 1946, a microscopic dinoflagellate had been identified as the culprit up the coast in Venice. However, the fundamental grouping, or levels, of chemical compounds or elements in the environment that must come together to trigger these infrequent environmental disasters is not fully understood to this day.

Taking a long shot, I applied for a fishery technician position. My expertise in the fishery field was limited, but I did have some level of background in wildlife biology. Also by this time, I had published another paper — on indigo snakes — and was listed as an authority in the recently published *Handbook of Snakes*. I underwent an oral interview and took a very difficult written test. I was sure I had scored well orally, but I was uncertain as to how I did on the college-level written exam. Back in those days, a person could be hired at a higher grade, and ultimately attain a higher salary level, if the combination of experience, knowledge, and skills was sufficient. It was almost equivalent to a college degree.

By this time, I had left the Everglades Wonder Gardens and was working full time, in a union apprenticeship program, in a woodworking shop in Naples. I was also moonlighting in my own commercial art business. I received a call from the red tide lab director and was asked to come by his office whenever it was convenient. Wow, I had been selected for the position!

A week later, I reported for duty. I was hired as a fishery technician and assigned to assist and be trained by a bright Hungarian-born fishery biologist named Alexander Dragovich. Alex took me under his wing, teaching me the new job.

My duties were varied. On a regular schedule, I drove to established water sample collection sites between the Myakka River to the north and 40-Mile Bend out on U. S. 41 to the southeast. There I collected surface and bottom water samples. The samples would be analyzed in-house by chemists, biologists, and technicians. As part of a rotation system, I was also assigned to serve on the sample collection crew aboard the *Kingfish*. The boat routinely traveled the Gulf between Marathon and Tampa Bay.

After I had been sufficiently trained to a high level of competence in the principles and techniques of microbiology, I spent most of my laboratory time peering through stereo microscopes. Samples of both estuarine and Gulf water were divided, part for chemical and the other for biological analysis. I had to not only identify microorganisms, but also make acceptable estimates of their populations per liter of water. At first, this aspect of the job was very satisfying and educational; however, prolonged exposure to a microscope's eyepieces made me and the other technicians restless. Supervisors knew this, so when one of us approached temporary burnout, we were sent into the field for a respite.

I had the opportunity to be assigned to a lengthy Gulf cruise aboard the *Gerda*, a research vessel operated by the University of Miami. The boat left Fort Myers Beach and traveled in a gigantic hourglass-shaped course across the Gulf of Mexico to the Gulf of Campeche. I was the bottom sampler, so had to man a series of electric winches to collect water samples from the Gulf of Mexico, whatever the depth. This trip was my first opportunity to observe cobalt blue seawater, giant sharks, pelagic dolphins, and seabirds.

In the spring of 1957, a girlfriend and I had been on a trip around Lake Okeechobee on a snake-collecting expedition and were returning to Naples. The Florida Department of Transportation was rebuilding U. S. 41 through Bonita Springs, and we had to detour around the Oak Creek bridge, approaching close to the Williams place. There, sitting on the porch of a neighbor's house, was Jean. She had kept in touch with me and I with her, but she never told me she was coming home. What a surprise!

I slowed the car and remember yelling loudly out the open window, "Hey, Yankee!"

In about an hour, I was back in Bonita Springs cruising up and down the street in front of her house, gunning the engine until she noticed my car. Cautiously, she snuck out her bedroom window to catch up with me. There was no way I was going up to that door — I wasn't ready to face Duke Williams!

4

LOOKING TOWARD THE FUTURE

During my tenure with the Bureau of Commercial Fisheries, I met William Duane "Tommy" Wood. "Tommy" was a nickname he picked up while a student at the University of Virginia. He was a seaplane pilot and also the refuge manager of the Sanibel National Wildlife Refuge. With the establishment of the red tide field laboratory in Naples, the U. S. Fish and Wildlife Service increased the scope of his duties and instructed him to devote part of his work week to assist in collecting water samples along the lower Gulf coast. He flew a Government-owned Piper Tri-Pacer on floats. I began to spend several hours a week aboard seaplane N787, flying to inland waters at such places as St. Petersburg, Lake Okeechobee, and Shark River. Tommy would artfully set the aircraft down on the water at established collection stations, and I would step out onto a float to collect both surface and bottom water samples, and the temperatures of each. I especially enjoyed the flights when Tommy would turn the aircraft's controls over to me and I would become his student pilot.

The trips to Marathon, in the Florida keys, aboard the *Kingfish* were usually three-day jaunts. We ran our collection grids in the Gulf, beginning at a point to the west of Gordon Pass, Naples, down to Shark River. There we would anchor for the night. We allowed some samples we collected to remain as a liquid, but others were quick-frozen aboard the vessel. The second day out consisted of running another grid, making periodic collections along the outer periphery of Florida Bay, and ending up for the night in Marathon. Tommy would fly to Marathon ahead of us, spend the night on the *Kingfish*, and leave early the next morning loaded with our liquid and frozen samples bound for the Naples laboratory.

Tommy was born August 20, 1903, in Ozona, Florida, a small coastal town near Tarpon Springs. As a young man, he became interested in aviation and soloed in 1927. His flying career was then underway. He became a barnstorming pilot in the midwest and owned his own air charter service. At the outbreak of World War II, he enlisted in the U. S. Navy and saw service in the Pacific theater. There he piloted flying boats and attained the rank of Lieutenant Commander. After the War, he settled in Key West where he operated a seaplane charter service. Later, enticed by his friend Jack Watson, a famous Federal law-enforcement officer, he took a vacant position with the U. S. Fish and Wildlife Service as a laborer-patrolman assigned to the Key West and Great White Heron National Wildlife Refuges. (Tommy had discovered that Jack had also been born in Ozona, but they had no recollection of ever meeting before Tommy made his move to the Keys.) Jack later became the refuge manager of the National Key Deer Refuge. In early 1949, Tommy was offered a position on Sanibel Island.

President Harry Truman established the Sanibel National Wildlife Refuge in 1945. Immediately postwar, all the national wildlife refuges in South Florida were administered as the Everglades National Wildlife Refuge and were headquartered in Dania, Florida. This included some lands that would eventually be transferred to the National Park Service when Everglades National Park was authorized in 1947. At about this time, the U. S. Fish and Wildlife Service decided to create a permanent position at the new refuge on Sanibel Island.

In 1947, Gerald Baker, refuge manager of the Everglades National Wildlife Refuge complex, commented, "Law enforcement on Sanibel does not appear to be difficult. There is active public interest and support for a successful wildlife refuge."

Two U. S. Fish and Wildlife Service employees, both of whom were classified under laborer-patrolman positions, had earlier been assigned to the post. From 1938 to 1943 and from 1946 to 1947, William C. Lehmann functioned as a transient officer. During the latter period, his patrols included Sanibel Island along with other Federal refuges as he traveled along the Florida coastline from his home and headquarters in Mango, Florida. In his premilitary assignments (from 1938 to 1943), Bill was not only responsible for the Florida Islands National Wildlife Refuges, but also routinely patrolled east coast refuge lands and waters. This included the nation's first refuge, Pelican Island National Wildlife Refuge, which was established in 1903 by President Theodore Roosevelt.

Early in 1943, Bill Lehmann visited Sanibel Island for the first time when he was sent to inspect Federal lands as the process to establish the Sanibel National Wildlife Refuge began. Later in 1943, he entered the U. S. Navy, served in the Seabees, then resumed his duties with the U. S. Fish and Wildlife Service after the War. Bill Lehmann came to Sanibel more frequently for law enforcement patrols and wildlife censuses until his transfer in 1947 to become a U. S. Game Management Agent.

Sanibel resident Jake Stokes was hired in 1947 as the U. S. Fish and Wildlife Service's first local laborer-patrolman, but he chose not to make a career of the position. Instead, he became one of the area's early fishing and shelling guides, a school boat operator, a carpenter, and later a restauranteur. Up until the mid-1960s, Jake's offshore live-shell dredging trips were very popular.

Tommy Wood was selected to fill the vacant position, which had been upgraded to refuge manager/pilot to fit his specific skills. He reported for duty on Sanibel Island on April 30, 1949.

In mid-1957, the U. S. Fish and Wildlife Service suddenly announced plans to relocate the Naples red tide field station to St. Petersburg Beach. The move was to be made before the end of the year. Some of us assigned to the lab were eager to transfer to the new, larger facility. However, several of us, including me, did not want to leave the area. So I began to look around for another job.

In July 1957, I applied for a position with the Florida Game and Fresh Water Fish Commission. I went to the city of

Okeechobee, where their regional office was located, and successfully passed their written test. A few weeks later, I was asked to travel to Tallahassee for an oral examination.

When I was being interviewed by the director and his staff, I was asked, along with a variety of other job-related questions, "In what branch of our program are you interested in becoming employed, should you be selected for a position?" I told them that I was interested in pursuing a career in wildlife or game management, not wildlife law enforcement.

A few weeks later, Luby Kirkland, a Florida wildlife officer assigned to the Naples area, came to the lab to see me. He said, "Charles, I've been sent to see you to let you know that you've been selected for a position with the Game Commission — if you're still interested."

I answered, "Yes, I certainly am very interested." But a little later during our conversation, I chanced to ask, "Where do they plan to assign me, and with what branch?" Remember, I was not really interested in leaving the immediate vicinity.

Luby said, "After you're trained, you'll be assigned as a wildlife officer, like me, but in Immokalee."

"Immokalee!" I said to myself. "Why would anyone in their right mind want to move to Immokalee?" In 1957, Immokalee was still frontier-like and was not settled by the most conservation-minded inhabitants. "A good place to get myself shot," I thought. And to boot, this job offer wasn't in their Game Management division. I told Luby, "I'll think it over and get back to you in a couple of days."

At that point, I had just about made up my mind. Not only was I *not* going to St. Petersburg, I wasn't going to work in Immokalee either! After procrastinating for a day or two, I telephoned Luby to let him know I had changed my mind and would not take the job. After this our first of many conversations, Luby Kirkland remained in Naples as a wildlife officer for many years. My sister, Natalie, would eventually marry his son Robert, and my youngest brother, Laurence, would marry his youngest daughter, Peggy.

I resigned from the U. S. Fish and Wildlife Service on August 23, 1957, and went back into the woodworking business with my father. That year, I published two additional research papers, both on crocodilians. It became perfectly clear to me that my interest in the wildlife field, and my intention to remain in southwest Florida, would be key elements in my future. At this point I made two decisions: I would (1) ask Jean to marry me and (2) ask Lester Piper for my job back at the Everglades Wonder Gardens. The first decision was not taken too seriously and received no immediate response. But the second resulted in being hired — with a pay raise. After the fifth time I proposed, Jean agreed we should get married.

Now we had to run this idea by her parents. My mother and father had known Jean for a couple of years and were excited for us. Jean introduced me to my future in-laws at their home in Bonita Springs in July 1957. I had dreaded the moment, but it worked out well, with civility and cordiality. I think we got their blessing.

As we were leaving the Williams' home, Duke said to me, "Charlie, yesterday's history, tomorrow's a mystery, and today's a gift — That's why they call it the present. 'Cap'n' is your present and your future. Treat her good son, and don't let her burn your biscuits."

We were married on New Year's Eve 1957 by Reverend Tracy Day Spencer, a Presbyterian minister, at my parent's home in Naples. Other than immediate family, only my friends Richard Beatty, who lived next door to my parents since 1956, and "Sonny" Marine attended.

We rented a one bedroom apartment on 8th Avenue South in Naples and took up residence there after a short honeymoon in Fort Myers. Our bedroom had a thin common wall with the bedroom in the adjoining apartment. Our neighbors were our high-school friends, Jimmie and Sue Jones, who had married just a few months before us.

In April, Sue took Jean to the doctor because she wasn't feeling well. My wife came home an expectant mother.

In early June, I received a telephone call that would, in time, change our lives. I hadn't been home from work long when the telephone rang. Jean answered and called me to the phone, saying, "Its Tommy Wood from Sanible."

"Hello, Tommy, how are you?" I said.

He answered, "Just fine, Charles. I've got something to discuss with you that may be of interest. I've received approval to hire someone here at the refuge on Sanibel, on a full-time basis, and I'd like you to apply for the job."

After a brief moment of excited silence, I responded, "Thanks for thinking about me, Tommy. I really appreciate it. You better believe I'm interested!"

He asked when I would have a chance to come over to the island to meet with him and discuss the job.

"How about this coming Friday?" I said, Friday being my regular day off.

Tommy said, "Okay, I'll meet you at the Sanibel ferry landing at 8:30 Friday morning."

Jean and I could hardly sleep that night as we imagined what this phone call might mean to us. Without much rest, we both overslept the next morning despite a loud alarm clock buzzing next to my head.

I didn't remain asleep long though, because I heard an angry Jimmie Jones pounding on the wall next door and yelling between blows, "Get up! Shut off that damned alarm!"

When I arrived late to work, I learned that a mule had been struck by a train at the U. S. 41 crossing just south of Bonita Springs the night before. Lester had been notified by the Sheriff's Department and he and his son, David, had gone down and destroyed the mortally injured animal. The mule was brought to the Wonder Gardens slaughterhouse to be butchered, its meat to be stored in the walk-in cooler to feed the large collection of Florida panthers and other carnivores.

During the skinning and butchering process, in one of his rare gleeful moods, Lester asked, "Does anyone want some steak, after I quarter it?"

Someone spoke up and said they did.

I asked, "Is it any good?"

Lester replied, "It's better than horse and some cows I've eaten."

I thought, "Think I'll take some home and invite Jimmie and Sue over, sort of as a peace offering, for waking them up this morning." "I'll take a couple," I said aloud. Lester expertly cut two nice-looking $1\frac{1}{2}$-inch-thick steaks, wrapped them in newspaper, and passed them to me — his idea of a bonus.

That night, we invited the Jones' over for dinner. Jean had informed me earlier that she wanted no part of eating mule. Sue made it clear she didn't either. They decided to prepare something of their liking. Thus forced into doing our own cooking, Jimmie and I pan-fried and consumed all the steak. It was very good, and through the years of our long friendship, we would often talk about our mule feast, remembering it as some of the finest meat either of us had ever eaten.

5

RETURN TO SANIBLE

This time, I walked across the loading ramp and onto a nine-vehicle steel ferry, named the *Rebel*, headed for Sanible. I had parked my car at Punta Rassa because Tommy Wood planned to meet me on the other side.

Crossing San Carlos Bay brought back memories of my first trip. I had seen the island from a distance a few times since 1952, but it was always from the air in a floatplane or from the water aboard a Government-owned motor vessel. As we approached closer to the shore, I was certain the skyline hadn't changed at all over those six years. As I walked off the ferry, I noticed the refuge sign was still there, but now in need of major refinishing.

Tommy was waiting for me just beyond the sign. Sitting behind the wheel of an old military jeep, he was swatting mosquitos with an Australian pine branch thick with needles.

"Hello, Charles. Get in before these damn mosquitos carry us off!" he exclaimed.

I jumped into the open vehicle as he put it in gear and started to drive away. We hoped the breeze would dislodge the mosquitos that, having found us both, must have been overjoyed and bloated. He continued, "We'll go to my place first, have a cup of coffee, then I'll show you around the refuge."

We soon passed Bailey's General Store and followed the narrow road along the shore of Pine Island Sound, heading out toward Woodring Point. We finally stopped at an older, somewhat familiar looking two-story house that was situated on the outermost point of land at the entrance to Tarpon Bay. Here was the Government seaplane. But this was not the same plane of our red tide days. This was a brand new Piper Super Cub!

I was introduced to his wife, Louise, who served us coffee and homemade cookies. She explained to me that they had purchased this home in June 1953. "We don't live in this house on a regular basis. Tommy and I usually stay in one of the buildings at the lighthouse, but drinking water has become a problem. Since we have a good supply here in this cistern, we decided to move here temporarily until the rains start and refill the lighthouse tank."

After our refreshments, we ran to the jeep to beat the ever-present mosquitos, then retraced our way back toward the main road.

As we passed Bailey's Store, Tommy told me, "Bailey's has just about everything we need here, and if they don't, Francis Bailey will get it for you. Louise goes to town every payday — you know, every two weeks — to get a few things. I usually stay put here on the island, unless I have to take the aircraft to St. Pete for servicing. Then Louise goes with me to visit our son Bill in Clearwater or my mother in Ozona."

Located at the junction with the main road was a Standard Oil gas station, and I learned, "This service station is owned by the Bailey's and is where I usually buy fuel for the refuge and personal vehicles. I also special order 55-gallon drums of aviation fuel for the seaplane."

The ride down the road was pleasant. The overhanging canopy of vegetation and the absence of buildings along the way gave me the impression that this place hadn't really changed very much. It looked almost the same as it had six years before. At the end of the road, we turned left and entered a large marsh and savannah area. After about a half-mile, Tommy turned right at another refuge sign, which identified the land as refuge and also as the Frank P. Bailey Tract.

After leaving the paved road, Tommy turned and said, "Just after I came here, the Fish and Wildlife Service purchased these hundred acres from Mr. Bailey for 50 dollars an acre. Before that, we leased it. Mr. Darling, the famous cartoonist who stays on Captiva in the winter, managed to buy a one acre piece of the leased land and had a 4-inch well drilled on it to provide water for wildlife during the dry season."

Tommy parked the jeep near a small observation tower he called the Bird Tower. We walked over to an artesian well that flowed into a little pool, then turned into a rivulet which ran south into the open areas of the nearly dry marsh. "This is Mr. Darling's well," Tommy informed me.

Back in the jeep, we drove north, passing a large stand of red mangroves that were strangely growing in what seemed to be a fresh-water environment. Pointing toward the mangroves, Tommy said, "That's the mangrove head. It's a rookery and a night roost for several thousand colonial nesting birds — mostly ibis, egrets, and herons."

We passed another flowing well on our left, a 6-inch well I was told, and I could hear the sound of heavy equipment working ahead of us.

We turned back toward the west, onto a somewhat leveled grade, and came upon a well-drilling rig on our left. "This is another 6-inch well that will help maintain some water in the impoundment to our left," Tommy told me. Ahead and off to the right, I could see the boom of a dragline bobbing above the marsh grass.

He continued, "The dragline contractor is completing another dike that will impound the marsh on our right. A few years ago, we used dynamite in the low sections of the Sanibel Slough — this Bailey Tract is about the widest part of the slough — to try to produce areas that would retain permanent, year-round water for fish and wildlife. I blasted several dozen holes out here, but most of them sloughed back in, and it ended up to be too shallow to meet our management objectives."

He talked a few moments with the well drillers about their progress and checked their drilling log. Because the dike top wasn't graded beyond the well site, we walked over to the dragline. I could see the operator of the machine was digging out the grass and topsoil, creating a shallow ditch, and was using the spoil to create a continuation of the dike.

We drove away from the Bailey Tract, back-tracking again.

Tommy told me, "We'll go on to headquarters so you can look around at the quarters and we can discuss the job."

As we proceeded east, I asked him a question about a subject that perplexed me. I had noticed years ago that whenever he talked to me about "Sanible," he pronounced it differently than most folks did, even the kids that I had gone to school with and Jean's dad. When Tommy uttered the word, it came out "San-i-bell," not "San-a-bul or San-i-bull." I had often thought to myself, "Why is the word sometimes pronounced so differently?" So, this being my opportunity, I asked.

Tommy answered, "Most people who were born or raised on the island, or even in southwest Florida, seem to generally prefer to pronounce the word as 'San-a-bul.' Like most recent newcomers and visitors, I got into the habit of saying 'San-i-bell.' In the early 1800s, the island's name was actually spelled 'S-a-n-y-b-e-l' and pronounced 'San-ee-bell.'"

The road to the lighthouse went off on an angle from the main road just south of the post office. The lighthouse road was divided where it passed through the Kinzie property. When it came up to the boundary of the lighthouse reservation, the division stopped. From where it left the main road by the post office, its entire length was shell surfaced. Small coconut palms and oleanders covered the median between the traveled way. When the median strip ended, the road curved to the right and continued south to a point close to the Gulf beach. The road paralleled the beach until it ended at the lighthouse complex. As we came into sight of the buildings, I could see that the area had changed. It appeared to me that the beach had eroded considerably since Christmastime 1952. As we drove up to and under the first building to park beneath it, waves were actually sweeping up beneath the other building which was closer to the water.

I told Tommy, "This place looks just as it did when I visited here back in '52, except the erosion out front looks a little worse."

"Yes, nothing much has changed here, although I did have the shop and garage built in July 1953," Tommy said as he pointed to a small concrete structure north and to the west of the lighthouse tower. He continued, "I also contracted for Quarters 1, where I live, the office building, to be covered with asbestos siding in 1955. It certainly looks better; the cypress siding was a constant painting headache. Let's go up to the office."

I followed him up the stairs of the building under which we had parked. We entered a room that apparently served as the office. It contained a desk, a filing cabinet, a few chairs, and a table covered with a variety of papers. The walls were adorned with a few nautical charts and wildlife photographs.

"Charles," Tommy said as he sat down at his desk, "I've finally convinced the powers that be at the regional office in Atlanta that I need some full-time help here. I can't keep up the place the way they expect it to be maintained anymore, as well as take care of all the other responsibilities the regional supervisor keeps putting on me. The Sanibel Refuge was once under the administrative control of the former Everglades National Wildlife Refuge, but the Fish and Wildlife Service gave independent status to the staffed stations in south Florida — Loxahatchee, Key Deer, and Sanibel — a few years ago. We're all directly supervised by the Division of Wildlife Refuges in the Atlanta office.

"It looks as though, at least for the short term, the new position will be classified as a maintenance man, but I expect to upgrade that in the not-too-distant future. The starting pay is $1.87 per hour. The position description will require, as a condition of employment, that the person selected lives on the station, actually in Quarters 2 next door. Rent will be charged and deducted from the person's salary, and the employee is responsible for his or her own electric service. We have a telephone in the office, but there are no personal phones available here at the lighthouse.

"Water is a major problem almost everywhere on Sanibel and Captiva. We have a shallow well that provides water which is not really potable but is sufficient for bathing and laundry. The toilets are supplied by another shallow-well system, but that water is brackish. Bottled water can be purchased, but Louise and I use cistern water as long as the supply is adequate. Of course, our supply depends on the rainfall. You've been exposed to a hint of our mosquito problem today. They aren't as bad as they can be. Wait until it *does* rain!"

He continued, "There's not much to do here at night. I have a saying: 'The shellers go to bed at seven, and the hellers go to bed at nine.' We have one Fort Myers television station, WINK, but the reception is lousy. The ferry runs only in the daytime. If someone needs a special ferry at night, maybe for an emergency, Kinzie charges $25.00. We do have a part-time doctor in the winter. He's actually retired, but he does see patients. He lives up at Henderson Cove. The person who is selected for the job will have to deal with these lifestyle changes, and accept a great deal of responsibility. Do you think you're interested, based on what you've seen of the place and what I've told you?"

My reply was simple, "You better believe I am, Tommy. I'd like to take a look at the living quarters so I can tell my wife about them. When is the closing date on applications for the job, and when is the starting date?"

Tommy said, "We haven't pinned down all those details yet, but I sure hope to have someone onboard before the end of the year."

I asked, "How much is the rent?"

Tommy replied, "My rent for Quarters 1 is $4.50 per pay period; it works out to be a little over $9.00 a month on an annual basis. My rent is reduced, from a higher base rental fee that's established by the Division of Realty, because the office is located in my quarters. If you get the job, when we complete your Quarters Occupancy Agreement, we'll show that you have a transient or official guest room in Quarters 2 and you'll pay the same as me."

We went next door to Quarters 2. Tommy explained, "This was originally the assistant light keeper's residence. When the Coast Guard personnel, who were assigned here at the lighthouse after the War, left in April 1949, the Fish and Wildlife Service negotiated with the Coast Guard to acquire Point Ybel for refuge purposes. We signed a revokable permit on June 21, 1949, which allowed us to use all the buildings and grounds except the lighthouse structure and the small brick kerosene storage building, or oil house, next to it. The Service later subleased Quarters 2 to a U. S. Public Health Service employee who was assigned to the Sanibel Mosquito Investigative Project for the last quarter of 1949.

"Later, between 1950 and 1953, Jim Haeger and his family — he was an employee of the Florida State Board of Health — lived in this building and used it as an operational base while he conducted further mosquito studies on Sanibel.

"When they left, Paul Stahlin and his family — they're private citizens to whom the Fish and Wildlife Service rented the quarters — moved in for a couple of years. Paul operates the J. P. Carter Company. They transport freight to the islands, including merchandise for Bailey's and construction materials for island contractors. It has been the Service's position to have someone in residence here, in the event I'm detailed somewhere else temporarily, simply for fire protection and security. The quarters have been vacant for a few months now and do need some work and renovation before anyone moves in."

Looking around, I told myself, "It sure does — lots of it!"

The two quarters were identical, except they were mirror images of each other. The main sections of both Quarters 1 and 2 consisted of four identical-shaped rooms, one of which in Quarters 2 had recently served as a kitchen. The extended wing on the eastern side of this building contained a long utility room, a bathroom, and a bedroom. Tommy's quarters were laid out identically, but were oriented differently and had other uses. The main section contained the office plus living quarters. His kitchen was still in the original location, in the wing that extended off to the west. The bathroom was located in the same relative position as the one in Quarters 2.

Tommy gave me a Standard Form 57, the Application for Federal Employment, and suggested that I complete it and mail it to Atlanta soon. The Regional Refuge Supervisor would make the selection and hire the candidate who could fill the new position. Somehow I felt that Tommy would have some input too.

We walked around the lighthouse grounds, battled the ever-present mosquitos, and talked about the work he wanted to see done at the headquarters and elsewhere on the refuge. We left the lighthouse point and traveled west along Lighthouse Road. As we passed a driveway leading off to our left, I caught a brief glimpse of a small cottage out on the beach.

Tommy said, "That's where our closest neighbors live, James and Snooky Williams[1]. They've been here for many, many years. James is quite a guy — You'll enjoy meeting him."

Further west, on the main road again, Tommy pulled into the parking lot of a building located next to a Gulf Service Station. He

---

[1] Formerly Kathryn Shanahan, daughter and granddaughter of former Sanibel light keepers Webster and Henry Shanahan and stepniece of Clarence Rutland.

announced, "This is Reisinger's Restaurant. We'll get a sandwich before I take you back to the ferry landing. My treat!"

The trip home was full of thoughts of Sanible — correction, Sanibel — and how much I had enjoyed being there again, visiting with Tommy and seeing parts of the island I hadn't seen before. In my mind, I began to complete the application, looking for ways to enhance it so that its ultimate reviewers would receive the best presentation of my qualifications, skills, and experience. Just a few days after my Sanibel visit, I mailed, with crossed fingers, the completed application and supporting documents to Atlanta.

A few weeks later, I invited my parents, brothers, and sister to make a day trip to Sanibel with Jean and me. Jean wanted to see first-hand the place that might become her new home. Earlier, I had telephoned Tommy to ask if he had received any feedback on the position selection. He hadn't. When I mentioned Jean wanted to see the place, he suggested that we come over. Everyone was captivated by the location.

In her mind, Jean already began to decorate the enormous house. When she walked around inside, she commented, "I can't believe that whoever lived here last painted every wall pink! That has to go!"

The wait and anticipation began, and things soon returned to normal. In 1956, I had been granted a permit from the Florida Game and Fresh Water Fish Commission to capture, tag, and release American alligators in Collier County. That same year, along with Richard Beatty, I had formed a small group — the Collier County Herpetological Society — and we made it our mission to investigate the life history of alligators in the Big Cypress ecosystem. I also continued my loggerhead turtle studies. By the fall of 1958, we had caught and tagged over 1,500 alligators in western Collier County.

Weeks and months went by. Then in early October, I received written notification from the Regional Refuge Supervisor, Lawrence Givens, that I had been selected for the job. I was to work out a reporting date with Refuge Manager Wood. I called Tommy to discuss my new appointment and schedule a starting date. I told him I really preferred to wait at least six weeks, because we expected our first child shortly. There were problems with our apartment lease as well. Tommy was very amiable and we came to an agreement. I would move into Quarters 2 in late December, and January 5, 1959, would be my first official day on the job.

Our daughter, Leslie Estelle, was born in Naples Community Hospital on October 17, 1958. Our apartment lease would expire on December 31st, so I notified the landlord we would be moving. On December 15th, I alerted Lester Piper that I would be leaving his employ on the 27th. I had introduced him to my friend George Weymouth a few weeks before. George was a naturalist, very knowledgeable, eager, and wanted to fill my position. Because Lester had a replacement for me, I left the Wonder Gardens with his best wishes for a great future.

Richard Beatty and one of our alligator-tagging friends from Bonita Springs, Mert Snow, agreed to help me move to Sanibel in Mert's pickup. We loaded the truck on Sunday the 28th and headed for Sanibel. I figured I could pack the rest of our belongings in our car the following week.

We arrived at the lighthouse and discovered that the Woods were again living in Quarters 1, but Tommy was away that weekend. With Louise's broom, I swept out the house before we began to unload the truck.

Taking an inventory of what the house had for appliances, I found it had no stove, refrigerator, hot water heater, kitchen sink, or cabinets. Concluding that these were my responsibility, I noted the floor dimensions and approximate locations where each would go. A few years later, I learned that these items should have been furnished by the Government, but the refuge budget must have been slim at that time. Tommy never mentioned to me that the Fish and Wildlife Service should have provided the appliances and had them installed in Quarters 2 before our move.

After unloading the truck, we decided to walk around the lighthouse point, look for seashells, and check out the catch at the fishing pier. We had packed a picnic lunch and decided to go to the Bailey Tract to eat. We climbed up the observation tower, had lunch, and then I decided I would show the fellows the Bailey Tract. In Mert's truck, we drove north from the tower until I saw the mangrove head. For some unknown reason, I told Mert to turn left on a trail I was totally unfamiliar with. After he swung left, we immediately bogged down in the mud up to the axles. Every effort we made to dig out the pickup failed. So I walked out to the paved road and hitchhiked back to the Standard Station to see if someone there could help us. When I reached Tarpon Bay Road, a few cars passed, but then a man in an old grey Dodge sedan stopped and offered me a ride.

I told him who I was, my dilemma, and the fact that I was moving to the island to work with Tommy Wood.

Shaking my hand, the man said, "My name's Clarence Rutland. Tom Wood's a good friend of mine. I've lived on Sanible almost all my life. Believe me, I've been stuck a few times out in the river slough myself. Hell, I once had a team of mules buried ass-deep out there trying to get a wagonload of tomatoes to the house!"

I wondered to myself, "Why did he use the term 'river'?" To me the interior of Sanibel Island looked like an expansive wetland system — a large marsh. I certainly would have to ask Tommy about this.

At the Standard Station, I pleaded for help — Richard, Mert, and I had to get the truck out in time to make it to the ferry landing. One of the men who worked there had a jeep and offered to pull us out for $10.00.

I explained, "I don't think we have ten bucks between the three of us, but I'll make up the difference next week."

A trusting soul, he agreed, drove me back to the Bailey Tract, hooked a chain onto Mert's truck, and after some cussing and tugging managed to get the vehicle free. We made the very last ferry leaving the island that Sunday.

The next day, Jean and I drove up to Fort Myers and made arrangements for a bank loan that would provide funds for the needed appliances. We also needed bedroom and livingroom furniture. My father offered to build some kitchen cabinets to hold the sink we bought. Things began to fall into place, and we decided to make the final move on New Year's Eve day — our first wedding anniversary. Our first stop on the island was the Standard Station to pay off my debt.

Instead of the three of us moving directly into Quarters 2, Tommy waived the normal rental fee ($2.00 per night) and we were temporarily lodged in Quarters 3. This unit was a small two-bedroom cottage that I saw when I first visited the island. It was built by the U. S. Coast Guard just after the start of World War II and was currently being used as a guest cottage for visiting or vacationing employees of the U. S. Fish and Wildlife Service. Some time after I first saw the lighthouse grounds in 1952, a concrete block cistern had been built behind the cottage.

We moved into Quarters 3 fully expecting to remain there only for the time between our arrival and my official reporting date. Although Jean and I worked on Quarters 2 day and night, we were unable to finish and had to remain in the cottage for another week after my starting date.

Finally we succeeded in making Quarters 2 comfortable, and we spent our first night there on January 12th. My further education on Sanibel Island — its history, lifestyle, lighthouse, wildlife, refuge, and special environment — was about to begin.

6

SANIBEL ISLAND LIGHT STATION

A few nights after we moved into Lighthouse Quarters 2, Jean and I were relaxing on the Gulf-side porch before retiring. She said, "Charles, can you imagine what it must have been like living here a hundred years ago?"

Amused, I responded, "It was probably just about the way it is now, except maybe for the electricity."

As we talked, we both noticed how dark and quiet it was. Even the air wasn't moving. The only electric lights we could see were dim, three or more miles away at Fort Myers Beach on Estero Island.

Suddenly, Jean said, "Look — out there on the beach. Whenever the light in the tower flashes, it lights up the waves, the beach, and the trees around the compound."

I hadn't noticed this before, probably because we hadn't been outside much after dark. Up to now, we had stayed inside to finish painting and making the place comfortable. As I watched, I roughly timed the light's flashes as they reached the ground. When I really concentrated, I could hear the bell buoy slowly clanging, in the low undulating swells, nearly five miles to the southeast. And before each flash of the light, I could hear a faint sound coming from the very top of the tower. This was the illuminating gas exploding at the mechanism's orifice, ignited by the perfectly timed pilot light.

The first inhabitants of Sanibel Island were the Calusa, a fierce-ly aggressive group of Native Americans whose culture was the dominant social force among the aboriginal peoples of the lower Florida peninsula. In the early 1500s, Spanish explorers landed in southwest Florida and attempted to establish settlements on Sanibel and nearby islands. The most notable of these adventurers was Juan Ponce de Leon.

None of these early colonies was successful. Many factors pre-vented permanent, large-scale European occupation of southwest Florida. At the close of the 1700s, the Calusas had disappeared. Only a few tough individuals and small family units — Spanish, Indian, or a mix of the two — began to move into the area. They developed seasonal fishing villages, called "ranchos," or attempted to farm.

In 1778, British maps of east and west Florida documented the location of Sanybel Island, and 1845 Dutch charts identified the island as Sanybell.

In 1831, a group of New York investors learned about Sanybel Island and somehow acquired title to the island. The consortium called their land speculation venture the Florida Land Company and platted the island in June 1833.

An interesting map depicting this company's future develop-ment plans for Sanybel Island was discovered for sale in 1977 at an estate auction in New York. The map was acquired by a couple familiar with modern Sanibel Island and was later published and sold as a limited edition print.

On this map, the eastern point of Sanybel Island is identified as a common and is further delineated as the "intended site for a light-house." By 1833, the first American settlers arrived to occupy Sanybel.

At night in the early 1800s, the Florida Gulf coast was indeed dark — very few regularly occupied dwellings were located between Tampa and Key West. Those that existed were illumin-ated at night by wood fires, candles, kerosene lamps, or gas lamps. It would be a century or more before electricity would arrive in the coastal communities of southwest Florida.

Near-shore coastal navigation was a daylight endeavor; only the most foolish of mariners attempted to enter the uncharted inland waters after dark. The New York developers knew that a lighthouse was a critically important element if their scheme to permanently settle Sanybel Island was to succeed.

Only a few decades before, in 1789, the new United States Congress empowered the Treasury Department to assume control of all aids to navigation and lighthouses. The next year, the Treasury Department established the Revenue Cutter Service, and in 1848 launched a program of constructing strategically located coastal life-saving stations under control of the Revenue Cutter Service. In 1878, the life-saving stations were placed under the jurisdiction of the newly created U. S. Lifesaving Service. Congress created a nine-member Lighthouse Board in 1852, and in 1910 established a new Bureau of Lighthouses, transferring control of aids to navigation to the U. S. Department of Commerce.

Another major administrative change occurred in 1915 when the Bureau of Lighthouses, the U. S. Lifesaving Service, and the Revenue Cutter Service were all merged into the U. S. Coast Guard. In 1939, the U. S. Lighthouse Service was eliminated, and those career personnel who elected to do so became members of the U. S. Coast Guard when that agency took over operation of the lights.

Soon after creating Federal control over lighthouses and their operations, Congress made further changes. In 1820, lighthouses and other navigational aids became the responsibility of the General Superintendent of Lighthouses. In 1833, the Sanybel settlers petitioned the General Superintendent of Lighthouses for approval and funding of their planned lighthouse. Approval for a Sanybel Island lighthouse was a long time coming, and when it finally did many years later, the first American settlement of Sanybel had faded into history and was forgotten.

The outbreak of the Second Seminole War occurred in 1835. The subsequent attack by a Seminole war party on the customs office on Useppa Island, in upper Pine Island Sound, led to the death of the customs officer assigned there.

The threat of Indian attack, coupled with difficult living conditions and the inability of the immigrants from the north to cope with the harsh new environment, led to the abandonment of the island by 1836. That year, a military force that was chasing Seminoles along the coast reported there were no Indians occupying Sanybel Island, nor where there any white settlers. Another

Government force found the island deserted in 1837. By 1844, the American military implemented a program designed to discourage settlers from establishing permanent residences on the island. The military didn't want anyone to establish trade with the few remaining coastal Seminoles who refused to be relocated to the Indian Territory, now a part of Oklahoma.

By this time, the deep-water entrance to San Carlos Bay leading to the mouth of the Sanybel River had attracted coastal dwellers, and a small fishing settlement was formed at Punta Rasa (now Punta Rassa). Today, the Sanybel River is known as the Caloosahatchee and flows from Lake Okeechobee to San Carlos Bay.

In 1838, a military installation was established at Punta Rassa. Known as Fort Delaney, the facility was enlarged in 1841 to house more troops for the Seminole campaign. Because Punta Rassa was practically on the mainland, it began to develop into a seaport, and commerce steadily grew at this hub. A trail was created through the dense mangrove forest, and later a narrow causeway was constructed to improve accessibility. In the years immediately preceding the outbreak of the War Between the States, shipments of produce and cattle burgeoned at Punta Rassa, and it continued to thrive during the Civil War.

In December 1856,[1] the Lighthouse Board finally made an official request to the Federal agency controlling public domain real estate. The Board asked that Sanibel Island be withdrawn from the public domain and reserved for lighthouse purposes. Again, beaurocrats stonewalled the application for approval and construction of the light on Sanibel's eastern tip. Later a second request, further justifying the need due to the importance of the port at Punta Rassa, reached the General Land Office in December 1877.

In 1883, Congress appropriated $50,000 to construct a lighthouse complex on Point Ybel, the modern name for Sanibel's easternmost projection. The third-order lens required to light the new facility alone had a value of between $5 and $10 thousand (in 1883 dollars). Today, one of these original lenses is worth about $3 million.

On August 29, 1883, the U. S. Lighthouse Establishment contracted the Phoenix Iron Company in New Jersey to fabricate parts

---

[1]   About this time, the word "Sanybel" was replaced, on documents and as a colloquialism, by the modern name "Sanibel."

for the Sanibel light tower. However, before actual construction of the light station could begin on Sanibel, a land title problem arose.

A few years after Florida had entered the Union in 1845, Congress enacted the Swamp and Overflowed Lands Act of 1850. This act conveyed fee-title ownership of certain Federally-owned lands to the states for drainage and reclamation purposes.

A cooperative governor, William D. Bloxham relinquished Florida's jurisdictional claim to the designated property, and Sanibel Island became a lighthouse reservation. Withdrawal of the necessary lands from the public domain took place by an Executive Order issued on December 19, 1883. Through the years, the United States has whittled this reservation down in size and has disposed of it piecemeal as surplus property.

The Sanibel Island Lighthouse Reservation was downsized considerably after the middle and western portions of Sanibel were released for homesteading in the late 1880s. By 1902, the western boundary of the reservation ran across Sanibel Island two miles west of the lighthouse, about where Bailey Road intersects with Periwinkle Way today. That year much of the remaining reservation land was surveyed into 10- and 15-acre lots. These would later be sold at public auction. By late 1923, the reservation had been reduced to its present size.

On October 31, 1923, the present boundary was approved by W. W. Himeritt, Superintendent of Lighthouses for the Seventh District, in Key West. The Coast Guard-controlled property, the Sanibel Island Lighthouse Reservation, now extends from the water's edge at Sanibel's eastern tip westward to the Gulf-to-bay north-south boundary. For cadastral surveying purposes, the tract's legal description places the line 1,000 feet to the west of the center of the lighthouse tower.

In March 1884, an advance construction crew arrived on Sanibel Island to build a 160-foot-long T-shaped dock on the deep-water bay side of Point Ybel. When this pier was completed, the wrought-iron pilings and lumber for the two keepers' quarters, as well as a variety of accessory structures, arrived from Key West where they had been in storage. To maintain an orderly flow in the light station's development, the craftsmen then proceeded to build the keepers' quarters (for short-term workers' housing), the station's water system, and the foundation which would later support the light tower.

The lighthouse structure, which consisted of prefabricated wrought-iron parts, was delivered to Sanibel Island aboard a schooner. About two miles off Point Ybel, the sailboat went hard aground, wrecked on a huge shoal that still extends offshore to the south-southeast from the point. The vessel broke apart, and some of the components of Sanibel's future lighthouse fell into the Gulf of Mexico.

Two lighthouse tenders, vessels stationed in Key West, were dispatched to the scene. A hard-hat diver was aboard one of these boats. It has been reported that all the missing parts except two small fittings were salvaged by the diver and tender crews, with the assistance of the U. S. Lighthouse Establishment's project engineer and the contractor's construction team on Sanibel. Although the light tower assembly was off-loaded on Sanibel behind schedule, actual progress on the station was not affected. The light tower was completely assembled, the water system filled and operational, and the light tested by mid-August 1884.

Some published works and other sources give this date as 1885. An official Coast Guard publication quotes the following passage from the annual *Report to the Lighthouse Board–1885*:

> "This structure was commenced in March 1884,
> and on August 20, 1885 was completed and
> lighted for the first time."

The above excerpt contains a typographical error(5). My review of a more complete copy of the 1885 report verifies the 1884 date is historically correct.

The flashing beacon of the Sanibel Lighthouse, the focal plane of which is elevated 98 feet above sea level, was first illuminated by a kerosene lamp. The lamp, its size matching the order of the lens, contained three concentric wicks located inside a rotating third-order lens.

The lights of major aids to navigation, like lighthouses, had lenses that fell within a seven-order range. A lens fitting the first-order category was a monster — up to 12 feet tall, 6 feet in diameter, and with the greatest candlepower — these were used for seacoast lighthouses. Sixth-order lenses were the smallest and had the dimmest illumination — these were used on harbor buoys. The design group of seven orders of lenses also included a three-and-one-half-order lens, and there were different classes or lens designs in each of the seven orders.

These intricately ground lens designs were the brainchild of Augustin Jean Fresnel (pronounced "Fray-nell," 1788–1827). He was a French physicist who developed the advanced optics technology that has been used in most lighthouses around the world. Five manufacturing firms in France produced Fresnel-designed lenses for the world's aids to nautical navigation.

Sanibel Light's third-order lens measured 5 feet $2^1/_4$ inches high and 3 feet $3^1/_2$ inches in diameter. The weight of a fully-assembled third-order lens, minus its rotating pedestal assembly, was about 900 pounds.

Once lit, the lamp, housed inside the third-order lens atop the Sanibel Light, burned constantly through the dark hours. Its lantern produced a constant, fixed, 7,300-candlepower light. The original lens of the Sanibel Lighthouse rotated around the centrally-located lamp which housed the burning wicks.

To anyone viewing it, the slow-turning, brass-mounted glass lens assembly appeared to create a flash. Actually, a series of magnifying bullseye prism optics which were ground into the panels and centered at the focal plane created the flash. These flashes generated 41,000 candlepower and were mechanically timed by the lens' speed of revolution and the number of bullseye prisms spaced as panels within the total circumference of the lens.

This delicate mechanism produced a 6.4-second duration flash of light, then 120 seconds of low-intensity light, followed by a 6.4-second flash of light, again followed by 120 seconds of low-intensity light, etc. This interrupted pattern continued throughout the night. This regular flashing sequence was the specific identifying element of the Sanibel Lighthouse.

The light pattern, known as the "characteristic," along with the tower's construction style and color, set it apart from other lighthouses. The characteristic and other pertinent information were published in the U. S. Lighthouse Establishment's *Light List* and on nautical charts of the day as: `FFlev.120sec98ftvis16M`.

This designation means: white light, fixed, flashing every 120 seconds (the preceding is the "characteristic"), center of light 98 feet above sea level, and visible from the horizon at sea level a distance of 16 miles.

The Sanibel Light is a seacoast landfall light. This means that it was never meant to specifically caution mariners about hazardous bottoms or impending dangers. Seamen who were sailing or steaming along the southwest Florida coast were able to see the flashing Sanibel Lighthouse more than 16 miles at sea. This range was line-of-sight from the center of the light out to sea level. The higher a person stood on a vessel, or on the "hill" (a mariner's term for dry land), the further the beam could be seen. Based on the specific characteristic, a vessel's navigator would time the light's frequency of flashes, review his or her nautical charts to determine the identity of the light, and immediately know the vessel's relative position.

About ten years after completion of the Sanibel Island Light Station, the U. S. Lighthouse Establishment installed range light towers in the upper reaches of San Carlos Harbor. When range lights are aligned with the rear light exactly behind the front light, a vessel's pilot knows the craft's course is properly following a designated channel. One of these towers, the 45-foot-high rear range, displayed a 160-candlepower light and was positioned immediately south of Fisherman Key. The 30-foot-high front range also generated a light of the same candlepower and was a few hundred yards to the south of the rear range, opposite Punta Rassa, near what later would become the ferry landing.

A large sea buoy marked the entrance to the port of Punta Rassa and San Carlos Harbor channel. This was bell buoy number 2, anchored 4.75 nautical miles to the southeast of the lighthouse. Once an inbound vessel's pilot located the lighthouse or its flash, he/she next searched for the bell buoy marking the entrance, staying well to its east. The next act of navigation was to locate the front and rear range lights.

Before the range lights were built, a 250-foot-long cattle boat had difficulty negotiating the channel leading to the cattle docks. Once the vessel's helmsman could see these critical lights or their towers and distinguishing daymarks, guided by the harbor pilot, the helmsman would steer a heading to maintain perfect alignment with the ranges. Namely, the rear range was aligned visually so that it stayed constantly directly behind the front range as the vessel moved. In this way, mariners could safely negotiate the 12-foot-deep channel to reach Punta Rassa or the entrance to the Caloosahatchee. Later the Caloosahatchee would have its own set of range lights.

In 1895, the characteristics of the range lights were: front, fixed red; rear, fixed white. Like the lighthouse, these were fueled by kerosene. However, the range lights burned day and night. About once a week, the light keepers from Sanibel would launch their small light tender and cross San Carlos Bay to clean the lenses, service the lamps, and fuel these lights.[2] They were fitted with a kerosene reservoir which surrounded the lamp chimney well above the focal plane of the lens.

In 1923, the Punta Rassa range lights were fitted with acetylene-fueled flashers and their candlepower increased. The front light produced 750 candlepower and the rear produced 2,500 candlepower.

In the 1940s, the range lights were converted to battery power, and their characteristics changed. The front range flashed green every second, and the rear range had a one-second flash of white light every ten seconds.

These prominent range lights were extinguished and their supporting towers dismantled in 1963 when their usefulness to navigation ceased. The lights on the Sanibel Causeway's drawbridge now function as range lights.

Originally, the Sanibel Lighthouse was accessible by one of four staircases, two on each quarters (one on the front and one on the back) leading from ground level up to the porches. Two separate stairways, one from each building, led to a platform at the lighthouse entry door. The staircase from the Quarters 1 porch was located at the structure's northeast corner, and that leading from the Quarters 2 porch was at the northwest corner of that building. This design allowed entry from either residence to the lighthouse. During severe storms and tidal flooding at Point Ybel, the crossover stairs permitted keepers to access the light tower to service and maintain the light. They also allowed families to visit back and forth in inclement weather, or perhaps reach the safety of the light tower's secure staircase tube during severe hurricanes.

---

[2] This is why the lamp apparatus on the front and rear range lights were also known as eight-day post lanterns.

The Sanibel Lighthouse lamp was ignited, timed, and went permanently on-line the evening of Wednesday, August 20, 1884. The keeper on duty hand-wound an intricate clockworks with complex gears and a heavy counterweight. When engaged, the counterweight caused the lens to revolve around the stationary, hand-pumped, air-pressurized kerosene lamp. As the clockworks unwound, the counterweight, which weighed close to 75 pounds, slowly dropped down through the pipe-like center stair support inside the light tower.

The keeper remained on watch throughout the night and rewound the clockworks every two hours. After sunrise, the lantern was extinguished and the revolving mechanism disengaged and rewound. The counterweight was then set on a support to avoid fatigue to its cable, and the lamp's wicks were smoothed to ensure a uniform flame the next time they were lit. The keeper simply rubbed a finger around the wick; they were not trimmed with a cutting instrument. Wicks were replaced according to a written schedule.

The keeper filled a two-gallon container of kerosene from the large tanks in the oil house and had to lug it up the series of staircases. The air-pressure lamp used in the Sanibel Light's third-order lens burned slightly less than two gallons of kerosene every night, or more accurately, 685 gallons of fuel per year.

Every facet of the lens and glass lamp chimney was then carefully cleaned of fuel residue and soot. The keeper had to wear a long white linen apron so his buttons, belt buckle, or rough clothing wouldn't scratch the glass prisms. Following this standard daily cleaning procedure, the lens was covered with a soft white linen lens cover.

Ten storm panes made up the glass-walled enclosure, called the lantern room, at the topmost level of the lighthouse. Khaki-colored, well-fitted cloth curtains were hung from hooks above the storm panes. The curtains protected the glass lens components from sunlight — direct exposure could heat the glass enough to actually crack the delicate and expensive-to-repair prisms.

Light keeping at Sanibel Light was equally shared between the primary keeper and the assistant. At dusk, the assigned keeper would enter the central cylinder of the light tower, climb the 127 steps inside to reach the lantern room, remove the lens cover and curtains, ignite the lamp, and release the turning device. (To reach the lantern room from the oil house, the keeper had to climb even more steps — 15 from ground level to the porch, 19 from the porch to the lighthouse entry deck, one step up into the tube, then 127 more to the lens level — a total of 162 stair treads in all.)

After timing the light's characteristic with a stopwatch and making any necessary adjustments, the keeper would remain in the watchroom. This was a non-windowed room beneath the storm panes and was surrounded by the walkway platform and set of railings. During the watches, the keeper inspected the lantern frequently to ensure that the continuity of the light was not compromised. Then the keeper rewound the counterweight mechanism on the required schedule. In this manner, the light's characteristic and brilliance were maintained night after night, year after year.

In 1912, the air-pressure wick lamp was replaced by a new incandescent oil vapor lamp. This system was very similar in operating principle to today's Coleman camp lantern. Again by hand-pumping, kerosene was forced into a pressure chamber where the fuel became vaporized. The gas then passed through small orifices to reach the burning mantle.

The first appointed permanent light keeper at the Sanibel Island Light Station was Dudley Richardson. He was already an employee of the U. S. Lighthouse Establishment and was promoted to serve as primary keeper of the Sanibel Light.

A keeper's job was tenuous at the time; the rate of resignation was high. In 1884, the Lighthouse Board finally issued dress and fatigue uniforms to their male lighthouse keepers. But it wasn't until May 6, 1896, that light keepers became part of the classified Civil Service and more permanency filtered into the position. The last full-time resident light keeper at the Sanibel Island Light Station was U. S. Coast Guard Chief Bosun Mate William Robert "Bob" England, Jr. Bob and his wife, Mae, along with two enlisted men, were quartered at the Sanibel Light Station from 1946 until 1949. Then, because of damage to the facilities and Quarters 2 during a 1948 hurricane, the Coast Guard determined that the site was unsafe for resident personnel. So on April 19, 1949, the light was designated as fully automated, and unwatched, and would no longer need constant care. The protective lens cover and the lantern shades would never be installed again.

Bob and his crew moved to the newly created Fort Myers Light Attendant Station on the Caloosahatchee, just east of present-day downtown Fort Myers. By the mid-1950s, this became a two-man station charged with maintaining the aids to navigation. By the late 1960s, the Fort Myers station was phased out and the Aids to Navigation Group at the St. Petersburg Coast Guard Station assumed direct responsibility for navigational aids in the area — including the Sanibel Lighthouse.

In 1923, the Lighthouse Service's decision to phase out kerosene at its Sanibel facility and use acetylene gas required major changes to Sanibel Light's illumination source. For the Sanibel light keepers to take advantage of this improvement, complete refitting of the light and its mechanism was necessary. However, lighthouse keeping would ultimately become a little less labor intensive.

The first task was to replace the original rotating Fresnel lens and its bullseye prisms with a fixed non-rotating lens without bullseye optics in the central arrangement of lens panels. The fixed lens, still a third-order, would accommodate a true flashing mechanism and produce a 360-degree flash.

To accomplish the change, first a storm pane had to be removed. Through the opening, a long extending arm was secured, to which a block and tackle was attached with its proper rigging lines. Then, sections of both sets of railings, the upper one around the lantern and the lower unit around the watchroom, were removed. The individual lens panels were then unbolted at their brass-framed supporting partitions and door frame. After disassembly, the delicate lens sections were slowly and carefully lowered to the ground.

The original geared rotator pedestal, with its remarkable set of ball bearings, was left in place with no connection to the fixed replacement lens. The pedestal would turn no more, except when moved by a curious official visitor, or maybe by a painter doing regularly scheduled painting on the structure. The light tower is sandblasted and repainted about every 12 years.

At the time of refitting, the flasher unit was one of only ten such units in existence. It was a very progressive design that was state of the art at the time. Six cylinders of acetylene gas (a highly flammable, poisonous, and colorless hydrocarbon) were hoisted to the base of the lighthouse staircase cylinder. The stairway begins its spiral just inside the entrance door to the left. The tanks were positioned just inside the entrance door to the right of the central stair support which runs from the foundation, through the tube's base, and up to the top of the tower, ending at the antique rotation pedestal.

These acetylene-gas tanks, each weighing 225 pounds, were connected in groups of three to two manifold assemblies. At any one time, three tanks were active and three were on a standby manifold. A copper tube led from the distribution (active) manifold to the upper reaches of the tower and connected to the light-burner equipment. The gas supply tube was installed in the pipe through which the counterweight once slowly dropped.

Three new full tanks had to be installed, in rotation, every six months. For a few years after I arrived at the lighthouse, I assisted the Coast Guardsmen in hoisting the heavy gas cylinders up to the platform.

When their permanent personnel (Bob England and his assistants) left in 1949, the Coast Guard had virtually abandoned the buildings to the elements. The staircases leading to the lighthouse from each quarters had deteriorated and were removed in 1951 by the Coast Guard. The Seventh Coast Guard District, headquartered in Miami, would not spend a dime to make any repairs to either of the light keepers' quarters until 1982.

By the time I was assigned duties as a light keeper, access to the lighthouse entry door required a climb up a vertical, 12-rung wooden ladder to a wooden platform. A Coast Guardsman would toss a heavy hemp rope from the platform over a higher horizontal member of the light structure, then firmly tie one end to the cylinder and the other end to my military jeep. Then I would pull the full tanks up to the platform and lower the empty ones to the bed of their truck.

During this period, the Coast Guard officer-in-charge issued me a key to the lighthouse — just in case someone, in an official capacity, should ever need one. By working on the lighthouse, I actually became the last resident light keeper at the Sanibel Island Light Station.

A sun relay photocell was the main component of the light's acetylene illumination technology. Called a "sun valve," this apparatus was clamped to the upper gallery railing on the southeast side of the structure and connected to the ignition apparatus inside the lighthouse. This device was the pre-computer-era "brains" of the light's ignition; it automatically turned on the gas flow at twilight and off at dawn, and it permitted the supply of fuel to reach the flasher unit. At dusk or during foggy conditions, the valve allowed the gas to flow into the appropriate flasher chamber. Then the pilot light ignited and exploded the regulated volume of acetylene. Thus began the characteristic's all-night cycle. Then at dawn, light from the rising sun would close the valve and prevent the gas from traveling up to the flasher chambers.

The flasher had three chambers. The upper chamber regulated the duration of the explosive flash, and the two lower chambers regulated the frequency of the flashes.

These flash units were very delicate instruments. They could be very frustrating pieces of equipment, especially when they failed to maintain a perfectly regulated characteristic. The characteristic would never really be far enough out of synchronization to matter, but most light keepers were perfectionists. Small wedges would control the valves easily enough, but it could take hours to set the pressure regulator properly. If it wavered out of kilter somehow, the keeper would have to turn and re-turn the small adjusting screws, sometimes for hours on end, to get the flasher perfectly synchronized.

When all adjustments were correct, the acetylene light would flash $1/2$ second, be off (eclipse) $11/2$ second, flash for $1/2$ second, eclipse $71/2$ seconds, flash for $1/2$ second, eclipse $11/2$ second — and so on through the night.

Knowing that the Sanibel Causeway would soon be completed and 24-hour accessibility to the light would become a reality, the Coast Guard decided in 1962 to electrify the Sanibel Lighthouse. Personnel from the Coast Guard unit at St. Petersburg arrived at Point Ybel with another lens and all the necessary fittings and equipment to make the changeover. The magnificent third-order fixed Fresnel lens was replaced with a much smaller 500-millimeter drum lens which had been used on a lightship.

As lightships were being phased out, these costly lenses were recycled for use on seacoast aids to navigation.

They had one major problem, however. The Coast Guard didn't have a key to the lighthouse; they had forgotten it. To their surprise, I climbed up the ladder, pulled my keychain out of my pocket, and unlocked the door. Tommy had always told me to cooperate to the fullest extent with the Coast Guard, and for this lighthouse-related project, he instructed me to assist in changing out the lens.

The methodology, discussed earlier, which was used to remove the original rotating lens system was also applied to this replacement project. Later, in the early 1980s, the lightship lens would be traded out with a 190-millimeter beacon — the fourth lens assembly to shine at Sanibel Light.

After electrification, the composite group flashing characteristic of the Sanibel Light remained the same as in its acetylene-fueled days. Today, nautical charts code its characteristic and other information as: `Fl(2)6s98ft13M`. Also, the wooden ladder and landing at the lighthouse's entry were replaced with metal counterparts. Following electrification, the light's performance was plagued with problems. A series of standby batteries were included in the electrical circuitry because of anticipated frequent power outages. However, failures of such simple equipment as mercury switches and battery chargers resulted in the unattended light being occasionally completely inoperable for days and even weeks. Such is the price of automation.

The gong of Number 2 bell buoy was also silenced and replaced with a new structure and flashing light at the same position. Its characteristic and other data now are: `FL2.5s40ft7m`.

Out of the blue in October 1972, the U. S. Coast Guard announced plans to extinguish the Sanibel Light. They had determined that the light was no longer necessary as a navigational aid. As a licensed motorboat operator and a sailor, I could appreciate where the Coast Guard was coming from. From offshore, the Sanibel Light was no longer discernable due to the multitude and magnitude of lights on Fort Myers Beach and Sanibel Island. Modern coastal illumination had basically rendered the lighthouse beacon invisible. From five miles at sea, a pilot couldn't even find the lighthouse to locate the entrance to San Carlos Bay. The horizon sky virtually glowed with these coastal communities. Coupled with the intensity of the lights from Fort Myers and Cape Coral, this caused the Sanibel Lighthouse's flash to be completely obscured, even a few miles seaward of the light.

Public hearings were held. Many Sanibel and mainland folks voiced their opinions, arguing that the historic lighthouse should remain operational. As a subconscious tribute to the men and women lighthouse keepers of the former U. S. Lighthouse Establishment, as well as those of the U. S. Coast Guard who came later, the hearing officers agreed with the public's sentiment. The Sanibel Island Light Station continues to "burn."

In the early 1970s, because of the light's significance to the history of Sanibel, the island's historian at the time, Elinore Dormer, nominated the Sanibel Lighthouse and keepers' quarters for official historical recognition. She was successful. So, on October 1, 1974, the structures were officially listed in the *National Register of Historic Sites.*

7

DRINKING WATER — HEAVEN-SENT

The coffee was different! Not only did it have a strange taste, it also had a new color.

I asked Jean, "Is this the same brand of coffee we used in Naples? Did you make it in the drip pot?"

She replied, "I fixed it the same way for the past year. It must be the water."

Water is indeed an important factor in making good, flavorful coffee. In my childhood, I drank the nation's best-tasting water — that from the fresh, clear, cool reservoirs in Massachusetts. But after arriving in Florida, I was introduced to sulfur water. This was deep artesian well water that was full of ghastly sulfur dioxide gas, and it gave the water a distinctive rotten-egg odor. During her years on Marco Island, Jean had been raised on rain-produced cistern water, and more recently she had used unaerated sulfur water from her parents' well in Bonita Springs. For the past year, both of us had been spoiled by "city water" in Naples.

We drank the coffee that cool New Year's Day morning, our first on Sanibel, despite both of us complaining that we didn't like the taste. When Tommy dropped in the next morning to see what my planned work schedule was for upgrading Quarters 2, I told him about the coffee.

He explained, "Guess I forgot to tell you. The tap water in the houses is supplied through a shallow well. It's really not too bad and can be used for drinking. If you'd rather, you can do as Louise and I do. We use cistern water for cooking and drinking and restrict our use of the well water for laundry and bathing. Y'all have a choice of either purchasing bottled water or getting a container and filling it from the cistern spigot in our kitchen. That's the only cistern we have, which is operational at present. Once you have your quarters ready, we'll do some plumbing and make a few changes."

At lunch, I explained the drinking water situation to Jean. She said, "Leslie and I are going to Bailey's Store later to buy some groceries. I'll get a 5-gallon jug of water. We'll use that, then you can refill it over at Tommy's."

That evening, I sat in my favorite outside chair on the Gulf side porch listening to a chuck-wills-widow in the buttonwood strand to the west of the lighthouse. I was reviewing the day's events and noting them in my required field diary. I thought to myself, "Look at all the water out there, and all we have to drink is either a few feet underground or next door in a round, cypress-clad cistern."

For generations, urban Americans have taken fresh, potable drinking water for granted. All a city dweller has to do is turn on a faucet, which taps into a municipal supply, to draw water for a bath, cook meals, wash dishes, and even water plants. And with hydrant systems available in most large communities, the means to extinguish a fire quickly is at hand.

For many suburban and rural dwellers, however, water has been a little more difficult to obtain in volume, yet it is available from a variety of sources and for similar uses. But only if adequate pumps are available can this water be used for fighting fire.

On most coastal barrier islands, Sanibel-size or smaller, adequate supplies of potable water were a luxury for residents. Inadequate supplies restricted or even prevented settlement and development. However, Sanibel was unique from most other barrier islands because potable water was an available, easily used, and almost reliable natural resource.

Prior to permanent settlement of Sanibel in the 1880s, year-round surface fresh water, hydrologically known as the water-table aquifer, was very restricted. It was hydraulically connected at the surface only during, and for a few months after the end of, the summer rainy season. By mid-winter, the surface volume of sweet water had receded and fresh water existed only at a few scattered, shallow ponds. By late spring, when drought conditions prevailed, the only fresh water left existed in a few deep alligator holes located in the small open areas subject to annual seasonal rain flooding.

A few of these flood-prone areas were later named Fitzhugh, Stewart, and Mitchell Ponds. Scattered about the island were less than a dozen small to moderately-sized isolated alligator holes. Those located in the central interior marsh usually contained permanent fresh water, even during the driest part of the year. The annual fluctuation between high and low levels in the water table aquifer was, and still is, about three feet.

Alligator holes are established in natural marsh systems when an adult alligator of either sex establishes a territory and a den or cave. Island surface-water levels are seasonally reduced due to overflow, evaporation, plant transpiration, and percolation laterally through the porous shell soil or slowly downward to recharge the deeper, more saline layers of water. Dropping surface-water levels trigger alligators to use their powerful and agile bodies, tails, and even mouths to move soil away from deepening water areas they excavate as their den sites. Permanent fresh water is essential to alligators and their first cousins, the caimans. However, it is not so critical for most of their more distant relatives around the world, the more salt-tolerant crocodiles.

On Sanibel, the water-table aquifer penetrates the Earth's crust to a variable depth, depending on how deep the nearly impermeable clay deposit is at its base. The maximum depth of this supply of surface water is around 25 feet below the island's surface. Recently, this aquifer has been referred to as a "lens" of fresh water, and its very existence means that Sanibel is nearly unique among barrier islands.

Still deeper, below the surface water, there are other layers (aquifers) of water that are saltier. This means that they have higher sodium chloride and other salt concentrations. The uppermost of these is called the shallow artesian aquifer. This layer lies below the clay layer and atop a limestone stratum. Sometimes referred to as bedrock, the limestone layer varies in depth, but generally the uppermost level of this deposit lies between 29 and 34 feet beneath the island's surface. This limestone, some of which is water-bearing, varies in thickness and is believed to totally underlie Sanibel. In some areas, it extends to a depth of 130 feet. The clay layer is a barrier, positioned above the shallow artesian aquifer. Unless it is penetrated, by wells or excessively deep surface excavations, it prevents the brackish artesian water from intruding into the upper fresh-water "lens."

Several hundred feet below the shallow artesian aquifer is another stratum of water known as the deep artesian aquifer. The uppermost part of this is called the lower Hawthorn aquifer. The two artesian aquifers are separated by a variety of limestone, clay, phosphatic sand, and marl deposits. Marl is a mixture of several of these soil types. Still deeper are other water-bearing formations, but they are beyond the scope of this discussion.

The deep artesian[1] aquifer is under such extreme subterranean pressure that water is dispersed vertically and horizontally through the porous limestone earth. If this water-impregnated layer is penetrated by a well, the well is supplied by pressurized water that is ejected up to a level, or artesian head, that is often a considerable number of feet above the Earth's surface.

All well-constructed residences on post-1900 Sanibel Island (that is, those that were not simple palm-thatched dwellings, as many were) included one or more cisterns. These cypress-staved or shell-concrete tanks[2] were connected to the structure's roof by gutters and downspouts.

Precipitation falling on the roofs was the source of water, unless the roof-supplied cistern water could be augmented by pumping potable water from a well.

Two major types of shallow wells penetrated the ground at selected locations into the surface-water aquifer. The first were permanent shallow pits that were hand-dug by those homesteaders who were fortunate enough to have houses on high ridges where cabbage palms grew in abundance. The presence of these trees meant to the pioneers that fresh potable water existed just a few feet below. The pits, some of which were 6 feet square and 5 feet deep,

[1]   The term "artesian" is based on the geographic location of the first man-made well in Europe. It was drilled in the part of France now known as Artois in the year 1126.

[2]   Before today's premixed concrete, builders on Sanibel and Captiva Islands routinely used seashells as their aggregate when mixing concrete.

were lined with brick or concrete to prevent the soil from slough-ing in. Having percolated through the permeable soil, fresh water from the water-table aquifer would seep in, filling the excavated hole and maintaining its level in these shallow wells. Some homes had windmill-driven pumps to force the water into raised wooden water storage tanks. These tanks were usually separate from the cistern system. Others used more economical hand pumps to dis-tribute well-originated water into their tower tanks, or even their cisterns, during periods of drought.

Later, well-point water systems were introduced. These were pointed metal pipes perforated by hundreds of tiny holes and cov-ered with a bronze-mesh screen which served as a simple filter. The screened point prevented large particles, such as seashell frag-ments, from entering the pump device and blocking the intake. Today, well-points are still in use and are available in a variety of lengths, diameters, and materials.

Customarily, the well-builder digs down with a post-hole dig-ger until surface water begins to seep into the hole. Before the operation proceeds any further, the water is allowed to settle for a few moments and is then tasted. If the water doesn't taste good, the exploratory well-digging operation is abandoned and moved to another site.

Typically, well-points are fitted with a length of compatible-size pipe and a drive coupling to prevent damage to the threaded ends when the pipes are driven. The labor-intensive driving may be done using a common heavy sledge hammer or a modified dri-ver such as that used on Sanibel for decades by Nave Plumbing. This implement is made from the guts of an automobile differential with the axle shafts still attached. One shaft is placed inside the vertical pipe, and the opposite shaft is raised. The gear assembly is then slammed down, striking the drive coupling and hammering the well-point into the ground.

Usually, well-points are driven with the pointed end down, but they can also be dug down and placed horizontally. Their final installed depth is based on the well-driver's local experience. Depth is also determined by the season of the year and by the depth of the water-table aquifer below grade at the well site.

Turn-of-the-century residents and farmers who could afford it had wells drilled into the deep artesian aquifer. Under ideal conditions, the pressurized water first entered an aeration tank to help remove the sulfur dioxide gas. Before electricity came to the islands and electric pumps were available, the water was forced by windmill or hand pump into an elevated tank which supplied gravity-fed water to the buildings.

With water originating from the heavens (rain) or from just a few feet below the Earth's surface, water conservation was always an important element of island living. Generations of people were raised on Sanibel and Captiva Islands guided by one simple doctrine: "On this island in the sun, we don't flush for number one."

When the Sanibel Island Light Station was completed, it included a state-of-the-art water system (at least for lighthouse complexes established on remote subtropical barrier islands). A 4,000-gallon elevated cistern was located on the Gulf side of each quarters where the kitchen wing joined the house. The bottoms of the tanks were raised about eight feet off the ground on stout, round, thick brick bases.

These water reservoirs were made of full 2-inch-thick, 4-inch wide, vertical cypress staves. Each board was expertly beveled at its joining edges so when fitted together, they formed a perfect water-tight circular tank. These were bound in place with seven $1/_2$-inch-round, adjustable metal straps around the cistern. A similar, slightly larger 5,000-gallon cypress tank was built and held together in the same manner. It was placed at near ground level on driven foundation pilings between the buildings.

In those days, the light station's potable water was indeed heaven-sent. Each downspout allowed rainwater, falling on the roofs and carried about by the guttering, to flow into the cisterns. There were two downspouts running into each tank, and each had a moveable butterfly valve. During dry times when rain was imminent, these valves were adjusted so that the rain was diverted from entering the cisterns. After sufficient rain had fallen to clean the roofs, gutters, and cistern-connecting pipes, the valves were repositioned so that the rainwater entered the tanks again. This technique washed away any bird droppings, dead insects, or any other undesirables that had fallen onto the roofs since the last cleaning.

During the summer rainy season, with almost daily rains, the butterfly valves remained adjusted so rainfall entered the system without precleaning the roofs.

The only potable running water serving the dwellings was supplied via a direct line from their respective cisterns into the kitchens. The 5,000 gallon tank was a backup system. Its contents could also be pumped up to either of the raised cisterns when necessary. From time to time, water was brought to the station aboard regularly visiting lighthouse-tender vessels and pumped to top off the tanks. From 1884 until 1923, there was no other plumbing in the quarters.

Privys (outdoor unplumbed pit toilets), which were used every day, were located on the upper beach on the Gulf side of the dwellings. Each quarters also had a privy closet. These were located on the outer Gulf-side part of the structure not far from the corners where the elevated cisterns stood. These were boxed all the way down to a pit in the ground by a wooden vertical chute. These primitive toilets were used when weather or mosquitos made it impossible to leave the buildings.

Then in 1923, major improvements were made to the light station's quarters and plumbing facilities. Prior to that time, the kitchen wing was separated from the four-room section by an open breezeway. Remodeling included closing in the breezeway and constructing screened porches on the bay side of each building. I removed both screen enclosures in the mid-1960s.

"Real" bathrooms were installed in each quarters in an area that formerly was a combination pantry and storage room. The fixtures included bathtubs, flushing toilets, and sinks. Two 25-foot-high elevated water towers were built between the houses. Each of these supported a 1,000-gallon cypress tank. The tank on the east was covered, as were all the cisterns; the tank on the west was unroofed and open. Immediately south of the base of the two towers, a small frame building housing manual pumps was built. One of the pumps was connected to a well-point buried a few feet deep in the water-table aquifer, which was saline, brackish water due to its proximity to tidal waters. Water from here was pumped up to the open tank. The other pump was connected to the potable water cisterns by means of a series of pipes and valves. The cistern having the most water was selected as the current source, and its water was hand-forced up to the covered tank. The elevated water then provided gravity-fed, pressurized water to the quarters on demand.

The brackish well-point water supplied the toilets, and the covered tank furnished water to the other bathroom and kitchen fixtures. Waste-water lines were provided for the toilets only. These drained into a 4-inch terra cotta sewer pipe which emptied into a single septic tank and drain-field system buried out on the Gulf beach. Effluent from a laundry tub, next to the old privy closet, and from the bathtub and sinks also flowed into piping, but these pipes simply led into the ground. This "gray water" was allowed to percolate into the shelly soil.

The Rural Electrification Act of 1936 funded electric service to rural areas throughout the nation. The Lee County Electric Cooperative, which furnishes electric power to our barrier islands, was organized soon after. In 1941, their electric power distribution lines reached Sanibel, Captiva, and Marco Islands. However, electric power on the islands was unreliable and subject to long-lasting outages, especially following hurricanes. Therefore, the Coast Guard continued to operate the Sanibel Light's lantern on acetylene gas.

The hand-force pumps in the light station's pumphouse were soon replaced with electric pumps. Along with a wooden poultry house near Quarters 1, this frame building was subsequently demolished by a hurricane. By late 1958, the pumps for filling the gravity tanks were relocated upon the eastern porch of Quarters 1. Only one pump, that which pumped the brackish water for the toilets, was still operable when I arrived to take up residence at the light station.

During the early years of World War II, when the Government was concerned with possible infiltration of German U-boat-borne saboteurs, the Coast Guard built coastal observation and patrol bases. These were responsible for guarding our coasts from such invasion. Therefore, in 1942, the Coast Guard constructed the cottage, Quarters 3, and a wooden observation tower out on the extreme tip of Point Ybel. The cottage was connected to the general plumbing system and had its own septic waste disposal unit.

Since the Sanibel Island Light Station already headquartered a three-man Aids to Navigation Unit, the Coast Guard constructed the cottage for crew quarters. It also built the observation tower, where submarine lookouts maintained surveillance of the channel. (Regulations prevented the lighthouse tower itself from being used for observation purposes.) This special detachment of Coast Guardsmen detailed to Sanibel also patrolled the beaches of Sanibel and Captiva by jeep, looking for enemy landings that were never encountered. U-boat traffic was real in the Gulf of Mexico, and it was reported that a German submarine sank somewhere west of Gasparilla Island, where Port Boca Grande used to be.

In 1944, a major hurricane destroyed the ground-level water tank between the structures, the elevated cistern of Quarters 2, and the septic tank and drain field. The Coast Guard replaced both cisterns with steel tanks and installed individual septic systems just north of Quarters 1 and 2.

Then a 1948 hurricane washed away the metal tank at Quarters 2 and the Gulf-side staircases of both structures. With reduced storage capacity, the Coast Guard had to transport more water to the station by tender. The Coast Guard also provided the light station crew with a 300-gallon water cart they would occasionally pull behind their jeep to Jake Stokes' residence. Jake had a high-quality artesian well and shared his water with fellow islanders when necessary. The water cart had a pump, and Bob England and the light station staff would top off the cisterns if their supply ran low during the dry season or before a tender was scheduled to arrive. At the time, this water cart was also the only piece of mobile fire-fighting equipment on Sanibel Island.

In January 1959, Jean and I began to use a shallow well for drinking water and general domestic use. The well was a considerable distance further inland from the point where the toilet water supply originated. It was adequate — once we were used to it. A jet pump with a pressure storage tank supplied water to all three quarters, but at times because of demand, the pressure could be very low.

It was my responsibility to climb the toilet water tank, inspect the fluid level, then operate the pump to keep the tank topped off.

I rigged up a float inside the tank and connected it to a gauge I had made and nailed to the outside. I could then check the water level from down below and avoid climbing the tower so often.

Several years before, in some hurricane, the conical-pitched roof covering the drinking water tank was blown away. It was later replaced by a flat cover with an open hatch. In December 1961, while I was up top doing some repair work to the toilet tank, I heard a commotion coming from inside. So I climbed up the tank-mounted ladder to see what was going on. As I peered into the dark cypress tank, I was startled as an adult barn owl flew out the opening, nearly striking me. On the bare bottom of the tank sat four cowering, downy barn owl chicks, looking up at me and frozen with fear.

Bob Sabatino and his family moved to Sanibel a few weeks after we did. We met, found we had a few things in common, and became close friends. I couldn't wait to tell Bob about the little owls. Soon, the two of us climbed the tower to check on their progress. Bob and I decided they were so cute, we'd each take one and raise it as a family pet. I kept mine for a couple of days, but it was so much extra work caring for it properly, I returned it to the tank. Luckily it was welcomed back into its family unit.

The Sabatinos continued to raise their owl and did an excellent job. All the necessary permits to cover its retention in captivity were obtained, and the bird lived a long and happy life as a local celebrity.

Bob named his barn owl "Hoot." For several years, this beautiful bird was the center of attention at the Sanibel-Captiva Audubon Society meetings, which were routinely held during the winter at the Sanibel Community House. Bob and "Hoot" made every meeting and put on quite a show. After considerable head-bobbing and wing-spreading — checking out, teasing, and almost milking the crowd — "Hoot" would leave Bob's arm and fly out over the audience. On its owl-silent wings, it flew just inches above the heads of the crowd. After making an inaudible and graceful loop or two around the small auditorium, "Hoot" would return to Bob's waiting arm like a trained falcon. It was impressive to say the least.

The barn owls continued to nest in the tank until we were ordered to dismantle the system and tear down the towers in 1968. In the meantime, "Hoot" moved to Captiva and lived with Bob Sabatino for a total of 14 years.

* * *

Early one Tuesday morning in the late summer of 1962, while Tommy and I were having coffee at his kitchen table, he said, "Charles, our days here at the lighthouse may be numbered."

"What do you mean, Tommy?"

"Yesterday, I met with two engineers from the Seventh Coast Guard District Headquarters who drove over from Miami. They showed me some impressive plans they're developing to eventually use all their land here at the point. Now that the damn bridge is almost done, if they can get an appropriation and everything else comes together, they'll turn the lighthouse point into a fully operational Coast Guard station. This will include quarters for officers, enlisted men, and dependents; recreational facilities; offices; communication and fueling systems; and some breakwaters and boat docks on the bay side. In time, they expect to base a 95-foot cutter, a number of smaller boats, and a helicopter here."

I was dumfounded and devastated. I couldn't imagine our quality of life being threatened any worse.

Tommy continued, "They have contracted with Miller Brothers, a well-drilling company in Fort Myers, to drill a deep well about 200 feet west of the light tower, over near this end of the center road. If the water meets their specifications, they'll begin construction of a water system first, after they work out some final details with the Lee County Commission. They'll fence off the point and prohibit public entry with a guarded gate."

"I can't believe it! After they abandoned this place to the elements, they'd take it back? Our Government's really screwed up!"

Tommy laughed and went on. "We'll just have to sit tight and see what happens. But in the meantime, you might want to look around, buy some land, and be prepared to build if this thing comes to pass. I'm sure they'll revoke the Service's permit."

When I told Jean about the situation that evening, she said, "Let's not worry about it. Everything will work out for the best."

But Jean and I took Tommy's comments seriously and began to look around the island for a building lot. After looking at most available properties in our price range, we selected a nice lot on Coquina Drive in The Rocks subdivision, the rear of which bordered on the "lake" excavated by the developers. We paid $3,000 for this "waterfront" lot.

The Coast Guard's well went ahead on schedule. It was a 6-inch well that was drilled to a total depth of 475 feet, down to the lower Hawthorn aquifer. To prevent contamination of the well's water source or other adjacent sources if the quality of the water was good (or bad), 335 feet of 6–inch steel well casing was installed. When completed, the well's artesian head was under greater pressure than any other flowing well that had been drilled before on Sanibel, and there had been scores of them. Water from the artesian pressure reached an altitude of over 33 feet above mean sea level, or 28 feet above the ground's elevation at the well site.

Unfortunately, or fortunately depending on your point of view, the well's water turned out to be less fresh than the Coast Guard's engineers had hoped for. The salinity was a little greater than 1,550 milligrams per liter (mg/l) of dissolved chlorides.[3] In comparison, "Ding" Darling's well in the Bailey Tract was 557 feet deep and produced water with 1,000 mg/l of chlorides. The high salt content of the well was a major obstacle to the planned development. Desalinization of such water was possible, but the technology at the time to produce potable water from such highly saline water was ultra-expensive and far beyond the budget appropriated to build a new station. So it was two strikes against the Coast Guard base.

The third strike came in 1963 when the U. S. Coast Guard requested that the Lee County Board of County Commissioners grant non-revenue status for its people and their dependents, who would ultimately be stationed at their new facility, whenever they crossed the Causeway. The Board refused to let them cross toll-free, and the plans of the Coast Guard were scuttled. Those of us residing at the Sanibel Island Light Station breathed a sigh of relief.

I was elated. I thought, "Wow! A salty well and the uncooperative County Commissioners have stopped the U. S. Coast Guard

---

[3]   Saline water is defined as water containing 1,000 mg/l or more of dissolved chlorides.

and saved Point Ybel. Generations of Sanibel residents and visitors will continue to enjoy its beach, open spaces, and historical significance."

Although slightly salty to the taste, the Coast Guard's well had value for the Fish and Wildlife Service. The abandoned well had been fitted with a large shutoff valve so it would not be free-flowing. We bought a roll of several hundred feet of black 1-inch plastic pipe, assorted clamps, and fittings and connected the pipe to the well head. I dug a shallow ditch from the edge of the light station's clearing over to the concrete cistern of Quarters 3 and laid the pipe. I elbowed the pipe up and let it discharge, under its own pressure, into the cistern. When the tank was full, I walked over to the well's valve and shut off the flow. Once the water was exposed to the air, the rotten-egg odor dissipated. And the aerated water really wasn't too offensively salty for the uses we had in mind.

By turning a series of valves closing off the intake line to the well point, we could then distribute the artesian well water from the cistern through the lines and into the plumbing system of the three quarters. During an earlier improvement, we had tied a $1/_2$-inch metal line into the cistern pipe at Quarters 1 and ran it between the buildings into my kitchen. This gravity-fed line connected drinking water directly into Quarters 2. This meant I no longer had to manhandle heavy glass jugs up and down the stairs.

In 1965, a group of Sanibel and Captiva residents formed the Island Water Association, Inc. Their aim was to operate a water supply and distribution system on the islands. They purchased water from an association on nearby Pine Island. This water reached Sanibel through a 10-inch, 9,500-foot-long pipe that ran along the bottom of Pine Island Sound from St. James City on Pine Island to Woodring Point on Sanibel.

By 1973, the Island Water Association constructed their own electrodialysis water treatment plant, and by 1975, the capacity of this plant had grown to 2,100,000 gallons a day. In 1980, a Sanibel-based reverse osmosis plant went on-line, and water is no longer purchased from the Greater Pine Island Water Association. The obsolete electrodialysis plant was shut down, and the reverse osmosis plant's current capacity is 4,800,000 gallons a day.

In 1966, the new water system's distribution lines reached the boundary of the lighthouse reservation, and the Fish and Wildlife

Service connected up. It took 1,300 feet of 2-inch plastic pipe to get us on-line. All at once, we no longer had to rely on heaven-sent drinking water.

8

"DING"

It was Thursday morning, December 3, 1959, and I was busy repainting the flagpole at the refuge headquarters. A car came around the bend and parked near the foot of the office stairs. An elderly man got out, took his cane in hand, and slowly walked in my direction.

"Good morning," he said. "You must be the new man. I'm 'Ding' Darling. Tommy told me you had reported for duty. He also told me you were interested in alligators, snakes, turtles, and birds. On my way down from Captiva, I saw a big, beautiful indigo snake cross the road by the Sanibel Community Church. Seems like I see more dead ones anymore than live ones. Too many damn cars on the road with too many dumb drivers."

"I've heard a lot about you, Mr. Darling," I responded shyly. "I remember that great cartoon you did a few years ago, about the key deer hunters, and I've read and looked through a few of your books that Tommy loaned me. He's up in the office, and I'm sure he'll be glad to see you. It's really been a pleasure meeting and talking with you."

He then turned and slowly made his way toward the office.

I went about my business and later, after I had cleaned the paintbrush, I heard Tommy yell out his kitchen window, "Charles, come on up and have a cup with us."

"I understand that you and Mr. Darling have met," Tommy said as I joined them for coffee.

"Yes, we met outside a few minutes ago."

Mr. Darling then proceeded to direct the conversation and its subject matter. He asked serious questions and expected qualified, no-nonsense answers. At first, his interest centered on what had been happening on the refuge since his last visit. Then he asked about certain individuals in the wildlife refuge system. He ended up with comments about a bridge.

Thinking to myself, "A bridge? I had never heard anything about a bridge before. One to Sanibel?"

Mr. Darling was wound up. He continued, "I don't think that bridge, which has been talked about for years, will ever be built, but that doesn't make me a prophet. The draglines and bulldozers are ripping the goozle out of what is left of Florida's natural habitat areas and nesting grounds. Thousands of little mangrove islands along the Gulf Coast of Florida are disappearing because of money-hungry, bloodthirsty real estate promoters."

Tommy agreed with him one hundred percent, and I, listening in awe, did also.

The discussion was emotional and meandered among a variety of subjects: the ruination of Sanibel and Captiva, the destruction of the environment and of the country in general, and the destruction of wetlands which had resulted in low duck numbers. Then the topic suddenly centered on loggerhead sea turtles, and I was all ears. Mr. Darling wanted to know how loggerhead eggs had fared against a growing raccoon population the previous nesting season.

Tommy told him, "Hatching success was much better than in '58, so it appears the raccoon population has decreased. Charles spent a great deal of time out on the beach at night this past summer. He's done a considerable amount of work with sea turtles down the coast at Naples and is very interested in developing a sea turtle conservation program, and some other studies, here on Sanibel. We'll develop a program over the winter and get out on the beach when nesting season starts next May."

"Good!" was Mr. Darling's reply. "Those little turtles don't have a Chinaman's chance in hell of making it. Charles, please, it's critical that you do everything you can to help and protect them.

Someone just has to! From my discussions with old friends, I know there's a considerable amount of interest to save little sea turtles on Captiva and Sanibel, if you need any help."

After finishing my coffee, I excused myself and went back to work. One of my greatest ambitions, a key to my life's master plan, was to work with sea turtles, and I had just had my work cut out for me by none other than "Ding" Darling himself.

A few days later, Tommy told me, "I'm doing a morning waterfowl survey tomorrow. I know it's Saturday, but I'd like you to get up early and come along. I want to be in the air just as soon as it's light enough to take off."

I hadn't flown with him much since my arrival, so this was a pleasant surprise. And it would be a surprise! Before the sun had completely climbed above the eastern horizon the next morning, we took off from Tarpon Bay where the floatplane was stored. We headed north, over the tidal mangrove-lined bays and bayous of Sanibel. The tide was nearly low, but ducks were still grouped in the area as we flew a few hundred feet overhead. When we reached Blind Pass, Tommy turned 180 degrees to the right over Pine Island Sound, heading back toward Sanibel. We flew over several huge rafts of lesser scaup, some of which probably contained 5,000 birds each. At the lighthouse point, he again turned around, this time flying just offshore from the western edge of Pine Island. Again, rafts of scaup and other waterfowl species were scattered among the small mangrove keys. By the time the sun had broken through the morning haze, we were flying across Charlotte Harbor.

Tommy said, "I'm going to set down over by Cayo Pelau. That's the large mangrove key ahead of us."

He did a flyover, checking the wind and water depth, then landed next to a large exposed oyster bar. I could tell that the oyster bed was usually covered with water, but the tide was exceptionally low. He cut the engine, hopped out onto a float, opened the luggage compartment, and took out a small anchor and rode. Then he stepped off into the cold water to push the aircraft off the bar before the aluminum floats hit the sharp oysters. He anchored the seaplane, returned to the fuselage compartment, and withdrew a couple of gunnysacks. He tossed one to me and said, "Come on, it's our day off. We're going to do a little oystering."

It wasn't long before our croker sacks were nearly full of large oysters. Tommy passed me one of his oyster knives, and I popped open about every third oyster I picked up. These were exceptional, fat, delicious oysters and made a great breakfast. When we each had a bagful, which we could barely carry, we walked back to the floatplane. Tommy used some rope he had aboard and tied on the oyster-laden bags, one to each float. I then climbed aboard while he pushed the plane away from the bar, positioning it for takeoff.

Once in the air, Tommy said, "Let's get a cup of coffee."

A few minutes later, we had again crossed Charlotte Harbor, descended, and landed at a small island called Cabbage Key. A tall water tower and a white house sat atop a high Calusa indian mound not far from where he tied down the plane to a small dock.

"I often stop here to visit a friend of mine," he said. He's an artist, lives here alone most of the time, and makes a great cup of coffee."

He removed a small sack from the plane's storage locker, filled it with a generous portion of the oysters, and started up the pathway toward the house. Tommy delivered his gift; we had coffee, visited for about half an hour, and soon were in the air again.

After we took off, Tommy turned the aircraft south again. Over the noise of the engine, he hollered, "That long island off to our right is Punta Blanca. It once had a good number of residents on it — even had a school. Back in '52, there were still a couple of families of commercial mullet fishermen living there. That year, they rescued and raised a young bald eagle with their chickens in an open pen. It was very tame as an adult, and they claimed, after it had gone off on its own, that it nested on LaCosta."

"We have one more stop to make before we head back to Sanibel," he yelled as he again banked the airplane.

A few moments later, we taxied to a stop on the margin of a huge mudflat behind LaCosta, now known as Cayo Costa, and anchored. This time, Tommy armed the two of us with plastic buckets and four-foot-long steel rods, each of which had a 90-degree bend at one end.

Tommy explained, "We need some stone crab claws to go along with our oysters. I promised Mr. Darling both. Due to his age and failing health, he'll be leaving Captiva next week for the last time, so I want him to have some of his favorite Florida seafood before he goes. Sure wish we had some lobster around here!"

The tide had just started to flow when he handed me one of the rods and a bucket.

"Follow me for a while and I'll show you what we're up to," Tommy said as he waded toward the mudflat.

He walked up to a small mound of white sand near what looked like a flooded burrow entrance, sort of like a very wet gopher tortoise hole. He bent down and stuck the curved end of the rod into the watery hole. In a moment, I heard a clanking sound when the rod contacted a solid object and stopped. Tommy slowly removed the tool from the burrow. Firmly attached to the metal with both of its powerful claws was an enormous — and irritated — stone crab. Tommy set the rod with crab attached down on the mud. The aggressive crab soon let go and tried to reach its burrow, threatening us by waving its claws in our direction. Tommy reached down and placed the steel section of the rod in the crab's path. The crab pinched the metal with both claws, and while it was preoccupied, Tommy bent down and grasped the crab with a claw in each hand and examined its bottom side.

"This is a male," he said.

I answered, "You sex them just as you do a blue crab, right?" "That's correct," Tommy replied and added, "Since it's a male, we can legally take both claws. If you catch a female, you can only take one claw. But I have an ethical problem with harvesting both claws on males, because it likely renders them incapable of defense and unable to feed properly. So we'll just take the crusher claw, the biggest one, off males and females alike.

"The technique in getting a crab out of its burrow is not to harm the crab by forcing it out; just let it grab hold and pull it out slowly. Once you've got one in your hands, break the claw off quickly and cleanly, like this." He neatly broke off the claw, then continued. "Studies have shown that stone crabs will regenerate their claws to full size after two molts. That's about one year."

After about an hour, the tide covered the flat with about a foot of water, so it became much more difficult to find the holes. We each had several pounds of claws, although I must admit Tommy's experience paid off. He had more claws than I did.

When we arrived back at the lighthouse, I went about some duties I had in the office, and Tommy went to his kitchen to boil and properly cool the claws. Suddenly, I heard a blood-curdling scream from the other end of the house. Startled, I dashed through the complex to find Tommy in the kitchen with a giant stone crab claw very tightly attached to his bleeding thumb. In picking up the claws to drop them into the boiling pot, one of them, because of some post-mortem reflex, had clamped onto Tommy's thumb. He was in great pain, cussing and trying to pry the claw loose with an oyster knife. He succeeded, but for days afterward his thumb was swollen, bruised, and painful.

"That's known as a crab's revenge," he would later tell anyone who asked.

In the afternoon, I learned that we would be going to Captiva to visit Mr. Darling.

* * *

Jay Norwood Darling was born in Norwood, Michigan, on October 21, 1876. As a young man, he was headed for a career as a physician, but at age 23, he took a job with the *Sioux City* (Iowa) *Journal* as a cub reporter. His drawing ability was a hobby, a sideline that he dabbled in basically for his own enjoyment. His hidden talent surfaced when a lawyer he was interviewing refused to be photographed. So, instead of a snapshot for the story, Darling submitted a caricature to his editor, who promptly published it. His first political cartoon appeared in the *Journal* on June 27, 1900. Six years later, after his marriage to Genevieve "Penny" Pendleton, they relocated and he joined the *Des Moines* (Iowa) *Register and Leader*. His first cartoon, entitled "Soft Coal," was printed on December 9, 1906. It was not well received by religious leaders of the day. So began "Ding" Darling's long career — on the cutting edge of controversial subject matter.

After five successful years with the *Register and Leader*, Darling accepted a position with the *New York Globe*. Management at the *Globe* tried to steer his creativity toward comic strips, but he resisted and his career stayed the course of an editorial cartoonist.

In February 1913, fed up with the Big Apple, he returned to Iowa and the *Register and Leader*. On his 40th birthday in 1916, he became syndicated through the *New York Herald-Tribune*. That same year, the *Register and Leader* became the *Des Moines Register*.

His signature, [1] which appeared on his cartoons, was neither original nor new to the Darling family. His father and brother had used the nickname before him, and he himself had used it in college. Originally, Jay N. Darling signed his wonderful creations simply D'ing, an abbreviation of Darling. This developed into his unique stylized signature that became known around the world. Years later, he embellished his signature to send a signal to First Lady Lou Hoover. During the presidency of his friend Herbert Hoover, Jay and Penny Darling often visited the White House. On one of these occasions, Mrs. Hoover asked Mr. Darling to somehow identify for her those cartoons which he actually produced by himself from beginning to end. (At this point in his career, he had taken on an assistant who would ink in many of Darling's pencil layouts.) So as part of this secret pact, he agreed to mark the cartoons that he personally completed, with a small "x" at the end of "Ding." [2]

"Ding" Darling was an ardent sportsman and waterfowl hunter, but he recognized early in his life that wetlands and wildlands were essential. His conservation-oriented cartoons illustrate this deep-rooted conviction that became a lifelong commitment. It has long been recognized that in those opinions which he graphically and vociferously conveyed, he was identifying his stance on vital issues. He was a pioneering environmental advocate almost a hundred years before his time.

In 1931, it was widely rumored that "Ding" Darling would run for the U. S. Senate from Iowa. This never materialized, but that same year, Joseph Stalin invited him to visit the Soviet Union.

In 1932, due to his political activism, he was seated as an Iowa delegate at the Republican National Convention. He distrusted Roosevelt; in fact, he confided to friends that he saw a welfare state coming. He was later appointed to the Iowa State Fish and Game Commission. To his astonishment, in 1934, elected President Roosevelt appointed him to serve on a three-man national commission to study threats to wildlife species.

[1]   Darling's trade signature.

[2]   Darling's trade signature w/X.

"Ding" Darling was appointed as Chief of the Bureau of Biological Survey on March 10, 1934, just four days after the President signed the Duck Stamp bill. He remained in this position only 20 months, but in that period, he developed a new direction for the Bureau's programs. Under the management of key people whom Mr. Darling hired, this Federal agency would later become the U. S. Fish and Wildlife Service.

"Ding" Darling designed the first Duck Stamp, today's Migratory Bird Hunting and Conservation Stamp, in 1935. Later that year, he developed the nation's most restricted waterfowl hunting season ever to ease the pressure on depleted populations of migratory waterfowl. Also this same year, he first visited 'Tween-Waters Inn on Captiva, a place recommended to him by his brother. "Ding" and Penny Darling fell in love with Captiva at first sight.

In February 1936, Darling was elected as the first president of the organization that became today's National Wildlife Federation. In 1942, he received his second Pulitzer Prize for a cartoon; he also completed a building project on (or I should say, very close to) Captiva. He had created a design for a piling-supported residence, completely surrounded by water, that would be very private. He even installed a drawbridge to prevent uninvited guests from disturbing him. He continued his editorial cartooning career, via the U. S. Mail, during his winter sojourns on Captiva until his retirement on April 24, 1949.

The Izaak Walton League requested that the Secretary of the Interior alter the format for Duck Stamp designs to allow the 1950–1951 stamp to bear a portrait of "Ding" Darling. Mr. Darling learned of this and wrote to the Secretary requesting, almost demanding, that such an innovation not be accepted. The Duck Stamp should remain as it was conceived, a waterfowl stamp that has raised millions of dollars for acquisition and preservation of critical wetlands — one of "Ding" Darling's hard-won battles.

In the mid-1950s, the Darlings sold their treasured piling home on Captiva. The house still stands today. For years afterward, he would lament that his advancing years and ill health caused him to give up his "fish house," and he sorely missed it. Thereafter, the Darlings returned to spend their winters at 'Tween-Waters Inn.

* * *

At 3:30 that afternoon, Tommy and I loaded up the car with the goodies we had collected that morning, along with some beverage of Tommy's choice. We headed for 'Tween-Waters Inn.

The Darlings were staying in one of the cottages on the southern part of the property. Mr. Darling was sitting on the screen porch when we arrived; Mrs. Darling was out.

"Hello, compadres! What brings you to Captiva?," he called as we stepped out of the sedan.

Laughing, Tommy said, "Charles and I did a biological survey this morning, and we collected some samples for you to examine."

We unloaded the car and carried the morning's haul up onto the porch and set them on the table in front of him.

"My God!" "Two of my favorites. Tommy, you know what seafood does for my asthma — but what the hell!"

Tommy brought out a bottle of whiskey, poured three stout drinks, and the festivities and conversation began. I learned many reasons why the two men had become such good friends: They shared a few common bonds. For example, like Tommy, "Ding" Darling was an aviator and was one of the first licensed pilots in Iowa. Each winter up until 1956, he would frequently fly around Florida with Tommy, and Tommy even checked him out[3] in the floatplane.

In the often one-sided conversation, Mr. Darling let us know in no uncertain terms that he was very concerned about the preservation and acquisition of wilderness areas. He insisted that, "Wild areas and shallow bay bottoms should be given a quick review and nailed down for sane management before those blood-hungry real estate promoters have taken their pound of flesh and moved on to other harvests."

I thought, "Here he is, 83 years old, and still pursuing his obsessive dedication to the conservation and preservation of our country's natural resources. What a unique, special, and endearing individual!"

"Penny and I will be packing up in a couple of days," Mr. Darling continued. "We're going up to Clearwater, where we'll be staying for our remaining winters, to be near our son, Doctor John — that is, as long as our health holds up. The years are catching up

---

[3]   Aviation jargon for approving a novice pilot's performance in a test flight and signing him/her off in the pilot's logbook for solo flying in that aircraft type.

with me. Hell, I was supposed to die back in 1925. Peritonitis damn near did me in. In fact, papers across the country had me on the brink of death. Some even printed obituaries. Probably won't be so lucky the next time around."

We finished off the oysters and crab claws, washing them down with a second whiskey.

When it came time to leave, Mr. Darling thanked us for the wonderful meal and said, "I wish I could have helped you two collect those specimens. Tommy, you and Charles come visit us. We'll be at the Fort Harrison Hotel. Charles, keep up the good work and stick with it! The Fish and Wildlife Service is a great outfit."

Tommy was mostly quiet on our way back down-island. During the silence, something suddenly struck me: "I have never heard Tommy address his old friend as 'Ding.' It was always Mr. Darling, always. What respect he has for that man!"

J. N. "Ding" Darling, probably the country's most significantly successful wheeler dealer, mover, and shaker ever to enter the conservation field, succumbed to a major stroke on February 12, 1962. "Ding" Darling had left us, and we were saddened. But his greatness would live on.

9

SKEETER HEAVEN

"Charles, get up! Come here and look at this window!," Jean yelled.

I jumped out of bed to find that the window screen in the hallway opposite our quarters bathroom was literally covered, like a black window shade, with thousands upon thousands of mosquitos. The window was on the leeward side of the house, and the insects had congregated there during the night.

"I believe that's the most mosquitos I've ever seen in one spot!" I exclaimed. I was in a state of disbelief. Even from several feet away, we could actually hear the humming sound generated by the tens of thousands of mosquito wings.

"There's quite a few there," Jean acknowledged, "but I've seen them thicker than that on Marco when I was little. They'd get so thick on us on the way to the school bus, we didn't swat them. We just took our hands and wiped them off."

It was May 1959, and heavy showers announcing the soon-to-arrive summer rainy season had just started. By this time, Sanibel was known the world over for its generous population of salt marsh mosquitos. Breathing in and fighting mosquitos had become a day and night fact of life on the island. One mosquito trap had collected so many in one night that Sanibel was established as the salt marsh mosquito capitol of the world. This record remained undefeated for 24 years.

The enormous number of salt marsh mosquitos was collected on September 15, 1950, at a New Jersey light trap station located just south of the Sanibel ferry landing. That night, 364,672 individuals were collected: 265,216 females and 99,456 males.

The New Jersey light trap is still used today. It consists of an all-night-burning, low-intensity light (25-Watt bulb), which attracts the night-flying nuisances, and a small fan, which diverts the bugs into a chemical-laced killing jar that doubles as a collection receptacle. The trap might have caught even more that September 15th, but the fan motor was shorted out by the insects, and the collection is considered to be incomplete.

Sanibel's record was broken in 1974 when one New Jersey light trap on Grand Cayman, Cayman Islands, British West Indies, caught 793,103 mosquitos in a single night.

A total of 26 different species of mosquitos have been collected on Sanibel and Captiva Islands since consistent record-keeping began in 1949. Another form, the 27th, was documented as being present prior to 1949. Of these, the black salt marsh mosquito (*Aedes taeniorhynchus*) is the champion nuisance.

In Florida, the salt marsh mosquito is a potential threat to humans because it transmits such diseases as St. Louis Encephalitis. In the Caribbean, the same species is known as a vector of a filarial parasite in humans. It is potentially capable of reaching Florida from the infected blood of Haitian refugees.

Sanibel's role as a major mosquito producer is linked to the wet/dry cycles of its interior fresh-water wetlands and the mangrove-forested areas which are subject to periodic tidal flooding. On Sanibel and Captiva, unflooded wetlands provide the ultimate sites for egg deposition by salt marsh mosquitos.

* * *

All barrier islands are dynamic, ever-changing, emergent lands and are subject to all the forces of Nature. Following the last Ice Age, Captiva Island was formed. It was a typical narrow, lower-Gulf-coast barrier island with a north-south orientation. Due to progressive changes in the Earth's ocean levels, Captiva likely rose to its present elevation about 10–15,000 years ago.

Up until the first quarter of the twentieth century, Captiva was about nine miles long. In 1921, a major hurricane began to divide the island in two, then storms in 1923 and 1926 made Redfish Pass a permanent feature. The Pass was created by tidal surge and scouring wave washover, and it now separates the two islands of Captiva and Upper (North) Captiva.

Soon after rising above sea level, prehistoric Captiva began to slowly develop a long, extended appendage of sand which curved off to the southeast. Over the centuries, this "leg" became Sanibel Island. The original leg, or ridge, is located within the boundary of the J. N. "Ding" Darling National Wildlife Refuge. Mature old-growth live oaks growing on its well-drained, ancient soils are evidence of the ridge's presence. Today, the more eastern part of this ridge is Sanibel-Captiva Road and has more recently been dubbed the Mid-Island Ridge.

A near-shore, or littoral, current prevails along the Gulf beaches of Sanibel and Captiva Islands. It passes by the beautiful shell-strewn outer shorelines in a southerly direction. Soils and sediments, which occur as suspended particles in the moving water column, are transported along the beaches by the littoral drift. Primarily the remnants of once-living marine organisms, these materials nourish and naturally maintain the integrity of the waterfront by continuously collecting in the intertidal zone and eventually on the beach dune system above. These soils and sediments are 90 percent biogenic.

This upland developmental process is known as **accretion**. However, other factors sometimes come into play and prevent suspended solids from coming to rest on the beaches. This results in erosion. Prior to the creation of Redfish Pass, the natural system worked well for Captiva, and over many centuries it supported the slow nurture and growth of Sanibel Island.

The water-borne soils were deposited on the Gulf side of the slowly maturing Mid-Island Ridge. Solids from the sea bottom or from submerged offshore sandbars were heaped against the growing uplands during violent hurricanes. Other storms also moved soils from the Gulf bottom to reach nearly the same positions as the ridges formed earlier. So over time, a series of almost parallel ridges formed, and continue to do so, along the length of Sanibel.

By anyone flying several thousand feet above Sanibel, this storm-produced ridge network is easily seen. The most recent ridges are those that parallel Sanibel's Gulf-front dune system from Point Ybel to Blind Pass. This ecological zone has been named the Gulf Beach Ridge. The spaces between each of the ancient inland ridges are often long, low, seasonally-flooded swales or depressions. Because they became isolated by subsequent major storms not long after they were formed centuries ago, most of these depressions have long-since partially filled with vegetative detritus. This occurred by means of a natural process called **eutrophication** — producing a thick blanket of fertile organic soils between the shell ridges. Originally, the swales were colonized by a variety of pioneering emergent aquatic plants and grasses.[1] Some swales are narrow and others approach a mile in width. Together they create variable-size "compartments" that are connected, infrequently and seasonally, by a high water-table aquifer during very wet summers.

This system of ridges and swales was named the Sanibel Bayou, or Sanibel Slough, not long after the first homesteaders arrived on these shores. More recently, this unique interior wetland system became known as the "Sanibel River." So, the land surface on Sanibel, situated between the Mid-Island and Gulf Beach Ridges, is a large reservoir of fresh water. Once saturated and flooded by precipitation, the rising water level temporarily brings the subterranean fresh-water "lens" to an elevation above the ground surface of the swale bottom and into view. When flood waters include sea-water storm surge, the ecology of the Sanibel Slough (my preferred name for the system, because it was originally marsh-like in character) is set back temporarily, but the system as a whole is soon regenerated and its uniqueness protected by periodic inundation by sea water. The elevation attained by high water levels in this basin-like floodplain is subject to the whims of rainfall or hurricane-produced storm surges.

Historically, when the Sanibel Slough flooded to capacity, it overflowed across the outer confining ridges of the basin and became the short-lived "Sanibel River." The water level crested and overflowed the ridges, creating a deep, gorge-like, large rill across the Gulf Beach Ridge. Through this rill, the contents of the Sanibel Slough swiftly discharged into the Gulf of Mexico. At the

[1]   Now of course, the severe invasion of exotic and noxious plants in the 1960s has changed these areas.

same time, the flowing fresh water produced a noticeable current as it discharged along its meandering course from the innermost reaches of the Sanibel Slough.

When the fresh water finally dropped below its flood-stage head, the breakouts (rills) were sealed by dam-forming accretion, a result of wave action in the Gulf of Mexico. Generally speaking, during summers that had normal precipitation patterns, the "Sanibel River" would breach the Gulf Beach Ridge about three-quarters of a mile west of the Sanibel Lighthouse. However, during heavy and torrential tropical weather, this one breakout was not enough.

When the Sanibel Slough was transformed into the "Sanibel River" but the rate of discharge through the lone opening could not keep pace with increased ongoing precipitation, as many as three additional breakouts could develop. One of these openings developed at Lake Louise, another at Stewart Pond, and a third near the island's west end. The third overflowed during very high flood levels and discharged into Kesson's Bayou.

Sheet flow was also common across the land near the present-day intersection of Tarpon Bay Road and Sanibel-Captiva Road, emptying into Tarpon Bay. The massive discharge of fresh water usually occurred in the fall, after normal summer rains, or following a tropical storm or hurricane. What little precious fresh water remained at the surface in the interior of Sanibel — water that had not flowed from the Sanibel Slough's basin — began to evaporate as the winter and spring dry seasons approached.

* * *

The pesky salt marsh mosquito is unique. The females never deposit their eggs on water as most species do. As adults, they can fly considerable distances to bother inland-dwelling humans, pets, and livestock. Sanibel-hatched salt marsh mosquitoes have been marked and collected as far as 50 miles from the island.

The life cycle of the salt marsh mosquito begins when the female deposits her eggs on damp soils. Each female can deposit egg clutches that exceed 200 eggs, and each is capable of producing two or three clutches during its brief lifetime. Because of the sheer gross numbers of adults, the eggs can reach extreme, mind-boggling densities.

Blood meals are not always necessary for the species to reproduce. It has been documented that in South Florida, as in other parts of the world, the salt marsh mosquito can reproduce **autogenously** — egg development without a prior blood meal.

Before the days of mosquito control on Sanibel, salt marsh mosquito egg counts commonly reached one-half billion eggs per acre of drying Sanibel Slough bottom. Some optimum production areas yielded 45,000 eggs per square foot, or two billion per acre. Normally rising water levels (due to regular monthly spring tides, infrequent winter rain storms, or normal summer precipitation) flooded the high swales of the mangrove periphery of Sanibel or its interior slough. Dormant eggs hatched in these areas to launch another generation of mosquitos. The cycle ultimately released mosquito broods at densities commensurate with the numbers of eggs deposited on the exposed slough bottoms.

With the establishment of the Sanibel-Captiva Mosquito Control District in 1953, serious mosquito control efforts started on the islands. By 1954, four separate districts had been established in Lee County; however, the tax base was not sufficient to support them all. Only the Fort Myers Mosquito Control District, which was organized in 1950, was sufficiently funded to operate at an effective level.

In 1955, the Lee County Commission was asked to establish a county-wide mosquito control program. However, they declined. Late that same year, the Florida Legislature passed a special act to establish the Lee County Mosquito Control District and fund the necessary equipment. However, no monies were made available to buy insecticide for mosquito reduction in Lee County. The State Board of Health also provided matching funds to local districts.

In November 1956, Wayne Miller was selected to administer the mosquito control program in Lee County. Before that time, officials from the State Board of Health had conducted extensive mosquito studies on Sanibel at their lighthouse-based field station. They had designed a Sanibel-specific protocol based on ecologically sound principles of biological mosquito control.

But the long-established trapping stations were still functioning, and nightly mosquito counts were still reaching 100,000 mosquitos two or three times a year.

Wayne Miller launched his program in early 1957. He moved state-purchased draglines to Sanibel, and his operators began to make channels in the Sanibel Slough. The project began near today's Beach Road and continued toward the west. By April 1961, the workers made the cut into Tarpon Bay. The District built a water control structure there, and by the middle of 1962, the draglines reached Stewart Pond.

The plan that the District had developed was primarily one of water management. In theory, the zealous scheme required that the slough-flooding water-table aquifer would be maintained as high as hydrologically possible without causing long-term flooding of developed lands. Maintaining as high a water level as possible as far into the dry season as possible would interrupt the salt marsh mosquito's life cycle. This flooding would cover up the once prime mosquito egg-laying habitat and prevent a return to former high levels of mosquitos by denying them their required habitat.

The Sanibel Slough bottom was excavated, and the myriad unconnected swales were tied into the main "Sanibel River" channel by a network of lateral canals. In general, all the swales were now interconnected at the surface of the water-table aquifer. Other than a few artificial spoil ponds from which fill was removed to raise grades at an increasing number of subdivisions, permanent fresh water had arrived on Sanibel. No longer were tiny populations of mosquito larvae-eating minnows confined to a few alligator holes during spring droughts. The new "Sanibel River" hosted a variety of small fish species that favored mosquito larvae. Now, when rising water triggered the dormant salt marsh mosquito eggs to hatch and billions of larvae began the metamorphosis to adulthood, the minnows moved about with the rising water and invaded every nook and cranny of the Sanibel Slough, gorging themselves on the newly hatched larvae. Biological mosquito control began to work, and Sanibel Island became more habitable and tolerable. Mosquito counts at the New Jersey light traps began to drop, and the tide of the mosquito war had turned.

The Lee County Mosquito Control District also used other tools in their arsenal of mosquito-fighting weaponry to deny superiority to their targeted enemy. In the early 1950s, the Sanibel mosquito control effort used a truck-mounted sprayer to discharge

DDT, a persistent toxin now recognized as hazardous. By 1958, when Malathion became the preferred adulticide, DDT was phased out by the Lee County Mosquito Control District. Malathion formulations resulted in dispersal of a reduced, less environmentally harmful quantity of active ingredients per acre. Malathion had also been found to be far more species-specific than DDT. Over time, however, adult salt marsh mosquitos began to develop a resistance to Malathion. Therefore, on July 2, 1965, the District began to use Baytex as its primary insecticide in the adulticide program.

At the same time as the adulticide phase of its operations were being conducted, the District also launched a larvicide program. In the early 1960s, they used a chemical known as Paris Green, and by 1971, they had sprayed 1.2 million pounds of this chemical on Sanibel and Captiva.

By 1971, Paris Green was no longer available, and the District adopted the larvicide Abate as their standard larval weapon. Today, Abate is applied primarily by helicopter and to a lesser degree by truck-mounted spray apparatus. But new compounds and technologies continue to be introduced as strategic components of the refined arsenal.

The work of the Lee County Mosquito Control District on Sanibel has been a success. Their efforts have effectively reduced the populations of the troublesome salt marsh mosquito to manageable levels. Their program has made the interior wetlands of Sanibel Island a better place for man, fish, bird, and beast alike.

In recent years, there has been some criticism of the District's mosquito program, in particular its continued use of certain larvicides. These larvicides are not fully understood relative to any actual or theoretical impacts to the local estuarine ecosystem. The District has to cope with a constant barrage of complaints from newcomers who yell and scream when a few thirsty mosquitos alight on their tender, exposed skins. Rather than moaning, groaning, and complaining, we all can do our part to help. Simply swat them! We no longer have to wipe them off!

* * *

By early August 1959, the draglines had almost reached Tarpon Bay Road. As plans were being developed for ditching to the west of this road, Tommy and Wayne Miller determined that the "Sanibel River" channel should follow a realigned route along the southern boundary of the Bailey Tract; namely, it should not follow the natural wide swale. The canal was to be excavated in a straight line and be much wider than the earlier ditching to the east of the Bailey Tract. This would allow Tommy to set down the floatplane at a new site away from corrosive salt water.

I was delegated the responsibility to find and cut three or four straight white mangrove saplings. These were to be used as end and center markers to delineate the proposed canal's course so that the dragline operators could align the ditch. After I cut the trees, we attached red flagging ribbon to the top end of each for better visibility. The canal was laid out without the advantage of instruments, and we used the southeast and southwest corner monuments of the Bailey Tract for the end dimensions. The center point, established as a working guide, was located when Tommy climbed a dragline's boom and tried to visually line up a pole with the mangrove staff we had installed at the western end. I held the pole about a half-mile away midway on the canal's northern bank-to-be.

The dragline operators doing the digging faithfully followed our stakes. That's why there's a bend in the canal. Tommy moved the aircraft from his Tarpon Bay home to the Bailey Tract Seaplane Canal on November 16, 1959.

* * *

Colon Moore loved three things in life: the U. S. Marine Corps, Busch beer, and operating a dragline. I never knew which was his favorite. He was a native of Arkansas, born there in 1907. He served as a "Leatherneck" in the Pacific Theater during World War II. Following the War, Colon ended up in Florida. One of his greatest personal achievements (the soft-spoken man seldom bragged) was that he had worked from beginning to end on the original Sunshine Skyway span that crossed Tampa Bay. In 1961, Colon arrived on Sanibel to work for a Fort Myers dragline contractor named Harold Pipkins. Later, in March 1962, he began work as a dragline operator for the Lee County Mosquito Control District. At that point in time, work on the ditching program had reached just west of Rabbit Road.

The decision was made to create a series of impoundments in the mosquito-laden mangrove forest west of Tarpon Bay and north of State Road 867, now called Sanibel-Captiva Road. The impoundments were designed in theory only, not on paper. Their acreage, dike location and elevation, and water management methodology would be developed later, as time passed and as field conditions dictated. The hope was that these impoundments would hold a sufficient amount of water to long-term flood the area known as the "Sanibel Sandflats." This would prevent the salt marsh mosquitos from laying their eggs.

On October 2, 1962, two draglines left the shoulder of the paved road and started through the nearly impenetrable mangrove jungle. One of the machines was under the skilled control of Colon Moore. Once they moved north of the Mid-Island Ridge, the progress slowed. Each machine had its own set of heavy, thick timber mats. Each mat had to be properly placed in succession and aligned under the dragline as it moved along to prevent the heavy piece of equipment from sinking into the mud.

It was a delight to watch Colon move ahead by skillfully manipulating the control levers and pedals from his operator's chair inside the dragline's cab. He was truly one with his machine. He artistically connected the cable eyes on the mat he was about to move with the hook on his drag cable and swing the wooden apparatus around into position. When he reached the mangroves, prior to moving out into the tidal system, he first had to dig enough spoil from the borrow ditch and place and grade it with the $^3/_4$-yard dragline bucket into a berm. Then he dug, moved mats, and "walked" the tracked equipment along on the mat-wide berm.

One dragline worked each side of the dike until they had gone just a few hundred yards beyond the first turn. Then other needs required that one machine be removed, so Colon worked on alone. We'll catch up with him later.

10

TURTLE TIMES

Tommy and I are supposed to make a beach patrol tonight," I told Jean at lunch on May 8, 1959. "He wants to show me the conditions of the beach, problem areas, and various trails to and from the beach. At least that's what he told me. I really think he wants to check me out in the jeep before he lets me go out on my own."

The jeep was a 1952 military Willys 4x4 with a hinged windshield and no top. It was equipped with a 24-volt electrical and ignition system and narrow, military-tread tires. It was the vehicle I routinely operated on workdays, but I never had a reason to drive on the beach much further west from Lighthouse Point than Lake Louise.

Jean and Leslie watched us from the porch as I cranked up. Over the noise of the jeep, I could hear Jean call, "Ya'll be careful out there. Hope you find a turtle."

It was a little after 9 o'clock when Tommy and I drove from under his quarters straight ahead and onto the beach. The tide was ebbing, and several yards of exposed wet sand below the high tide line made it easy to drive along in two-wheel drive.

Turning in my direction, Tommy said, "When operating below the high-tide line, always try to maintain a constant speed. Just in case you have motor trouble or begin to bog down, you'll have enough momentum to get up out of the wet sand and above high tide. Then if the jeep ever quits on you, a change of tide won't catch you too low and inundate the jeep."

I responded, "I was once in a jeep that a friend intentionally drove out into the surf, almost totally submerging it, on Bonita Beach. It was his father's jeep, and it sure didn't last long after that. The salt water ruined it — it was only a few weeks until it was a pile of rust. I like my job; I'm not about to ruin a Government jeep."

We arrived at the Casa Ybel, a cottage complex at Knapp's Point, which is Sanibel's southernmost projection into the Gulf of Mexico. A line of old pilings blocked our way. Because those farthest out were surrounded by waves, I couldn't drive out and around them, nor could the jeep fit between them. So, as I laced my way through the group of cottages, we were forced to drive up behind an old wooden bulkhead. We soon ran onto a familiar shell-surfaced road at the western end of the Casa Ybel. We followed the road and continued westward, headed for the Island Inn.

This was a long-established, Australian pine-lined, Gulf-front road located south of modern-day West Gulf Drive. For almost two miles, it followed the frontal Gulf beach ridge and connected the Casa Ybel and the Island Inn. Then in 1960, it was obliterated by a hurricane that changed the shape of the Sanibel Island outer beach.

As we drove along the beach, we passed other vehicles. Like us, some were driving on the beach, and a few others were parked while the drivers surf-fished. Vehicles on the beach were common in those days — a summer recreational, insect-escaping pastime. It was a normal everyday fact of island life until 1963, when the Lee County Board of County Commissioners passed an ordinance prohibiting it. Several cars and trucks were parked at a section of beach called "The Rocks." As we approached, I could see several fishermen standing out in the water several yards off the dry beach, which was littered with dozens of recently caught large snook. The fish, extra fishing poles, lanterns, and beer- and soda-stuffed ice chests nearly blocked our way.

"The Rocks" area of Sanibel consists of a parallel set of ancient limestone-based rock formations that run along the beach for a short distance. Some years, depending on beach-related erosion and accretion factors, some of the rock outcrops nearest the beach may be exposed or be covered with sand. Those offshore are always submerged. To this day, fishermen who know about this unpublicized fishing hotspot wade out to the farthest accessible rock formation, almost neck-deep, and catch impressive-sized snook. Today, however, the area is off-limits to non-residents, unless they are guests of residents or are tenants of the few nearby rental units. In season, it is a favorite place to find serious snook fishermen and at any other time a few thrill-seeking shark chasers.

More than just orienting me to the Sanibel beach, our patrol was also an enforcement effort. We would occasionally stop and talk to fishermen, most of whom we both knew, and Tommy would check snook sizes and limits. Although we hadn't seen any sea turtle crawls, which are the bulldozer-like tracks the females leave on the beach as they slowly haul themselves out to lay eggs, this was also a turtle-protection patrol.

Besides his Federal authority, Tommy had a State commission allowing him to enforce State wildlife regulations. In a pinch, he could also exercise general police power.

I was in probationary status at the time and would not receive my Federal law enforcement authority credentials until January 1960. Tommy then issued me, without any fanfare or training, a bronze U. S. Fish and Wildlife Service badge and an old military .38-caliber revolver. Now I was authorized to enforce the laws and regulations of six Federal acts pertaining to Federal fish and wildlife conservation laws. On August 30, 1961, I was issued Deputy Wildlife Officer Commission No. 75 from the Florida Game and Fresh Water Fish Commission. It would be three years before I would receive any law-enforcement training.

Once past "The Rocks," the beach became softer and I had to drop down into high-range four-wheel drive.

Tommy told me, "When you get to this area, you'd best stay up above the high-tide line if you can, unless you have to get on the lower beach to negotiate conditions. I usually goose the jeep until I can get up on top again. We can't go but a mile or more further, just a little past the Tradewinds subdivision. There's a lot of erosion this side of Blind Pass, and we'll have to leave the beach and drive through the woods to get there." The driveable section of beach, from the lighthouse to the Tradewinds, was about nine miles long.

Our trip back to the lighthouse was uneventful. The tide had turned, and most fishermen had caught their limits and left the beach.

A few nights later, Jean and I and Leslie went on our first turtle run together. Because it was a week night, there were fewer cars out on the beach. About two miles west of where Tarpon Bay Road met with the Gulf of Mexico, my straining eyes suddenly saw in the headlights a turtle crawling across the beach way out ahead of us.

"Turtle!" I yelled and quickly cut off the lights and stopped the jeep. I was looking at my first Sanibel loggerhead. Once our eyes had adjusted to the darkness, we could see that the loggerhead had continued to move across the beach, to a point nearly up to the outer edge of the pioneer vegetation and next to a recently planted coconut palm. A small cottage complex, which later became Beachview Cottages, was under construction on the upper Gulf beach ridge. There was little wind, so we could hear the turtle digging, tossing sand and shells aside as she removed dry sand from the beach surface. When she reached moist soil, she began to excavate her egg chamber.

Then the sandflies found us. Jean was prepared — she had brought long-sleeved shirts and a thin sheet to cover her and the baby. I put on a light nylon jacket and cap to keep them out of my hair and sprayed us all with a light mist of Gulfspray from a Flit gun. It didn't seem to help.

Sandflies, more correctly known as biting midges, are also called no-see-ums, although I never heard this term used on Sanibel until the late '60s. The word "no-see-ums" likely came from tourists visiting from the mid-Atlantic coastal states. These annoying insects are usually less than one-eighth inch long, almost invisible. They are overly abundant on Sanibel and Captiva Islands because of the vast acres of mangrove forests and marsh, their optimum habitat. Their cucumber-shaped eggs are like those of the salt marsh mosquito, in that they are deposited on wet mud, hatch after a three-day incubation period, and develop through a series of larval stages. Depending on the species, the larval part of the life cycle may take several months. The near-adult pupae stage is brief, lasting only two or three days.

Only the female sandfly bites, using special mandibular cutting teeth which line its proboscis. A small cut is made in the host's skin, an anti-clotting chemical is injected through the insect's saliva, and a minute pool of blood is sucked up by the tiny fly.

Seven species of sandflies are known to occur on the islands, and three of these are truly severe pests. Prior to the advent of air conditioning, life along the southwest Florida coast could be seasonally miserable for us humans because of mosquitos and sandflies. For our first ten years, we didn't have air conditioning at the Sanibel Island Light Station.

Suddenly, a gentle sea breeze came to our rescue and began to disperse the sandflies. With seven-month-old Leslie in my arms, Jean and I escaped the jeep full of starving bugs and slowly moved, crouching, toward the turtle. Pointing a small low-intensity pen-light to the area behind the reptile's shell, I could see that she was still digging. The rear flippers reached into the cavity and curled to trap about a half-cup of sand. She raised this soil to the surface and set it aside. With the opposite flipper, the turtle then flicked the sand, sending it flying off to the side. Using alternating flippers, the loggerhead continued to dig. When her flippers were at extreme extension and she could no longer reach the bottom of the cavity, the egg chamber was fully prepared.

In a few moments she stopped digging, and the dark turtle shape began to move up and down slightly and ever so slowly. I knew she was about to deposit her eggs. I knelt down and positioned my light to peek between her slightly parted rear flippers. I pushed some sand back from the lip of the flask, or pear-shaped hole, she had dug to see the egg cavity better. The pink ovipositor, a temporary external extension of the internal oviducts, was extended from the cloacal opening and swelled as she forced an egg, and more eggs, into the 18-inch-deep hole. Just prior to expelling an egg, the loggerhead would curl her rear flippers upward ever so slightly to signal that oviposition was about to occur. Each pliable-shelled, spherical egg was drenched with a heavy mucous-like fluid as it fell against another at the bottom of the chamber.

Initially, the eggs were deposited one at a time, but as things progressed, the ping-pong-ball-sized eggs dropped three, four, even five at a time. When it seemed the cavity would overflow, egg laying ceased. Then with her rear flippers, the turtle began to cover the eggs by reaching out and pulling sand over them. After the nest was covered with several inches of sand, the turtle paused to rest.

She had been oblivious to what was going on around her while she laid her eggs. During that time, while she was preoccupied and almost in a trance-like state, I walked around her in the darkness. This turtle was large — her shell was nearly four feet long. And as is typical for loggerheads, the shell was covered with a variety of animal and plant organisms.

I said, "Jean, watch this." I pressed my hand against the very top of the shell and quickly dragged it across the algae-covered surface. A bright white glow temporarily appeared. "That's bioluminescence — cold light — produced when my hand pressure-stressed the planktonic animals that are mixed in with the algae on her carapace. These are the same microscopic invertebrates that cause the waves to glow when they break offshore on dark nights like this."

"Come look at her tears," Jean said. "Poor thing, I'd cry too if I had just done all that work!"

Thick tears were indeed flowing from each eye. Folklore has a romantic explanation for the tears: Some people believe that turtle tears convey maternal sadness, a feeling of despair for the future of the offspring contained in the eggs buried in the sand. Another more probable explanation is that the tears keep the eyes moist and wash away particles of sand which may inadvertently land on them while the female does her sand-flinging routine. From a biological standpoint, because sea turtles live in the salt waters of our oceans and eat sodium-saturated foods, they have developed special salt-purging glands. These glands are located in the eye orbits and function constantly whether the turtle is at sea or on the shore during nesting visits.

The loggerhead began to move again. She reached forward with her front flippers and scooped up virtual flipper-fulls of sand. This was catapulted to the area beside and behind the turtle as she pulled herself forward an inch or so at a time. She continued this until the nest site was well camouflaged. Finding the eggs would be difficult for untrained humans but not for raccoons, which I'm sure were watching from the sea oats. The nest was high enough on the beach profile to be safe from normal tidal washout, so I decided not to relocate the clutch higher up as I had done so often in Naples.

"Look, Charles. She's missing part of her front flipper!" Jean exclaimed.

"Amputees are very common among loggerhead turtles. In fact, most that I've observed have part of one or more flippers missing or great crescent-shaped hunks out of their shells. Most of this damage is due to shark attacks. Turtles are very tough animals, but I'm surprised that they can survive such life-threatening injuries," I replied.

The three of us watched as the sand-covered loggerhead moved across the beach and disappeared into the Gulf.

"Daddy always told me that when loggerheads grow up, they come back to lay their eggs on the same beach they came from. Is that true?" Jean asked.

"I've heard that too," I answered, "but I don't know where that story started. It sure sounds good, sort of folksy romantic. I'll have to think that one over and check the literature."

From the time I first saw the turtle until she reentered the water, the whole event had taken an hour.

The windshield was lowered and resting on the hood, and the breeze felt great as we traveled northwest along the beach. We soon arrived at the section of beach close to Blind Pass, with its impassible barricade of fallen Australian pines. We stopped and star-gazed for a short time before resuming our family adventure.

During our return home, we occasionally noticed the glowing eyes of groups of raccoons reflecting from the jeep's lights. When the jeep came too close, threatening them, they scampered away and disappeared into the vegetation. Soon I saw the double crawl, created by our first turtle's up and down trip, ahead of us on the beach. As we came closer, I was disheartened to find that the 'coons had already discovered our turtle's nest. There were broken eggshells in several piles around the enlarged open egg cavity. I hand-dug into what had been a perfect egg chamber but found no surviving whole eggs. Then and there, my hatred for raccoons intensified.

Frequently throughout the 1959 summer, I continued to patrol the beach at night to mark loggerhead nests and test experimental techniques aimed at reducing raccoon predation. The latter was not easy, and in retrospect I did little to enhance the survival of these marked nests. I used ammonia and Clorox mixes, kerosene, dog repellents, and even burned dry cabbage-palm fronds around nests in hopes of counteracting the raccoons' exceptional ability to smell out the nests.

When torrential, frog-choking rainfall occurred during the rainy season, I found that the nests were not so easily pinpointed by these intelligent animals. The heavy precipitation washed away any odors associated with nesting and eggs. Therefore, eggs that were not depredated prior to rainstorms had a better chance of surviving, at least for the short term. However, I discovered that near the end of incubation, raccoons could once again sense the presence of near full-term, pre-emergent hatchlings several inches beneath the beach surface. It remains unclear if this feat is accomplished by the raccoons' olfactory response (their sense of smell) to odors emanating from under the sand or by the sound of hatchling turtles moving just a few inches below. About 60 percent of the loggerhead nests on Sanibel and Captiva were consumed by 'coons that summer.

In 1959, not much was known about the life cycle of loggerheads. From my viewpoint, it seemed that most of the biological information available simply wasn't accurate, was based on the behavior of other better-known species and was applied to loggerheads in generalities. The most accurate information was obscured by the time it reached the seacoast human population.

That summer, my long-range career plan was reinforced and implemented. I would remain on Sanibel, resist any move by the Fish and Wildlife Service to transfer me, and protect and intimately study my island's population of loggerhead turtles. Furthermore, I was determined that I would accomplish this under a program of my own design and control. My life's work was ahead of me and on track!

Later, my work with loggerheads would develop into a program with broad-based financial and community support. Through the years, the work took on a special element — it was always fun! It gave me such great personal satisfaction that I never tired of being out on the beach. On many nights in the '60s, I would be out on the beach alone all night long. On very busy nights during the height of the nesting season, I wouldn't arrive back at the lighthouse until dawn.

A few people delighted in making artificial nesting crawls along the beach to confuse me. These man-made tracks would lead from the water's edge up to the vegetation and were done with expert realism. The practical joker would usually lie down on his back next to the water, then push himself along with his feet up to the plant line or even into the grass. Two island men who thrived on tricking me were very good at this and could make crawls that truly appeared real. One was Donald Hiers, and the other was my former high school classmate Ralph Woodring. Several times through the years, I stopped and followed their tracks up and into the sea oats before it dawned on me what was going on.

One night I had a chance to get even. I was headed back toward the lighthouse and noticed another vehicle on the beach ahead of me coming in my direction. Suddenly, its lights went out and I no longer knew where it was. Shortly, I noticed the shape of a Model A cutdown parked high on the beach. It was partly concealed, but I could distinguish the silhouettes of three people sitting in it trying to hide. I continued on toward home and a cozy bed.

Less than a mile west of Tarpon Bay Road, contractors had dug a huge hole out on the beach as a source of fill for a motel complex under construction. In those days, digging spoil ponds out on the beach was a common practice to obtain fill. Over time, the pits would fill back in with sand carried by accreting wave overwash. The Lee County Board of County Commissioners outlawed this technique of land development in the mid-60s.

I drove a short distance past the flooded pit, stopped the jeep, and walked back to the pond. I too could make a darned good looking turtle crawl, and I did — a single, perfect one from the surf to the pond. I got back into the jeep, drove a few hundred yards further, and hid the vehicle up among the trees. I walked back, concealed myself near the pond, and waited.

I didn't have to wait long. I heard the engine first, then saw the Model A as it chugged along next to the water without headlights.

Someone yelled, "Turtle! She's crawled up and gone into the hole."

The cutdown stopped and three people hopped out. One took a flashlight and shined its beam across the borrow pit looking for the turtle. Their intentions were not good. These people were out "turtle turning," and any turtle they turned was destined to be hauled off the beach, killed, and cooked.

"I don't see her," one of the three muttered in a voice I recognized.

"Let's look," another shadowy figure said, and momentarily all three men where wading chest-deep in the water, feeling their way along trying to find the turtle.

Meanwhile, hunkered down in the bushes, I was literally cracking up. It was all I could do to keep from yelling out hysterically, revealing the joke, but I didn't. As I walked back to the jeep, holding my side which hurt from laughter, they were still looking. To this day, I have never let the cat out of the bag — until now.

* * *

In 1963, Blind Pass closed up at a point near the southern end of Bowman's Beach Road. There was no longer a separation between Sanibel and Captiva and I could patrol the whole beach. On nights during extreme low tides, I could leave the lighthouse and drive close to the water along the entire beach as far as the S-curve on Captiva, a distance of about 15 miles. I did this frequently until 1967, when erosion seemed to accelerate and fallen trees blocked most of the Captiva beach. In 1972, Blind Pass reopened at its present location at the Blind Pass Bridge.

The days that followed July 4, 1962, were eventful times. The 4th was a Wednesday, and as usual the community had its regular fish fry at the lighthouse. About 300 residents were on hand for this long-standing traditional event to enjoy the fried fresh mullet, hush puppies, and swamp cabbage. We all had a great time. It gave everyone living on the islands the opportunity to meet as a group and visit with old friends. Unfortunately, this was to be the last Independence Day community fish fry at the Sanibel Island Light Station. Times were changing, and the island comradery would soon begin to wane. Even now, the change was inching across San Carlos Bay from Punta Rassa to Sanibel. Later that same year, the

Labor Day cookout would be the last community fish fry the residents of Sanibel and Captiva would enjoy at the lighthouse.

My parents had driven up from Naples for the festivities and planned to stay until the following Sunday. Along with my family, I planned to take them out on the beach a couple of nights for turtle patrols. Jean's and my family had grown with the birth of our son, Charles R. (Chuck) III the previous October 30th. By this time, the old military jeep had been replaced with a newer Willys jeep station wagon. I didn't think much of it — for one thing, it didn't have a windshield that I could lower to enjoy the night air. Maybe that's why the inevitable happened.

When the six of us left the lighthouse, the tide was extremely low, about as low as it could go in the summertime. I had no trouble driving out and around the row of pilings at the Casa Ybel. Even the Gulf bottom beyond the farthest piling was exposed, though wet and soft.

We cruised along the beach toward Captiva. Then we found, chemically treated, and marked two nests that were still intact from the night before. Reaching the turnaround point, I drove off the beach and negotiated a soft, sandy trail that eventually brought us to the Captiva Road. I headed back toward the lighthouse on the hard road. We stopped at our house long enough to enjoy a cup of coffee before continuing westward along the beach again.

Shortly before midnight, we saw a loggerhead just west of "The Rocks." She was completing her nest, and we all enjoyed the stretch and respite from the bouncing jeep as we waited and watched close by. She completed her chore and safely made it to the water. Rather than drive off the beach to go home by road, and after checking the tide, I decided to turn around and drive along the beach to return to Point Ybel. I hoped to encounter another turtle.

The tide had begun to flow; it was on its way back in. Slowly it overwashed and flooded the offshore sandbars which earlier had been exposed and nearly dry. I had just driven around the Knapp's Point bend and began to carefully negotiate the jeep out on the wet sand around the outermost piling off the Casa Ybel. At the moment we were seaward of the piling, the jeep sputtered, died, and would not restart. I tried and tried, but the jeep refused. The rising tide soon lapped around the four tires, and the jeep began to sink into the bottom as the water and waves rose around it. We pushed and pushed, but to no avail. The jeep was inextricably stuck and stubbornly refused to start. I drained the battery trying.

"Damn it! What am I going to do?" I was about to panic.

We decided that Jean and my mother should walk up to the Casa Ybel, use the phone, and rouse some friends out of bed to assist us in another attempt at pushing the jeep out. "Maybe with enough help we can push it out — before its too late," I told her.

Within about a half-hour, a couple of friends arrived after futilely trying to get someone out with another jeep to hook onto the Government vehicle. We pushed without success. The jeep had sunk further into the bottom and by this time was resting on its running boards and axles.

"What about Martin Hier's boom truck?" someone asked. He continued, "I'll go get Donald. Maybe his father will let him use the truck."

It was now nearly three in the morning, and I watched in numb disbelief as the tide and surf slowly rose higher. Soon the water was rushing into the vehicle and breaking over it. Each time a wave struck or a swell surged below it, the jeep would rise in an eerie reaction.

"The jeep's lost, and my job probably is too," I thought as I waited, fighting back tears.

It seemed to take forever, but finally Donald Hiers arrived. As he fed cable from the winch, I waded out, hooked it onto the vehicle, and the slow pull began. Resisting for an instant, the jeep rose up from the submerged hollows where its tires had been embedded and slowly edged toward the dry beach.

Once the jeep was up on the beach and well above the water line, we connected a short chain to the two vehicles, and Donald pulled me out through the Casa Ybel complex and continued on to the lighthouse. My father rode with me, and our friends took Jean, my mother, and the children home to the lighthouse. I don't think Donald ever knew how much I appreciated him rescuing me. He died tragically on March 21, 1982.

In the small hours of the morning, I still had work to do. With a hose, I rinsed the jeep inside and out, trying to prevent the inevitable. After a few hours sleep, I drained and refilled the differentials, transfer case, transmission, and even the crankcase —

each of which was full of chocolate mousse-looking fluid — and dried all the accessible ignition components. But the jeep still would not start.

Tommy had been away for the weekend, and he buzzed the lighthouse in the floatplane early Monday morning. This was the signal for me to head for the Bailey Tract to pick him up. After we tied the seaplane down and pulled the dolly cradle up on its track, I nervously told him about what happened with the jeep.

"I knew it would happen sooner or later, Charles. It's happened to me — maybe not that bad. Let's tow it down to the service station later this morning and let them get it going. But let's stop at Coconut Grove first. I need a cup of coffee!"

That's the kind of supervisor Tommy was. He didn't chew me out; he understood the liabilities associated with operating a motor vehicle on a salt-water-saturated beach. Nothing more was ever said about the ordeal.

* * *

That same summer and later in the fall, my law enforcement responsibility was seriously challenged. The first time was on Sanibel and was related to loggerhead turtles. My friend Joe Redinger, who was the only Sanibel mail carrier in those days, joined me for a night on the beach looking for nesting turtles and harassing would-be turtle turners. We left the lighthouse soon after dark and drove along the beach as far as the Casa Ybel, where we decided a cold drink would hit the spot. The Casa Ybel had the island's only package store back then, and several customers were coming and going. Joe went to get our sodas while I waited outside in the still-running jeep.

From the shadow of the building, the shape of a large man appeared, staggering in my direction. As he drew closer, I recognized him to be an islander with a belligerent reputation, and I could tell he was nearly dead drunk. He had trouble standing, much less walking, in his condition. This person had never caused me any problem personally, so I spoke to him in a friendly manner, called him by his name, and asked, "How's it going?"

He muttered a few incoherent words as he was working his way closer, but now I heard him clearly as he said, "I'm going to blow you out of this f.....g jeep with my shotgun if you don't stay off the goddamned beach so I can get a turtle!"

The adrenalin kicked in. Thinking quickly, as Joe came out the door heading toward the jeep, I replied, "You'll only get one shot. If you want to be that stupid, you'd better shoot straight, because I promise you, you'll miss and I'll blow your head off with my first round!"

Joe was shaken and couldn't believe what he heard. But he jumped into the jeep as I turned on the lights and drove off, headed for the beach to spend the night doing my thing. From that time on, I never went on any turtle patrol without carrying my Government-issue revolver in the jeep plus a concealed .38-caliber over-and-under Derringer in my pocket.

The rest of the summer went along smoothly, without any further confrontations or pot-shots. I realized that alcohol had released the hostility on that June night at the Casa Ybel. It was sober business to me at the time, but later I didn't take it quite so seriously. However, for the rest of the summer and most of the next, I never stopped looking over my shoulder or scanning potential ambush spots ahead of the jeep.

* * *

In November 1963, Tommy and I were chosen for a temporary tour of duty at the newly established Merritt Island National Wildlife Refuge near Cape Canaveral. The Service was going ahead with plans for a duck hunting season, and the seaplane was needed for patrol purposes. Since the refuge, under newly appointed Refuge Manager Curtis Wilson, formerly of the Loxahatchee Refuge, had no employees other than himself, I had to fly over with Tommy and work on the ground with Curtis. Three United States Game Management Agents also joined us. The precursors of today's Fish and Wildlife Service Special Agents, these three were tough men who treated wildlife law violators severely.

The seaplane was needed more for a show of force than any tangible law-enforcement use, so after about three days, Tommy wasn't needed and flew back to Sanibel. I was left to work with the pros. It was a real education, and the teachers were cruel. I watched as a few hunters had their brand new vehicles seized for shooting ducks over the legal limit. I also saw expensive custom-engraved shotguns seized as evidence because they were unplugged (capable of containing more than the legal number of shells).

Late on November 29, Curtis and I were about to call it a day. It had been a long one when we heard shooting out in the marsh. It was definitely after legal hunting hours, so we proceeded in his refuge-owned jeep along a dike toward the general direction of the shots. Two or three rounds exploded as a group of blue-winged teal passed overhead, and two birds fell from the sky not 50 yards ahead of us. We reached the spot at about the time two duck hunters began to wade away from us toward their fallen prey. The two men retrieved the ducks, turned around and headed in our direction, but briefly halted when they saw us. After they exchanged a few words that Curtis and I couldn't hear, the two hunters began to come toward us again.

Curtis and I were sure they knew they had been caught red-handed. The general area around their shooting spot was littered with spent shotgun shells as well as several empty beer cans. We didn't have to call one of the nearby rocket scientists at the new space center to determine that these two were under the influence of alcohol. This can be a serious, even life-threatening problem in a hunting situation.

Curtis confronted them. "We're Federal officers, and I'd like to see your hunting licenses and duck stamps, please."

The younger man was carrying the ducks. He dropped them to the ground, and both reached into their vests and produced the documents. They were properly licensed and had in their possession the then-modern counterpart of "Ding" Darling's innovative duck stamp.

I had moved away from the jeep and was standing nearby, about ten feet away, when Curtis asked to see the closest man's shotgun.

"I'd like to inspect your gun, sir," and he reached for the firearm.

Without any hesitation, the pump shotgun was passed, and Curtis examined it to see if it was properly plugged, as required by Federal regulations. The gun passed muster and was handed back.

"May I see your shotgun?" Curtis asked the other man, adding, "Who shot the teal?"

"I got them," said the younger man, who continued defiantly, "Hell no, you cain't see this shotgun!" He went on, "This is my Daddy's gun. I borrowed it and you ain't going to confiscate it from me!"

Curtis was momentarily taken aback, and I slowly reached down closer to the rusty old .38 at my right side. The hunter was holding his shotgun with both hands but hadn't made a move to raise it and point it at either of us. So the situation was still under control.

Curtis cautiously replied, "Why would I want to take your shotgun?"

"'Cause it ain't plugged, that's why!" spluttered the now nervous and very fidgety hunter. "I ain't gonna let you wardens take it away from me. My Daddy will whip my ass!" By this time my hand was on my revolver.

Curtis expertly defused the situation when he said, "I'm going to charge you with taking waterfowl after hours and doing so with an unplugged shotgun, sir. We're also going to take your ducks as evidence, but I won't seize the gun. Fair enough?"

The hunter thought the deal over for a minute, then agreed.

Curtis repeated his request, "Now, let us see the shotgun and you'll get it back."

"You promise?" asked the duck hunter as he extended the gun towards Curtis' outstretched arm.

"I promise," Curtis replied sternly. He accepted the shotgun, examined it, then passed it to me. "Charles, take this and fill out a receipt with make and serial number and have the gentleman sign it. Then give him back his gun."

I moved my hand away from my pistol, took the shotgun, and filled out the required paperwork. After completing a field receipt for the ducks, Curtis took them too. The hunter signed both receipts, and we drove off into the twilight.

The incident could easily have escalated to a more serious level. Had the two been violent, there's no telling what could have happened. I never wanted to work in the field of wildlife law enforcement, and it sure wasn't part of my career plan. Such duties were involuntarily attached to my position over the years. Every day, police officers face threatening individuals, few of whom are armed. However, we in the wildlife law enforcement field have to face armed individuals every day we work a hunting situation, legal or illegal. On any average day, being a police officer during a routine drug raid in downtown Los Angeles is a much safer occupation than being a "game warden" working a baited dove field or conducting a field investigation in a campsite full of drunken, heavily armed deer hunters.

As my career slowly progressed, my primary duties changed. Periodically, I was temporarily assigned to law-enforcement detail at such refuges as the National Key Deer Refuge to try and apprehend key deer poachers, Loxahatchee Refuge to patrol at night for alligator hunters, and Merritt Island Refuge during duck hunting season.

In 1964, I attended my first law-enforcement training session in Deland, Florida. This basically covered Fish and Wildlife Service policy relative to the Federal acts we were authorized to enforce and how our State commissions were meshed into our general enforcement roles.

My next law-enforcement training was a week-long session in 1969 at the Regional Office in Atlanta, Georgia. Here, most of us received our very first formal firearms training. The firearms instruction included the Service's policy on the use of deadly force, safety aspects in the use of weapons, and qualification with revolvers. The weapons course and qualification procedures were held in a well-equipped shooting range in the basement of Atlanta's Federal Reserve Bank. We each qualified with revolvers, but we were also given advanced training in shotgun techniques. We each had the novel opportunity to fire a Thompson submachine gun.

Nearly ten years later, the U. S. Fish and Wildlife Service began taking the law-enforcement duties of its field personnel very seriously. In March 1978, I was one of the first Service-employed students to enroll in the Service's classes at the Federal Law Enforcement Training Center. This facility is located at the former Glynco Naval Air Station, once a dirigible base, on the outskirts of Brunswick, Georgia. It was an intense training program conducted by constitutional lawyers and Special Agents of the Department of the Treasury and the Fish and Wildlife Service. At any one time, 1,200 Federal officers are studying at this impressive campus.

Nearly every agency is represented, including the U. S. Coast Guard. However, employees of the Federal Bureau of Investigation (FBI) and the Central Intelligence Agency (CIA) train at other facilities.

I successfully completed the course, met all the qualification requirements, and received appropriate certification. I had new credentials, a shiny new badge, and a .357 Model 66 Smith and Wesson with appropriate leather gear. The old .38 Tommy had issued to me years ago was retired for good.

After the initial training in Georgia, each of us had to participate every year in a 40-hour law-enforcement refresher course. These courses and weapon requalifications were held at the Federal facility in Georgia and, in more recent years during my tenure, at the Florida Law Enforcement Training Center near Quincy.

11

THE SANCTUARY ISLAND

It was a magnificent sight! Buffeted by a strong northwest wind, the birds flew in from all directions. With black wingtips delicately controlling their flight, they skillfully maneuvered into position and landed to spend the night at the mangrove head in the Bailey Tract. It was almost dark, and over a thousand white ibis had settled on the red mangrove trees to roost.

This colonial species was significant as a food source for the early homesteaders and settlers of Florida. Had our evening observation occurred 50 years earlier, the arriving flocks of ibis might have flown a gauntlet of gunners as they approached their night roosts. More than once, as a youngster growing up on Marco Island, Jean had helped her father hunt these birds for his family's subsistence. As we watched the graceful flocks careening in on the shifting wind currents, she shared memories of her childhood with me.

"Daddy would take me and Sister down to the bird rookeries in one of his small net skiffs. He'd pole us around a key until the white ibis — we called them curlews — rose up and he'd shoot them with his shotgun."

After Duke had hit a few, he'd push the boat in close and the girls would get ready to jump overboard, wade up to the island, and try to collect the birds, which had fallen into the dense mangroves.

Jean continued, "Daddy'd say to Floy, 'Alright Cracker, you and Cap'n go fetch 'em,' and off into the water we'd leap like a couple of Labrador retrievers."

She went on, "He always tried to shoot the young birds, the brown ones, 'cause they were more tender. I guess Floy and I were little outlaws, 'cause I didn't know shooting curlews was against the law until I started going to Naples to school in the ninth grade. Mama usually fixed the breasts by breading them in flour and frying them. She cooked the rest of the curlew meat in gravy — we called it purlew stew."

This was the way things were in southwest Florida into and beyond the Great Depression and World War II. Sanibel was no different than Marco, at least when it came to how the residents used their natural resources. The inhabitants relied on a variety of wildlife to supplement cultivated crops and domestic poultry and livestock. Sanibel residents harvested white ibis and other resident birds year-round and migratory waterfowl during the winter and early spring. Other than mollusks, crustaceans, and fish which were always used for food, other wildlife forms included sea turtles, gopher tortoises, marsh rabbits, raccoons, manatees, and white-tailed deer.

Of these, only the deer is no longer found on Sanibel. The island deer were not key deer, the diminutive race that occurs in the Florida keys, but a larger Florida subspecies of the Virginia white-tailed deer. In one of our long-winded conversations through the years, Clarence Rutland told me that a major hurricane in 1926 destroyed the remnants of a once relatively large Sanibel deer herd. Clarence was prone to exaggeration, but in support of his deer tales, I once was shown the skeletal remains of a six-point buck that had been unearthed, in the mid-50s, on the Gulf beach ridge near the western end of West Gulf Drive. The bones were discovered as workmen were preparing a building site for Willis and Opal Combs.

The Migratory Bird Treaty between the United States of America and Canada was concluded in 1916. The Migratory Bird Treaty Act was adopted by Congress on July 3, 1918, and was later amended on June 20, 1936, to include Mexico as a treaty partner. The legislation prohibited the indiscriminate taking of migratory birds crossing international boundaries. Provisions of the Act regulated the hunting of certain species including migratory water-fowl. Later, other species would be added to the list. But despite Federal and later State protection (at least on paper), the taking of white ibis and other native and migratory birds continued as usual in most of Florida.

By the early 1930s, people who came to the islands to live and work had a different viewpoint on the harvesting of local wildlife resources than some of the long-term residents. The majority of Sanibel and Captiva residents soon viewed year-round hunting of protected species as wanton waste of a valuable resource, and a strong conservation ethic began to develop in the community. It would gather momentum after 1935.

"Ding" Darling spent his first winter on Captiva that year, and his reputation as a conservationist of national prominence came with him. Dismayed by the unregulated and unenforced taking of wildlife on the islands, a group of local people conveyed their concern and fears to Mr. Darling. Because he knew the system and the way to get things done in high levels of Government, he was drafted into spearheading the effort to curtail all hunting on the islands. His goal was to have Sanibel and Captiva set aside as sanctuaries, where migratory and resident birds and other native creatures could live free of mankind's disturbance.

Under "Ding" Darling's leadership, the group soon formed the Sanibel-Captiva Conservation Association to foster the concept of island-wide conservation and to promote wildlife protection locally, and in high levels of government. In time, the Florida Legislature responded and passed House Bill No. 1095 on May 25, 1939. This statute established a State Game and Fish Refuge on Sanibel and Captiva Islands and the Lee County Refuge Commission. This commission consisted of five members who were selected from nominated residents and appointed by the Florida Game and Fresh Water Fish Commission.

Within weeks, on July 1, 1939, the Bureau of Biological Survey, in the Department of Agriculture, and the Bureau of Fisheries, in the Department of Commerce, were transferred to a new agency, the U. S. Fish and Wildlife Service and were assigned to the Department of the Interior. Before this reorganization, lands managed as refuges and breeding grounds for native birds, migratory waterfowl, and other forms of wildlife were identified by the

Bureau of Biological Survey as migratory waterfowl refuges, or simply reservations. To distinguish Federal refuges from similar State operations, President Franklin D. Roosevelt proclaimed, on July 30, 1940, that henceforth, Federal refuges would be known as national wildlife refuges — not preserves, parks, or sanctuaries.

However, the battle was far from over. "Ding" Darling continued to engage his pen, wit, and personal contacts to boldly persist in his efforts to establish a national wildlife refuge on the islands. The Sanibel National Wildlife Refuge was finally established by President Harry S. Truman on December 1, 1945. At that time, the Refuge consisted of 2,392 acres of land which had been leased for refuge purposes under authority of the Migratory Bird Conservation Act of February 18, 1929. The U. S. Fish and Wildlife Service was now responsible for administering the mostly inaccessible mangrove-forested lands of the new Sanibel Refuge.

Even then, Sanibel and Captiva residents did not rest. The Sanibel-Captiva Conservation Association developed a petition and circulated it to property owners far and wide for signature. This document was postcard size and of similar weight card stock — individualized for mailing.

The executed petitions were tendered to the appropriate officials, and again the wheels of government ground at a snail's pace. Eventually, the people of Sanibel and Captiva were again triumphant when Presidential Proclamation No. 2758 was signed by President Truman on December 2, 1947. This proclamation designated a Closed Area on and around Sanibel Island and a small part of southern Captiva Island. The closure order, authorized by the Migratory Bird Treaty Act, extended beyond the original boundary of the Sanibel National Wildlife Refuge. The Closed Area prohibited the pursuing, hunting, taking, capturing, and killing of migratory birds, or attempting to take, capture, or kill migratory birds, within the boundary.

Once permanent staffing was approved and Tommy was assigned to the Sanibel Refuge in 1949, the Fish and Wildlife Service immediately implemented a resource protection and wildlife census program. This was soon followed by an underfunded attempt at habitat management. This activity began in 1950, when Francis (Frank) P. Bailey conveyed a one-acre parcel of wetlands just west of Tarpon Bay Road to the Lee County Refuge

Commission as a site for the artesian well financed by Mr. Darling. In 1951, an 80-acre tract of the Sanibel Slough, which consisted of land around the well site, was leased by the Fish and Wildlife Service from Frank Bailey. This became known as the Bailey Development Unit and gave the Service a site at which to apply experimental principles of wildlife management which were then untested in the subtropics. The land and wildlife managers of the refuge system hoped to demonstrate that if the duration of the flood cycle of the Sanibel marsh could be extended, the Sanibel Slough habitat could better support increased wildlife populations for a longer period each year. Eventually in 1952, the original 80 acres, plus an additional 20 acres, were purchased from the Bailey family by the Fish and Wildlife Service for a total cost of $5,000.00 — $50.00 per acre.

The islanders began to call the property the Bailey Sanctuary. In the early years, it was officially designated on refuge signage as the Frank P. Bailey Tract, but today it is known simply as the Bailey Tract.

After title to the property was conveyed to the United States, the lone employee, Tommy Wood, began the slow task of modifying most of the Tract's characteristics. During the lease period, some work had been accomplished with a small dragline and an entrance road, and some impounding dikes were put in place. With a bulldozer and operator, loaned from the South Florida National Wildlife Refuges (formerly Everglades National Wildlife Refuge, the complex headquarters on the east coast), the soil of the Sanibel Slough bottom along with marginal vegetation were pushed aside, forming long windrows of mud and marsh plants. The swales were cleaned out down to the top of the underlying white shell to an elevation of 3 feet below mean sea level. Many of these original man-made ridges are still well defined because of the types of upland vegetation that now dominate them. The deeper swales now held fresh water longer, because of the deeper grade which exposed a greater depth of the water-table aquifer. At the peak of the typical late spring drought, even the deepest of these pools would dry out and the exposed bottoms would crack. Years later, the excavation of the Sanibel Slough, for mosquito-control purposes, would bring permanent year-round surface water to Sanibel's freshwater wetlands. Later, individual ponds were excavated in a long-range cut-and-fill program in the Bailey Tract designed to make still more fresh surface water available.

The Bailey Tract's mangrove head was surrounded by a moat-like pool before the bulldozed dikes and dynamited holes were completed. Large alligators found the moat to their liking and moved in. They prevented any predators from successfully swimming across, further isolating the mangrove island. This isolation provided a safe haven for many nesting and roosting birds. The relationship worked well — that is, until poachers found and killed the alligators.

The absence of alligators allowed raccoons to move into the mangrove head, where they easily preyed on eggs and chicks. And because alligators were no longer there to maintain and patrol the open water, aggressive marsh plants invaded the moat. Finally, the colonial birds abandoned the rookery.

In an attempt to entice the birds to return, the moat was renovated in 1971. But no birds returned. Without the birds alighting on the "white-washed" foliage, the red mangrove canopy, stunted by years of bird excrement, began to grow again. By the time alligators reoccupied the new moat, the white ibis and other colonial birds no longer accepted the trees as nesting sites. Despite the Refuge's efforts at restoration, the mangrove head nesting rookery has never recovered.

When development began, the small parking lot and narrow dikes allowed the public to enjoy the Bailey Tract. It became a favorite area for bird watchers, especially in the evening when the ibis returned to roost. In 1954, local carpenters were hired to construct an observation tower. The Bird Tower was completed on July 1, 1954, and served the public until 1976. Then it was determined to be unsafe and not repairable. The popular tower was removed and never replaced.

Walking the low dikes in the Bailey Tract was a bird watcher's delight. Jean, the children, and I would spend considerable time there, that is, when we weren't out on the beach shelling. One Sunday morning, we put Chuck in a stroller and picked up Leslie from Sunday School at the Community Church. With Leslie carrying the too-large binoculars, we went to the Bailey Tract to look for the purple gallinule that someone had seen there just days before.

Leslie said, "Mommy, I hear a bullfrog out there."

Listening, we could hear the bass-pitched, grunt-like sound coming from the cattails of the mangrove head. Further off in the marsh, another frog responded with a similar series of grunts. "Those are sometimes called southern bull frogs, but their correct name is pig frog. Many people, even some who have lived here for a while, think the pig-like sound is actually an alligator grunting," I told my small audience.

I continued, "Pig frogs weren't found on Sanibel until about ten years ago. In April 1954, while he was detailed to the Loxahatchee Refuge, Tommy and some of the Refuge staff collected 20 pairs of these frogs. He flew them back with him, 39 survived, and he released them at several locations in the Bailey Tract the next day. They adapted well, multiplied, and can now be found all through the Sanibel Slough system. They provide food for wildlife and people."

* * *

With advancing age and amid personal frustrations due to changes to his beloved Sanibel, Captiva, and other parts of coastal Florida, "Ding" Darling finally threw in the towel. In disgust, he sold what little land he owned in the State. Government red tape (both State and Federal), poor wetland protection and acquisition records, liberal public land sales policies, and diminished public interest in his conservation ethic had defeated him — so he thought! However, after departing Captiva and Sanibel for the last time, he continued to remain very interested and was always eager to learn what was going on here. He was old, no longer antagonistically vocal, nor as quick to send a letter of criticism to some bureaucrat temporarily perched in a high place. Yet to the end, he would keep his hand on the pulse of the community and Refuge through frequent correspondence with Tommy Wood and personal reports from his daughter and son-in-law, Mary and Dick Koss, who continued to visit the islands each winter.

Once the Refuge and the Closed Area were established, Mr. Darling threw his total support into the creation of the Sanibel-Captiva Audubon Society. In time, following the dissolution of the Sanibel-Captiva Conservation Association, this became the lead island conservation organization. Affiliated as a chapter of both the National and Florida Audubon Societies, the Sanibel-Captiva Audubon Society was formed in the fall of 1953. On January 12, 1961, I was elected president of the organization and served the Society for five years. Not long after my shoe-in election (I was the only nominee), "Ding" Darling sent me a congratulatory note, through Tommy.

Following the death of Mr. Darling on February 12, 1962, a small group of his island friends and former associates in the Sanibel-Captiva Conservation Association banded together and formed the J. N. "Ding" Darling Memorial Sanctuary Committee. Tommy became a member of the Memorial Committee at its inception. At first I was his surrogate, an *ex officio* member, and attended meetings when he was unavailable. But later as the group evolved, I became a member.

At the same time, the J. N. "Ding" Darling Foundation was organized in Des Moines, Iowa, and the two widely separated groups collaborated to coordinate and advance the conservation aims of their late namesake. Having been organized as a foundation, the Iowa group served as a tax-exemption umbrella for the Memorial Sanctuary Committee on Sanibel and Captiva. Approximately $25,000 had become available to the local group from memorial contributions. This was held by the Des Moines foundation until it could be transferred to the Memorial Sanctuary Committee on the islands once a use for the funds had been determined.

In time, the use was identified — a major memorial to the life and achievements of Jay Norwood Darling would be created on Sanibel Island.

12

A FITTING MEMORIAL

"**D**ick Thompson will arrive late this afternoon and will probably be here for a couple of days," I told Jean at lunch. "I don't know what his schedule is, but we'll probably be in the field most of the time he's here."

Dick was the incumbent refuge manager of South Florida National Wildlife Refuges, headquartered at the Loxahatchee National Wildlife Refuge. The Sanibel Refuge was a satellite station under Thompson's direct supervision. He was Tommy's boss. His visits usually meant that we would first take care of some administrative chores, then inspect the equipment, facilities, and the Refuge.

In the office that afternoon, Dick told us that the purpose of this trip was much different from his earlier trips to Sanibel. "The residents on the islands must be getting to the right people in the Washington office. Larry Givens called a few days ago and told me to get over here and begin planning for a major land acquisition program. We must prepare a draft Refuge Development Plan and make recommendations as to what land would be included in an actual acquisition boundary. All this has to be up to the Regional Office in 30 days."

Tommy and I were elated. The hard work and lobbying by the "Ding" Darling Memorial Sanctuary Committee had accomplished what many of us in the Fish and Wildlife Service thought would be impossible. We certainly had our work cut out.

The "Ding" Darling Memorial Sanctuary Committee was ready to move ahead, to do something substantial in "Ding" Darling's memory and show memorial fund contributors that their monies were being wisely used. The group continued their unrelenting campaign to complete their mission. By 1966, the mission had been identified — creation of a unit of the Refuge to be named the J. N. "Ding" Darling Memorial Sanctuary.

The Fish and Wildlife Service moved slowly, but effectively, under the management skills of a group of people in the Regional Office who were committed to developing a lasting memorial to "Ding" Darling. To the long-time employees of the Service, "Ding" Darling was highly revered and known as "the best friend a duck ever had." The project reached priority status, agency schedules were juggled, and people responded.

In 1964, the Interior Department's Bureau of Land Management dispatched Dee Crain, a cadastral surveyor, from their Western States Office to do the required Sanibel survey work. His assignment was to determine ownership of certain lands located mostly to the north of Sanibel-Captiva Road. The properties were in the nearly impenetrable mangrove-forested tidal lands. By now, this huge expanse of Sanibel Island had become known locally as the Darling Tract or the Darling Sanctuary.

The J. N. "Ding" Darling Memorial Sanctuary Committee appointed Tommy as their "Chief Engineer," a voluntary position that had nothing to do with his duties as Refuge Manager. There was no official connection or input by the Fish and Wildlife Service into what was about to happen.

Even before the Sanibel Lighthouse was built, general Federally-sponsored land surveys of Sanibel Island, which were last conducted in 1876, were grossly in error. The new, accurate survey would confirm what local surveyors had known for years. Near the middle of Sanibel and westward, there was a quarter-mile overlap of townships. A township, which is a unit in U. S. land survey terminology, consists of an area totaling 36 square miles. No one knew where their property really was.

Crain and his survey crew soon located substantial parcels of public domain land that were mixed with State- and privately-owned tracts north of Sanibel-Captiva Road. In mid-1964, he identified an unmarked, unopened, 50-foot-wide public easement that ran north from Sanibel-Captiva Road and reached both Federal and State lands.

After learning that this easement existed, the membership of the "Ding" Darling Memorial Sanctuary Committee wanted to quickly claim it for the new Refuge — and soon they would. This easement is now Wildlife Drive and is located at the common boundary between land owned by the Lee County Board of Public Instruction, on their eastern line, and the Fish and Wildlife Service.

Dick Thompson and I stood at the intersection of Tarpon Bay and Sanibel-Captiva Roads. Dick said, "I believe this highway will make a good boundary. It certainly would be definitive and easily posted. What do you think?"

I replied, "Do you mean the Service will eventually acquire everything north of Sanibel-Captiva Road?"

"That's right," he said. "It's perfectly logical, it becomes a clearly defined Refuge boundary, and the waters of Pine Island Sound would be the northern property line. Now all we have to do is come up with the extreme east and west boundaries. What do you think about Tarpon Bay for an eastern limit?"

"No!" I quickly returned. "Let's include Woodring Bayous (now Lady Finger Lakes) and let Dixie Beach Boulevard be the eastern boundary." Continuing, I laughed and said, "Since it's up to us to make this major decision, I think we should include all of Wulfert Point too. Hell, let's go all the way to Blind Pass!"

Dick interrupted my brain-storming episode saying, "No, I don't think we should include Wulfert Point, at least not at this time, because of that little canal subdivision near the Indian mounds, where that bridge is. It would break up the continuity of the Refuge, and probably the land is too expensive anyway."

I jumped back in. "Dick, I think Wulfert should be saved too!" I lived here, I wanted it all, but I could tell I was going to be outvoted.

So, based on our discussion and approach to the problem, the acquisition boundary of the Refuge soon would be accepted by the Regional Office. To this day, whenever we get together, Dick Thompson and I reflect on what a great deed we did for Sanibel Island that day.

Our draft plan was completed on schedule and fine-tuned by the Regional Office staff. In August 1967, it was published as a prospectus, or concept plan, by the Fish and Wildlife Service with some financial help from the J. N. "Ding" Darling Foundation. Then it was publicly distributed to present the objectives, guidelines, and development proposals relative to the future operation of the Refuge.

Initially, land acquisition centered on Fish and Wildlife Service attempts to obtain title to the State-owned lands. Florida refused, but her politicians did agree to renew and extend the terms of the existing lease. On April 18, 1962, the Board of Lee County Commissioners passed a resolution supporting the wishes of the "Ding" Darling Memorial Sanctuary Committee, that State and school lands on Sanibel Island be set aside for wildlife refuge purposes. Five days after receiving County approval, the Memorial Committee met to develop strategy for a meeting, scheduled on the 25th in Tallahassee, with the Governor's committee on State lands.

On the 24th, with approval from the Regional Office, Tommy flew a seaplane-load of Memorial Committee board members (himself and three passengers) to Tallahassee.

First they met with John Evans, an assistant to the Governor. Tommy and I once worked with John when he was a fellow Fish and Wildlife Service employee at the Naples red tide laboratory. He agreed that a memorial to "Ding" Darling would be an appropriate use of Sanibel's State lands and promised to use any influence he had to bring this about.

On the 25th, the Sanibel-Captiva group met with the Governor's committee to discuss Sanibel's State lands. Again the officials were adamant — the Fish and Wildlife Service could not be granted title, but the State Park Board was instructed to draft an upgraded lease agreement.

Ultimately, the Service upped the ante. They offered other prime, Federally-owned properties in exchange for fee-title ownership of the desired State property on Sanibel. The offer would convey some exceptional property, potential State park lands, to the State, including Anclote Key National Wildlife Refuge near Tarpon Springs as well as other desirable tracts near St. Marks National Wildlife Refuge in northern Florida.

Finally, State officials woke up and realized what a deal they had been offered. The exchange was accepted and the land was deeded to the United States of America on January 30, 1970, duly executed by the State of Florida Board of Trustees of the Internal Improvement Trust Fund and the State of Florida Department of Education.

In the meantime, the "Ding" Darling Memorial Sanctuary Committee began to push harder. As "Chief Engineer," Tommy decided he had been pushed long and hard enough. So, without written official approval from his superiors, he met with Wayne Miller, Director of the Lee County Mosquito Control District, and worked out a ditching protocol for the leased area known as the Sanibel Sandflats. This plan would reduce mosquito production in the mangrove forest, but it would also provide access for wildlife refuge purposes. If implemented, the plan would also launch a series of projects by the "Ding" Darling Memorial Sanctuary Committee.

* * *

Colon Moore started his workday by driving as far out on the rough ungraded fill as his yellow jeep pickup could go. He would unload several cans of diesel fuel from the truck, place them in a small outboard-propelled skiff, and motor out into the borrow ditch until he reached his waiting dragline. As he moved his machine forward, he would level the most recent piles of spoil on top of the dike just enough to make them barely passable by his four-wheel-drive jeep. This prevented curious people in non-off-road vehicles from driving out onto the fill. When anyone wanted to visit Colon, they would have to walk some distance to where he was working on the dike.

At first, two machines worked together, one on each side of the dike. Progress was slowed when they started out across open water, because digging submerged bottom material was a soupy process and the drag bucket could not be retrieved with its full capacity of spoil. Later, one dragline was dispatched to another location, and Colon was left to finish the dike alone. By late May 1963, he had reached a point about two miles out from Sanibel-

Captiva Road. This area was constructed wider than the normal working width of the dike to accommodate the wishes and plans of the "Ding" Darling Memorial Sanctuary Committee. This location was selected for the first financial investment in the Refuge with memorial funds.

An observation tower, an exact duplicate of the old Bird Tower in the Bailey Tract, was constructed at the wide part of the dike in 1966. In 1967, this tower was named the O'Brien Tower in memory of Alice O'Brien. The O'Brien estate had made a substantial memorial contribution to the "Ding" Darling Memorial Sanctuary Committee for the tower. Alice had been a winter resident of Captiva and close personal friend of the Darling's.

Colon reached Hardworking Bayou, fittingly named years before, in early 1964. Every so often, Tommy would fly Colon over the dike and would select a not-to-distant landmark, such as a group of trees, and orient Colon in the direction he wanted him to continue the dike. Following one of these alignment flights, Colon began to cross Hardworking Bayou. He intended to dig and construct the dike straight across, and once reaching the northern side of the Bayou's entrance, he planned to meander westward along Sanibel's outer red mangrove fringe on the shore of Pine Island Sound.

He was out in Hardworking Bayou 150 feet or so, making slow progress, when his bucket quite unexpectedly began to strike hardpan and the water suddenly deepened. The hard material turned out to be a thick layer of coquina rock. Due to the nearly impenetrable bottom conditions and deep water, the planned route of the dike had to be modified. Colon backtracked and turned his machine westward through the dense mangroves.

Appropriately, we named this short dead-end spur of the dike, which went out into Hardworking Bayou, Colon's Point. It became a favorite fishing spot, and in 1966, when the "Ding" Darling Memorial Sanctuary Committee funded directional signage for the first Refuge canoe trail system, one of two floating dock trailheads was located at Colon's Point. I have always wanted to place a memorial plaque on this point to honor the man who almost single-handedly created the dike — now known as Wildlife Drive — that nearly a million people continue to enjoy every year. Perhaps one of these days it will come to pass.

In late 1964, Colon had reached a north-south section line that separates the western end of the Darling Tract from private property. This demarcation line was also the location of a private road for the residents of Caloosa [*sic*] Shores. Colon was instructed to build the dike in alignment with this road and proceed south, then cross the eastern end of Kesson's Bayou, and continue to dig southward until he reached Sanibel-Captiva Road. He started across the Bayou but again had to deal with excessive water depths that made digging and building impossible. He made a left turn, followed the Bayou's looping shoreline, and finally connected the dike to the private road again. The dike now had an end, but it was far from finished. Colon turned his dragline around and started digging back toward where he had come from but on the opposite side of the dike.

The impounding dike was completed in 1966. Then a second dike was started that led westward from the main dike and followed the mangrove margin just north of the Mid-Island Ridge. Originally, this was called the South Dike and would have eventually tied into the main dike near the loop at Kesson's Bayou. But the project was never completed. It has since been renamed the Indigo Trail.

During the construction, some concerned property owners began to raise serious questions about both dikes illegally trespassing on their holdings, and a growing number of people were threatening lawsuits. The Bureau of Land Management hadn't completed their surveys to indicate whose lands were whose, and land acquisition hadn't started. So dike construction was halted and the South Dike was left, and remains, a dead end.

Finally, to avoid title problems, the Fish and Wildlife Service contracted with a Fort Myers engineering firm to survey and sort out land ownerships in the Darling Tract acquisition boundary. To avoid long-term and major harm to the spirit of the project, and to avoid expensive litigation, a high priority was suddenly placed on the land acquisition program.

By March 1967, both the J. N. "Ding" Darling Foundation and the local Memorial Committee were concerned with the final name of the memorial sanctuary. As a tribute to "Ding" Darling, the Fish and Wildlife Service offered to rename the Sanibel National Wildlife Refuge, including all existing units within the original boundary, the J. N. "Ding" Darling National Wildlife Refuge. The Memorial Committee and the Foundation promptly concurred and voiced no major objections to eliminating the word "Sanctuary."

This recommended name change slowly inched along the chain of command, but the concept nearly died when it reached the Secretary of the Interior. Earlier, Secretary Stewart Udall had publicly stated that he was personally opposed to naming national wildlife refuges after people. But in the end, he made an exception to his strongly-held principle and signed the paperwork to honor "Ding" Darling. On August 15, 1967, the name change became official. The fitting memorial was real, but not yet complete.

To most of us who were affiliated with the "Ding" Darling Memorial Sanctuary Committee, our role was finished — until someone among us suggested that we not disband, but rather expand the scope of the Committee's purposes. Spearheaded by Emmy Lu Lewis, Ann Winterbotham, and Roy Bazire, the "Ding" Darling Memorial Sanctuary Committee decided to become autonomous on April 5, 1967. It was reorganized and chartered as the Sanibel-Captiva Conservation Foundation, Inc., a Florida not-for-profit corporation on October 31, 1967.

The Sanibel-Captiva Conservation Foundation (SCCF) has since evolved into the premier environmental organization on these islands, and its mission is supported by many of the residents of Sanibel and Captiva. The Foundation developed and coordinates a land acquisition program that has safeguarded vast wetland acreage along the corridor of the Sanibel Slough. They have directly purchased sensitive lands in the interior of Sanibel, constructed a Nature Center and a Native Plant Nursery, and continue to foster the ideals that we who founded the organization established so many years ago.

The U. S. Fish and Wildlife Service launched its Sanibel land acquisition program before the decade of the '60s ended. Ownership of privately-owned parcels within the approved acquisition boundary were conveyed to the Service via several methods. Many properties were directly purchased following negotiated settlements. However, other tracts had to be acquired through lengthy legal processes. Legal notices of condemnation, or Declarations of Taking, were filed, and some of these acquisitions were ultimately resolved in the Federal court system. By January 1973, the Refuge land acquisition program was essentially completed.

The fitting memorial to Jay Norwood Darling was now complete, and on February 4, 1978, the Refuge was officially dedicated as the J. N. "Ding" Darling National Wildlife Refuge in memory of this outstanding American.

* * *

A few months prior to the Refuge's formal dedication ceremony to honor Mr. Darling, I was asked to assist Bob Bridges, who had been sent down to Sanibel by the Atlanta Regional Office to conduct a biological inspection of Wulfert Point. Bob was the Service's Region IV Ascertainment Biologist for lands that were being considered as possible refuge acquisitions.

Bob and I drove out to the 415-acre Wulfert Point property on November 15, 1977. There we met with four people: retired dentist Harold Craig who was the resident caretaker, a visiting Chicago-based lawyer who represented the landowners, his client's hired ecologist, and an unidentified property owner.

At the outset, the lawyer recognized me. (On behalf of his Chicago clients, he had appeared before the City Council a few times during public hearings prior to adoption of the Sanibel Comprehensive Land Use Plan.) He pulled no punches, making it clear to Bob and me that he didn't want me to be part of the Fish and Wildlife Service ascertainment team; he didn't want me to set foot on his client's Wulfert Point property.

So I said, "Bob, I can leave, come back later, and pick you up?"

A little irritated at the attorney's demand, Bob said, "No, Charles, you're going to participate in this inspection." He then told the lawyer that I was necessary to his biological evaluation, that he had to rely on my expertise, and he insisted that I accompany the group in the walkthrough inspection.

The attorney reluctantly agreed and we were handed liability release forms for our signature. These legally authorized us to enter the land and I suppose to indemnify the owners should we be injured during the walk. This lawyer was working hard. Not only did he have an all-expense-paid trip to lovely Sanibel Island, he was going to justify his fee too.

The reason for the stiff legal attitude regarding my participation was because there was an active lawsuit between the City of Sanibel and the Chicago-based group of investors who had acquired Wulfert Point. The owners wanted to place 1,600 dwellings on the property, but the Comprehensive Land Use Plan I had helped adopt a year and a half earlier allowed a density of only 46 units. To say the least, they were very upset.

The land was like other well-drained upland island ecosystems that had been clear-cut for agricultural purposes. Much of this land contained remnants of once-productive key lime groves. It was also heavily forested with West Indian vegetation, but this habitat was interspersed with open meadowlike features. This open, sandy habitat was dominated by low shrubs and coarse grasses, ideal for gopher tortoises and eastern indigo snakes. Small ponds on the property were home for alligators, wading birds, and many migratory waterfowl in season. I also knew that a pair of bald eagles had nested on the parcel for the past several years. But when the subject was brought up during the conversation, the care-taker disclaimed the presence of eagles anywhere on the property.

Less than a month after this inspection trip, on November 29th, then Refuge Manager Del Pierce and I entered the property to pho-tograph the active eagle nest. We returned to the nest site on May 3, 1978, to inspect the nest again. On these trips into the private holdings on Wulfert Point, we legally entered the land within the scope of our Federal law enforcement authority as it relates to enforcement of the Endangered Species Act.

Over time, the Service continued to gather biological and appraisal data on the land, and several of us reviewed Bob's excel-lent inspection report relative to the property. It even established the final boundary for this proposed addition to the Refuge. However, shortly after all the field work was accomplished, there was a serious roadblock thrown up against the Service's acquisition of Wulfert Point.

The Service's Division of Realty in the Regional Office deter-mined that because of the ongoing litigation between the City and the landowners, the Fish and Wildlife Service could not negotiate a purchase, nor could it initiate condemnation proceedings to take the property for inclusion into the Refuge. Our hands were tied, so the issue was dropped.

When I was in Tallahassee on official business a few years later, Dick Thompson and I met and had a long-winded rambling conversation about recent events in the land acquisition program of the U. S. Fish and Wildlife Service. Bringing him up to date on recent events on Sanibel Island, I told him what had happened to the Wulfert Point tract. "We blew it, Dick! You should have taken me seriously back in '67. The Service should have purchased all of Wulfert then — and saved it."

13

DONNA

It was early in the morning on Monday, September 5, 1960. Tommy and I were on our way to the Bailey Tract, but as usual, we stopped first at the Coconut Grove Restaurant for a cup of coffee. A handful of island regulars were already there enjoying the homemade rolls or whatever else from John and Bella Kontinos' menu. Someone sitting at the counter spoke up, "I heard on the radio this morning that there's a good-sized storm coming into the Caribbean, and it may be heading this way."

It was hurricane season, so wherever people congregated on the islands, serious storms were popular topics of discussion. Most of us had gone through hurricanes before. My first, which I was too young to remember, was the 1938 hurricane that ravaged southern New England; my most recent was a brush by Hurricane Judith on October 18, 1959. The present storm was so far away that no one at the restaurant was overly concerned.

That evening at dinner, Jean said, "They've named the hurricane that's come into the Caribbean, Donna. They never had names when I was little. Why do they always have to name them after women? It's expected to stay on its present track for the next few days, and they seem to think that this course will bring it up into the Gulf way to the west of us. The last advisory from the Weather Bureau said the winds were already up to over a hundred miles per hour. What are we going to do if Donna threatens to hit Sanibel?"

"First," I said, "we should wait and see if the hurricane is coming toward us. Both Broward Keene and Clarence Rutland told me that we shouldn't stay here at the Lighthouse Point during a major hurricane. They both said that the buildings and the lighthouse likely will still withstand a severe storm, but our lives would certainly be threatened and our car likely ruined by rising salt water. We'd be wise to leave the point I suppose, but where we should go, I don't know, maybe to Bonita or Naples."

Like many Atlantic hurricanes, Donna had developed far out in the ocean near the African coast. On Friday, September 2, the National Weather Service's Hurricane Center in Miami issued its first hurricane advisory on Donna, when the storm was located about 700 miles east of the Lesser Antilles. By Tuesday, September 6, Donna skirted to the north of Puerto Rico, where her 135-mph sustained winds had done considerable property damage and many lives were lost. The storm was heading in a west-north-west direction, but on Wednesday the 7th, the course suddenly changed to almost a true west heading.

On the morning of September 6, what we should do was decided for us.

At first light, Tommy told me, "Louise is packing up some things and she'll be leaving the island today. I'm flying the seaplane to a hanger in St. Pete later this morning. I'll call you at the office tomorrow morning from St. Pete and let you know when to pick me up at the bus station in town. You can start securing things here and at the Bailey Tract. We'll finish up when I get back. I want you, Jean, and Leslie to get off the island if there's a real threat that Donna's going to hit us. I'll stay here to protect the Government's and our personal property until the storm passes and you return."

I began to argue, "Tommy, I want to stay here with you to help. I'll take Jean and Leslie to one of our folks' houses and come back and help you." I was actually feeling a little excited about the approaching hurricane and wanted to be where the action was. I would have loved to ride out a hurricane up inside the light tower — or so I thought in my younger days.

He countered, "No, Charles, your place is with your family. I'm ordering that once you get finished up here, you all are to evacuate if they forecast that Sanibel is in or near the hurricane's projected path."

At 2 o'clock on Wednesday the 7th, I was at the Trailways Bus Station in Fort Myers to pick up Tommy, and we were back at the lighthouse in time to hear a late afternoon hurricane advisory. As Donna began to move more to the northwest, the Hurricane Center issued a Hurricane Watch for southwest Florida. Later in the day, the Center upgraded this to a Hurricane Warning, the advisory that controlled whether we stayed or evacuated.

Securing meant tying down whatever would float or blow away. It also meant installing heavy wooden storm shutters on Quarters 1 and 2. Quarters 3 had no prefitted shutters so wouldn't benefit from anything we could do to protect it. I had everything under control by the first ferry on Thursday the 8th, that is, except covering the windows on the kitchen wings of Quarters 1 and 2. The shutters to protect those widows had to be installed from an extension ladder and I had to wait until Tommy returned from St. Petersburg to help me. Installation of the last group of shutters would make the quarters as storm-proof as possible.

In the meantime, to be sure we had drinking water when we came back, I filled three 5-gallon bottles from the cistern. Jean had packed up our important documents, a few days supply of clean clothing, and inventoried our canned food supply. In the event the storm was forecast to strike Sanibel and we were forced to evacuate, an available supply of food and water would be very important when we did return — if our quarters survived, that is.

By mid-afternoon on Thursday the 8th, Tommy and I finished securing the property, so we loaded our car and bade him goodbye — and Good Luck! Jean, Leslie, and I left the house and headed for the ferry landing, bound for my parents' home in Naples. As we drove away from the Refuge headquarters, we didn't know we had jumped from the frying pan into the fire.

Since we had no home telephone, I planned to use the pay phone at the ferry landing, the island's only public telephone, to call my parents and let them know we were on our way. We were the twelfth car in line, and there was a line of people, all fighting mosquitos, waiting to use the phone. Islanders and visitors were calling friends and relatives to let them know they were alright. It was anyone's guess if I would get to use the telephone before I had to drive onto the ferry, but I waited my turn. Nine of the vehicles ahead of us loaded and departed on the ferryboat. About 15 minutes later, I drove onto the next boat without having called anyone.

We stopped off at Jean's parents' house in Bonita Springs to see if they were secure. They were all boarded up and ready, when the time came, to head to a public hurricane shelter at the Bonita Springs schoolhouse. I called Naples from the Williams' — my family planned to weather the storm at home, and there was room for the three of us.

Friday morning the 9th, regular bulletins issued from the Miami Hurricane Center positioned Donna's center at 175 miles south of Miami, heading northwest. The storm was releasing energy equivalent to a hydrogen bomb exploding in the atmosphere every eight minutes — and it was strengthening. Its forward movement was also becoming erratic so its true direction was difficult to predict.

Early on Saturday the 10th, Donna's eye passed through the central Florida Keys, and Sombrero Key Light Station recorded a wind gust of 166 mph. Forecasters expected Donna's hurricane-force northeast winds to strike Everglades City around 9:00 in the morning. The storm's full brunt would arrive not long after, with high tides forecast to be more than nine feet above normal. At 8:30, the Weather Bureau's Miami radar showed that the eye was indeed approaching Everglades City and the hurricane's forward speed was 20 mph.

As dawn broke, we were all uncomfortably aware of what had been going on outside. No one had really slept. Throughout the night, the wind howled at a deafening and frightening level, objects struck the house, horizontally driven rain pummeled the windows, wind-borne gravel from the built-up roofs of houses sandblasted our cars, and electric power was lost throughout the city. We continued to receive weather bulletins with a battery-powered radio — until Donna knocked Naples' lone radio station, WNOG, off the air.

The wind continued from the northeast, and the barometric pressure in Naples reached a low of 28.0 inches of mercury just before noon. Then, the wind suddenly slackened and a peaceful calm prevailed — Donna's eye had arrived. An hour later, at one o'clock, the wind quickly increased again, but this time it was blowing from the southwest. This onshore wind would bring the highest tides and likely do the most wind-related damage. Later, we judged the eye of the storm to be about 20 miles across, easily calculated from the forecaster's report that the storm was moving ahead at 20 mph. Around six o'clock, the hurricane winds were noticeably diminished to gale force.

Collier County and City of Naples Civil Defense authorities had established their base of operations at the Naples High School auditorium. With the local radio station out, we had no way to find out what damage Donna had wrought as she moved northward toward Sanibel and beyond. In Naples, the roads were strewn with downed trees, electrical lines, pieces of roofs and other parts of buildings, and television antennas. The streets remained impass-able until early Sunday afternoon, when city and county work crews managed to reopen most of the main arteries.

We ventured out to assess the damage and hopefully find out what had happened to Sanibel and Captiva and our home. We arrived at the high school just as a news briefing was ending. Wind gusts in Naples were estimated to have reached 176 mph and the storm surge, when winds were out of the southwest, had reached 12.1 feet above normal in the Vanderbilt Beach area. Coast Guard helicopters and their flight crews had arrived from Clearwater ear-lier in the day, and on their way they had flown along the coast to assess the damage.

I walked up to a Coast Guard officer, introduced myself, and explained my concern. "I live up on Sanibel Island. I came to Naples to escape the storm, but that was sure a joke. I'm with the U. S. Fish and Wildlife Service and live at the Sanibel Lighthouse with my wife and daughter. Did you happen to inspect that on your way down? If so, were the houses still standing?"

He replied, "Yes sir, the houses are still there. It looked as though the tide had washed over Point Ybel, but the buildings appeared to be alright, at least from the air."

"Whew!" came my uncontrolled sigh. Now the question was Could we get home?

Like explorers heading into the unknown, we drove home Monday morning, September 12, in an adventuresome spirit. Devastation was everywhere along the way. In Bonita Springs, we found Jean's folks, younger sister, and brother at home and safe. But they suffered considerable damage to their residence and complete loss of two smaller outbuildings. Duke heard there had been one confirmed fatality and another person was missing in Lee County. There was no storm-related loss of life in Collier County. The Lee County victims were businessmen who had refused to leave their establishments on Bonita Beach Road just east of Bonita Beach. The missing man was "Lindy" Lindenheimer, whom I knew. Although under legal age, I had filled in as a temporary bartender a few times at his place, Lindy's Tavern, and often enjoyed his famous Limburger cheese and onion sandwiches. His body was found several days later floating in the nearby Imperial River.

Punta Rassa Road connected Punta Rassa to Barrett's Corner, and it was a shambles. Boats from Port Comfort Marina were scattered through the mangroves, and a few were even up on the road. Punta Rassa itself looked as though it had received a direct nuclear hit. The ferry slips were inoperable, so returning evacuees were being shuttled back to the islands by Jake Stokes, in his private boat, and aboard the *Punjab*, a 38-foot-long patrol boat owned by the Florida State Board of Conservation, the forerunner of today's Florida Marine Patrol. The three of us climbed aboard the *Punjab* for the trip across San Carlos Bay.

(Jean and I had been aboard the *Punjab* earlier. As a teenager on Marco, Jean sometimes babysat for Officer Jack Levins' young son. Jack operated the *Punjab* for the State at the time, and on one of his patrols down to Fort Jefferson and the Dry Tortugas shrimping grounds, Jean had the opportunity to go along. As for me, when the *Kingfish* was having new engines installed, the *Punjab* served as a substitute vessel for a few of my red tide trips. The excursion we were on now was certainly not as enjoyable as our first.)

The *Punjab* was precariously tied up at the mailboat dock at Bailey's General Store (or what was left of it), and we disembarked. The decking and most of the stringers on this county-owned pier had disappeared, but someone had put boards down as a walkway to make unloading less difficult. We had no choice but to strike out toward the lighthouse afoot. Bailey Road was nearly impassable. Trees had been knocked down and blown about by the powerful wind, and other debris had been washed inland by the tide. Our trip back to the lighthouse was exhausting, since we had to negotiate our path through or climb over the many barricades Donna had left in our way. The hike toward home seemed to take forever. Jean and I took turns carrying Leslie and our lone piece of luggage and a shopping bag.

Finally, we made it to the lighthouse. And indeed, the quarters were still standing. But the lighthouse point looked like a war zone. Trees, mostly Australian pines which had severely impeded our trek home, were snapped into a maze of pieces. Our beautiful, mature coconut palms were almost denuded, and the trunks of a few had actually snapped off in the ferocious wind gusts. The ground all around the Sanibel Island Light Station was covered with a fresh layer of sand and shell.

As I started to climb the stairway to Quarters 2, I noticed something partly imbedded in the new soil that covered most of the second stair tread (the first was completely buried). I stooped down and picked up a beautiful Scotch bonnet, a lovely seashell, which I still have. It is the first and only specimen of the species I would ever find.

From ground level, the light tower seemed to be completely unscathed, and the three quarters were relatively undamaged. However, there were pieces of steel guttering, which had not been torn completely off, hanging loose from their facia boards. Everything looked to be intact inside our quarters except a hallway window. Rain had blown through several broken panes and damaged some of my best books in a nearby case. In the main part of the building, the floor and carpets were damp and strewn with fine sand and shell fragments. Nearly an inch deep in some places, this sandy mixture had apparently blown up off the beach and under the Gulf-side doors. While inspecting, I noticed that the bottom corners of all the outside doors had been partly chewed away. Apparently, frightened rats must have tried to escape the rising water. The gnawed holes in two doors of Quarters 2 were big enough for an adult rat.

Tommy was nowhere in sight, nor were either of the two Refuge vehicles. Jean and I began to shovel and sweep the sand out of the house when I saw Tommy coming along the beach in the jeep. I went down to meet him.

He said, "I'm glad you all are back safe. It was quite a blow here. How was it in Naples?"

"Rough," I said. "I'm glad I didn't stay here after all."

Tommy continued, "I waited out the hurricane at Golden Sands Restaurant with a few people. It wasn't much fun here either. The main road isn't passable. The damn Australian pines are lying across it like pick-up-sticks, so to get around the island, everyone is driving on the beach. In the morning, there's a meeting at the Community House that you and I should attend before we start cleaning up. We'll work with everyone else in the community to get the main road open first."

In retrospect, Donna's aftermath was far worse than the few hours her winds and tides raged all around us. At the meeting, Paul Stahlin was elected Civil Defense Coordinator. Electric power, telephone service, and our special link with the mainland no longer existed, and we had no idea when any of these would be restored. There were a few privately-owned portable generators available, and it was decided that they would be rotated to businesses having the greatest need to keep their refrigeration systems functioning. Gasoline was rationed too — the available supply would have to meet everyone's needs until the ferries were running again. Ordinary gasoline-powered centrifugal pumps pumped fuel from the underground storage tanks at the Standard and Gulf Service Stations — not very safe, but a means to an end.

Several islanders who had various military and law enforce-ment experience volunteered to patrol the near-island waters to stop looters coming to the islands. This was serious work. In the elite neighborhoods of Naples, the National Guard had been dispatched early to protect property. In 1960, the affluent people on the main-land considered Sanibel and Captiva Islands to be the low-class communities of Lee County. So we had to take matters into our own hands.

Everyone at the meeting the next morning agreed that the first order of business was to get the roads open. All able-bodied islanders were expected to help, and they all did. I was assigned to a morning shift and used the Government jeep to pull chunks of trees aside to open the roads. About every half-hour or so, I'd have to stop, crawl under the jeep with wire cutters and pliers, and remove telephone wires that had wrapped up in the drive shafts. In 1960, aerial telephone wires were attached to poles along the north side of Periwinkle Way and to power poles on the south side. During the hurricane, the power and telephone lines were smashed down by falling Australian pines. These infernal trees were the real cause of our long-term problems, insofar as the total absence of electrical power was concerned.

It took just under a week to open Periwinkle Way fully to two-way traffic. Once the road was open, my work began full-time at the lighthouse. Those islanders who could commit time to the project began to clear the powerline right-of-way which parallels Periwinkle Way. When the ferries began to run again and workers from the Lee County Electric Cooperative were able to get to us, part of their toughest workload was already done for them. The Sanibel and Captiva residents had knocked several days off the schedule to restore electric power, because the electric line right-of-way was already prepared for new poles and wires.

In 1960, only one electric transmission line crossed Pine Island Sound to supply Sanibel and Captiva. This line still runs from St. James City on Pine Island to a point just east of Woodring Point on Sanibel. Today, a second power line crosses Pine Island Sound, crosses Wildlife Drive in the J. N. "Ding" Darling National Wildlife Refuge, and ends at a substation on Sanibel-Captiva Road.

A week after Donna's direct hit, the ferry landing was functioning again. Electrical and telephone repair personnel could now reach us and begin restoring the utilities. It would be five weeks before electric service was again operational and three months before telephone service was restored at the Sanibel Lighthouse. Other parts of Sanibel and Captiva were back on-line a few days before us.

Our first night back home was like taking a giant stride back in time — this trip lasted five weeks! Were it not for Jean's heirloom kerosene Aladdin lamp and a few ordinary hurricane oil lamps, we would have been completely in the dark.

"Thank goodness we bought a gas stove and hot water heater," Jean breathed.

I replied, "The stove will really help out, but the hot water heater won't. We don't have any water except the direct line to Tommy's cistern. When I find the time, I'll reroute some plumbing to the hot water heater so we can shower. There should be enough gravity force from the cistern for enough of a dribble to bathe."

We heard all kinds of unusual noises in the dark house that night. But finally we drifted off to sleep watching the regular flash of the acetylene-gas-fueled lighthouse glow against the few tall trees still standing outside our bedroom window. The next morning, my suspicions were confirmed. Rats!

On Wednesday morning the 14th, Tommy and I went across to Punta Rassa, where my car was parked, aboard Jake Stokes' boat. Then I drove Tommy to the Trailways Bus Station in Fort Myers so he could travel to St. Petersburg and get the seaplane out of storage. Before he left Fort Myers, he telephoned the refuge supervisor in the Regional Office to advise them of post-hurricane conditions at the Refuge. He was instructed to pick up the aircraft, then proceed south to the Keys, pick up Refuge Manager Jack Watson, and assess storm damage to those refuges.

While flying around the outer islands of Key West National Wildlife Refuge with Jack, he and Tommy rescued a stranded boater who had been marooned on a small key for nearly a week. They saved his life!

Regional Pilot Ted Ball was to fly to Sanibel from Atlanta on Friday the 16th, pick me up, and we'd inspect areas that the Regional Office wanted checked in southwest Florida. This seemed a strange way to do things, but our Government sometimes works in mysterious ways.

Ted Ball buzzed the lighthouse early Friday afternoon. He was flying a Service-owned Cessna 180 and I drove to the Casa Ybel airstrip to pick him up. He should have been on floats — the entire grass airfield was still covered with about ten inches of water when he set the plane down in a shower of spray.

Ted had been asked to inspect the Refuge and check specific items on our major property inventory. One item was FWS128, our 28-foot Chris Craft patrol boat, the *Tangerita*. The vessel was berthed at Port Comfort Marina on Punta Rassa Road. I had completely forgotten to check on it when Jean, Leslie, and I were on our way home, and Tommy and I forgot it on Wednesday. Tommy was hellbent to get back in the air.

I offered to arrange a boat ride to Punta Rassa and then drive my car to the marina. But Ted insisted we fly over — he planned to land on Punta Rassa Road. The Cessna slipped, slid, and tenaciously resisted breaking free from the flooded airstrip, but finally we were in the air. A few minutes later, after several passes over Punta Rassa Road to check the landing conditions, Ted changed his mind. Better to land on the narrow road on Connie Mack Island instead, he decided. After a couple of tippy flyovers and an uncertain approach, I found I was tightly clutching the edges of the seat, my knuckles white. The landing site appeared clear enough, but the road had a jog in it, much worse than our seaplane canal on Sanibel. We touched down, bounced a little, maneuvered around a close tree, and taxied toward the marina. I wasn't looking forward to the return flight at all.

The *Tangerita* was still securely moored. We were delighted she had suffered very little damage. Just a dented gunwale and a section of broken railing.

I was right! Going home, the takeoff and landing were just as scary as I'd thought.

On Sanibel, things began to return to normal despite the harsh living conditions. Before Periwinkle Way was fully open again, Tommy and I drove along the beach to check out the changes to the Sanibel Gulf front. We saw thousands of loggerhead turtle eggs lining the beach or floating in tidal pools like stranded seashells. They had been washed out of the sand and ruined by the heavy surf Donna generated.

We also saw scores of injured sea birds — pelicans, cormorants, gulls, and terns among others. They were injured from being blown about by the winds, unable to control their flight. It was anyone's guess how many others had been knocked down into the vegetation further inland and were hidden.

Tommy and I conjectured that bird mortality at the rookeries of our satellite refuges was extremely high, and tremendous wildlife losses probably occurred everywhere along Donna's path. Since there were no wildlife rehabilitation facilities anywhere near Sanibel, we had to humanely put down those birds that were mangled or slowed down enough for us to capture.

At Point Ybel, Donna dumped a huge triangular pile of debris on the beach. Beginning directly in front of and almost under our quarters, this mountain of decomposing plants and animals extended nearly a hundred feet out into the water. This heap included sea grasses, palm trees, and Australian pines along with a conglomeration of dead creatures — birds, crabs, fish, and shells.

In time, this heap began to rot — and how! Its stench was almost unbearable, and a breath of air from the right direction would gag even those with the strongest of stomachs. Finally, it became downright unhealthy for Jean and Leslie to remain at home. Leaving me to fend for myself, they went to Jean's parents' home. In two weeks, after wind, tide, precipitation, and time had finally diluted the stench, they rejoined me in my primitive lifestyle.

A week before the ferry service was restored and occasionally thereafter, a handful of us on the road-clearing crew would congregate at Clarence Rutland's house every evening to rehash the day's events. Each day, Clarence would make a trip to Bailey's Store to meet the mailboat and buy a huge block of ice. Later, we broke the ice into small pieces, filled some tall glasses, and added a generous portion of bourbon. Clarence had the ice and someone else usually brought the whiskey. The Rutland house had a two-drink limit.

Two days after my family and I returned to Sanibel, on Wednesday, September 14th, the war against the invading rodents began. That morning, I discovered their droppings in every room of the house, especially the kitchen. The old evidence had been swept outside with the sand and shells. They had inspected any soft-packaged food in open cabinets and demolished our only fresh loaf of bread. I had no idea how many were in the house.

That evening, we closed our bedroom doors so any rats there could not escape. I stayed inside to carefully inspect the room and furniture. Two rats had established residence in a dresser drawer. I frightened these out of their hiding place and shot them using rat-shot with my trusty Ruger Single-Six .22 caliber revolver. The culprits were roof rats — sometimes called barn or palm rats — and they were enormous, almost the size of squirrels.

Closing the bedroom door behind me, I slowly moved through the house using the same method.

Before dark, I had already killed six rats. I plugged their entry holes in the doors and planned to resume the battle later that night. After dinner and dark, with Jean and Leslie safely in the bedroom, I stalked the house, a flashlight in one hand, cocked pistol in the other. I investigated any tiny noise I heard. I dispatched another three rats. I'm sure the tiny holes the shot made are still in the floors and walls of Quarters 2. But we won the war!

* * *

A few days after the ferry service resumed, the two Coast Guardsmen from the Fort Myers Light Attendant Station arrived to inspect the lighthouse. They had their work cut out for them — Donna had destroyed most of their aids to navigation. But the light tower was basically unharmed. A few panes of glass were missing from the small windows in the stairway tube, but the light was continuing to burn properly and its characteristic remained true. The only major damage, which I hadn't noticed from down below, were three cracked storm panes on the western side of the lantern. The storm panes were about $5/_{16}$ of an inch thick, and over time, sunlight had turned them a light shade of green. I still don't know if these panes were original equipment, but if they were, they stood up remarkably well over 75 years of such abusive weather.

In a few weeks, a Coast Guard-contracted glazier arrived from St. Petersburg with new glass panes and hoisting tackle. But no helper! No key! Under the umbrella of "other duties as assigned" (part of my position description), Tommy instructed me to lend a hand. So for a couple days, I changed hats and resumed my light keeper duties. I took my key, opened the tower, helped carry up the block and tackle and associated rigging, and helped remove and lower the old glass. From the ground, I hoisted up the three new modern-style, inner-wire-reinforced glass storm panes. I then climbed back up the light tower to help the glazier position and fasten the panes in their frames.

For many years following the establishment of the Sanibel Island Light Station, Point Ybel and the deep anchorage of San Carlos Bay afforded protection to boats and sailors. They could reach the well-known harbor safely before a threatening tropical storm caught them offshore. Frequently, Cuban fishermen sought safe refuge in San Carlos Bay and occasionally even in the Light Station buildings. Some of these fishermen died when their fishing vessels were wrecked and sunk by hurricanes. Through the years, a few were even buried on Sanibel Island.

The Cubans fished in international waters in motorless sailing schooners called smacks. About 125 feet long, these vessels were unique; however, their uniqueness resulted from necessity. Before man-made ice was readily available and modern marine refrigeration was unknown, the fishing vessels that sailed the subtropical seas for long periods of time were usually smacks. The hulls of these utilitarian boats were nothing more than huge live wells. Fish that were caught by the hand-line and net crews were immediately dumped alive into the well. Seawater freely circulated through the well so that their catch could be processed (most were salted), and some fish might survive until the vessel returned to Cuba.

The smacks usually came relatively close to our coasts, into waters that seldom exceeded 15 fathoms deep. Grouper, which was and still is a much sought-after species, like to frequent variably deep, usually rocky bottoms. When caught in waters greater than six fathoms, some grouper and other deep-water species are completely puffed up, about to burst, when they reach the surface. Their eyes are bulged out, and the fish sometimes literally explode when they are brought to the surface too quickly. This happens because of the differences between the atmospheric pressure at sea level and the water's ambient pressure at the depth the fish were caught.

On one occasion, crew members from a Cuban smack helped save my quarters and maybe the adjacent buildings. Somehow, sometime, prior to 1941 (I have no definitive record), a fire started under or spread beneath Quarters 2. Broward Keene, a Coast Guard assistant light keeper from 1941 to 1944, told me that some kerosene had been stored beneath the building and had somehow ignited. At any rate, the building's floor joists were engulfed in flame, and light station personnel were frantically fighting the fire with their limited equipment and water supply.

At the time, a Cuban smack was anchored in the bay. Seeing the smoke, the crew responded and helped with the hand-force fire pump. Other crewmen formed a bucket brigade and dipped water from the Gulf of Mexico to fight the fire. The valiant efforts of Americans and Cubans working together saved the buildings.

In 1974, most of the undersides of both quarters were covered with plywood to reduce the amount of paintable surface and the time required for periodic maintenance painting. With their tell-tale burned lower corners rounded and charred by the flames, most of the floor joists are no longer visible. The outermost Gulf-side main support beam, which rests on the iron pilings, and the uncovered joists beneath the adjacent porch still show signs of the fire. Charred wood is visible where the paint is peeling.

By 1960, the Cuban fishing fleet was modernized. The new fishing vessels were motorized and had ice-storage capacity. The most recently built ones (likely with Russian money) had on-board refrigeration units.

In times of imminent danger from hurricanes, Cuban fishermen no longer sought safety behind Sanibel in San Carlos Bay. This was primarily due to the uneasy political situation that existed, and sadly still does, between Cuba and the United States. In 1948, the crew of a hurricane-damaged Cuban smack was given shelter at the Sanibel Island Light Station by the Coast Guard team stationed there at the time.

The last time a Cuban fishing smack sought refuge from a storm in San Carlos Bay was on September 30, 1950. The 30 crew members spent the night in Quarters 2. Tommy allowed the boat's captain to use the Refuge telephone to notify the vessel's owner in Havana that the smack and crew were okay. Of course, the call was made collect!

The Sanibel Island Light Station is located at 26 degrees, 27 minutes latitude and 82 degrees and 01 minute longitude. During a storm's passage, hurricane advisories are transmitted periodically. Using actual coordinates to plot a hurricane's changing positions can provide an interesting baseline assessment of a severe hurricane. For my baseline, I selected a storm from back in the days when they were neither named nor numbered. This mighty Category 5 hurricane struck the vicinity of Sanibel Island on October 15, 1873. On this date, this storm produced the flood-of-record at Punta Rassa.

Falling within a five-category intensity range, computer-modeled tropical cyclones have been created based on the submerged and terrestrial coastal topography of southwest Florida. Under certain scenarios, this modeling projects just what force a hurricane and interrelated atmospheric phenomena can produce. The storm elements related to flood elevations are: (1) winds, both sustained and gusts; (2) the wind's direction, in relation to the system's overall forward heading; (3) tides, in synchronization with periodicity and amplitudes of normal tidal events; and (4) the anticipated height of a storm-caused tidal surge, which is the wind-heaped water forced against the land mass. The official flood-of-record at Punta Rassa in 1873 was 14 feet above mean sea level.

The U. S. Geological Survey has marked the elevation of the land surface at the base of the Sanibel Lighthouse, above mean sea level, with a fixed brass benchmark. Now covered by a few inches of sand, this monument is stamped on its uppermost surface as having been measured 6 feet above mean sea level. In relation to this and as points of reference, the floor level inside the bottom of the light tower is 25 feet above mean sea level. The bottom edge of the main horizontal beams of both quarters, which rest on the pilings, are 11.5 feet above mean sea level. And the top surface of the quarters' cypress-decked porches are 13.5 feet above mean sea level.

To bring storm surge into perspective, I later measured, with a transit, the high-water mark on the concrete block wall of the Refuge shop at the lighthouse. This indicated a storm surge elevation of 8.7 feet above mean sea level. During Donna's strike, 2.7 feet of sea water surged across Point Ybel.

Over time, many violent tropical storms and hurricanes have directly hit Sanibel and Captiva Islands. In the future, many others will do their part in shaping these islands. During the major hurricanes of 1910, 1926, 1935, and 1944, light keepers and their families were joined by a handful of island families who had fled to the lighthouse for safety's sake. During the most severe part of the storm surges, in 1926, 1935, and 1944, water was lapping against the main beams of the buildings.

At their wit's end and fearing for their lives, men, women, and children crawled on hands and knees up the exterior stairs which led from each porch to safety inside the light tower. Along the way, their bodies were pelted by painfully stinging torrential rain and whipped by the powerful wind. By some accounts, the tower swayed in the violent screaming wind in 1944, although it was not designed to do so. If the Gulf waters did indeed reach the support beams of the quarters, the tidal surges of the 1926, 1935, and 1944 hurricanes must have been very close to 11 feet above mean sea level. It has been said that seawater completely inundated both Sanibel and Captiva during the 1926 storm. Had the light station's buildings been in place on Point Ybel during the flood-of-record hurricane in 1873, they would have been knocked down and swept away.

The Coast Guard's old submarine lookout tower was left leaning more than ever after Donna. Despite its expected plunge to the beach, the wooden structure still stood. Island teenagers often dared one another to brave the precipitous angle. Therefore, Tommy and I decided that it should come down, before it did so on its own, and kill someone in it or walking near it.

On a cool January morning in 1961, Tommy asked me to climb the tower and inspect the contents of the cubicle at the top. I discovered a cache of old comic books. (These were the days before *Playboy* became so popular.) When I came down, Tommy and I soaked the four corner support pilings with kerosene and torched them. These were well-creosoted pilings; they burned very hot and a lot of thick black smoke billowed up. It wasn't long before this former wartime observation tower came crashing to the ground. It was slightly under 20 years old at the time of its demise. During those two decades, not one of its occupants had ever sighted a submarine — that is, outside the covers of an adventure comic book.

PHOTOGRAPH SECTION

Don Carroll (left) and Charles LeBuff, June 1952. *Photo from the author's collection.*

This photograph was taken at my boyhood home in Medford, Massachusetts, when I first met Don Carroll. He was a man's man adventurer who convinced my parents that our family should move to southwest Florida.

Left to right: Laurence LeBuff, Don McKeown, Carl Williams (no relation to Jean), Charles, and Laban LeBuff, Bonita Springs, Florida, March 1953. *Photo from the author's collection.*

Charles LeBuff and Jean Williams on our engagement night, June 14, 1957. *Photo from the author's collection.*
This photograph was taken near Bonita Springs inside a commercial fisherman's one-room shanty. The friend's dwelling could be reached only by mullet skiff or other small craft or by foot after crossing a narrow double-plank-wide boardwalk that meandered through the dense red mangrove forest.

The LeBuff Family: Charles, Jean, Leslie, and Chuck, June 1962. *Photo from the author's collection.*

In June 1959, *Popular Mechanics* magazine featured an article on how to build an antique car replica. I decided to order the complete plans and built the vehicle over a two-year period.

It was powered by a 3–hp Briggs and Stratton gasoline engine, had an automatic centrifugal clutch, and even a simple differential that I had to fabricate from scratch. Top speed of the car on a level grade was 23 mph.

It became a true family car. We would use it to ride the beaches when we went shelling and picknicking, or drive it to Bailey's General Store on the bay to purchase groceries. Twice we trucked it to Naples where Jean and the children drove it in the annual Swamp Buggy Parade.

Soon after the opening of the Sanibel Causeway (and a few beers), a friend and I drove it from the lighthouse, crossed the bridge, U-turned at the toll plaza, and paid the $3.00 toll to get home.

Jean and I continued to use it for another year or two, then sold it to the owner of a Sanibel dress shop.

W. D. "Tommy" Wood. Good friend and first refuge manager of the Sanibel (J. N. "Ding" Darling) National Wildlife Refuge. *Photo from the author's collection.*

Jay Norwood "Ding" Darling, as he appeared close to the time I met him. *Photo courtesy of the J. N. "Ding" Darling Foundation.*

Greeting card to Tommy and Louise Wood from "Ding" Darling, Christmas 1950. *Photo of original from the author's collection*
  When Tommy retired, he gave me this unique "Ding" Darling ***color*** original. It has since been acquired by the J. N. "Ding" Darling Foundation to be displayed in the Visitor Center at the J. N. "Ding" Darling National Wildlife Refuge.

"UTOPIA," one of "Ding" Darling's best conservation cartoons. *Cartoon courtesy of the J. N. "Ding" Darling Foundation.*

Darling's inspiration for this rendition may well have been his beloved Captiva and Sanibel Islands. It is an appropriate piece of artwork and supports his concept of what would eventually happen to these seashell islands. Despite his own words, *he was* a prophet!

PROPERTY OWNERS

PETITION TO CLOSE, BY EXECUTIVE ORDER, all shooting, trapping or other molestation of birds and wild life on Sanibel and Captiva islands and adjacent island rookeries and feeding grounds, subject to the management and supervision of the U. S. Fish & Wild Life Service of the U. S. Department of Interior.

Signature _J. N. Darling_

Address _Captiva, Fla._

"Ding" Darling's signed petition requesting an Executive Order to protect Sanibel and Captiva, circa 1938. *Photo from the author's collection.*

The Sanibel Island Light Station, circa 1933. *Photo from the author's collection.*
    This early aerial photograph shows the well-defined light station compound. Note the small, well-trimmed Australian pines lining the walkway from the station to the pier.

The Sanibel Island Light Station, circa 1942. *Photo from the author's collection.*
Note the ground-level wooden cistern and the staircases which span from the
porches to the lighthouse landing. A major hurricane in 1944 swept away the
water tank, and the unsafe stairways were removed in 1951.

The Sanibel Island Light Station, circa 1943. *Photo from the author's collection.*
Note the fixed third-order lens is in place, as are the water towers and pump
house. The pilings in the Gulf are the remains of a temporary wharf. Building
materials were unloaded onto this pier to build the wooden observation tower
and the small cottage which housed the Coast Guard's beach patrol personnel.

Quarters 3, at the time of completion, 1942. *Photo from the author's collection.*
This two-bedroom cottage was our first Sanibel residence. By the time we arrived on the island, however, hurricanes had raised the land elevation around the building and the concrete foundation was just inches above the sand. Repeated salt-water soakings eventually caused the internal rebar (steel rods) in the foundation and pilings to rust, expand, crack, and break away the seashell aggregate concrete.

The fixed third-order Fresnel lens which occupied the lantern room of the Sanibel Island Light Station, from 1923 to 1962, November 24, 1950. *Photo from the author's collection.*
This is a poor photograph of the second lens used in the light tower. The first lens, a rotating third-order lens with bullseye optics, functioned in the lantern room from 1884 until 1923. Note the leaning observation tower and the cottage.

Aerial view of Point Ybel, Sanibel Island, November 1958. *Photo from the author's collection.*
    This photograph was taken a few weeks prior to our move from Naples to Sanibel Island. The canals to the left of the light station compound are mosquito ditches, and the road is an evacuation route during the frequent times the Gulf-front road was underwater due to storm-related tidal flooding.

The former lightship lens, circa 1983. *Photo courtesy of David Meardon.*
    The station's third lens system, this was a 500–mm drum lens, which I helped to install in the lantern room in 1962. It has since been replaced with a modern beacon and is scheduled to be displayed at Sanibel's Historical Village and Museum near City Hall.

Manatee care-givers: Leslie, refuge employee Ray Carner, and Chuck, 1969.
Photo from the author's collection.
Ray is holding our orphaned manatee.

The first Sanibel City Council, 1974. *Photo from the author's collection.*
Seated: Zee Butler (left) and Francis Bailey (right). Standing: Porter Goss
(left), Vernon MacKenzie, and Charles LeBuff (right).

Reenactment of my position during my tractor accident of December 17, 1979. *Photo from the author's collection.*
    I was able to get to my feet and walk away after the dual tires crossed my body. I consider my survival a miracle.

A loggerhead turtle with the author.   *Photo courtesy of Ed Phillips.*
    I dedicated 38 years of my life to field research and conservation of this threatened species on Sanibel and Captiva Islands and southwest Florida.

14

CARETTA

When the summer of 1968 rolled around, I was still using a Government-owned jeep for my loggerhead turtle investigations and conducting the summer field work mostly by myself. The commitments of time and personal resources were taking their toll on me, and I began to realize that the management objectives of the Refuge and its manager would soon change. The Refuge's participation in my sea turtle work, which had no clear connection with my official duties, was likely to be eliminated. Worse still from my point of view, the program could even be absorbed as a Refuge-controlled function. Because I had developed the protocol for the program entirely on my own, I had no desire for any interference by some future supervisor or any other form of Government control. I had already made a long-term personal commitment, so it became clear to me that my sea turtle conservation efforts would have to be restructured.

By this time, I had published more papers on the herpetology of Florida and had been promoted to biological technician. Also, I had thwarted two attempts by the Fish and Wildlife Service to transfer me to other units in the National Wildlife Refuge System, far away from these islands I had grown to love. Despite these attractive advancement opportunities, I resolved to remain on Sanibel and play out my plan.

One evening, I told Jean, "I'm going to write up a series of objectives for a sea turtle conservation program here on the islands. It'll be a privately financed new project without any formal ties to the Refuge. I'm going to call it Caretta Research and bring in some people to share the load."

I took the name Caretta from the scientific name of the loggerhead turtle, which is *Caretta caretta.*

"Good," she responded. "Maybe then we can take summer vacations, like normal people, and do something with the kids instead of you spending every night out on the beach!" Jean had become a "turtle widow" by now and really wasn't happy about the present arrangement.

The Caretta Research project was launched with a well-attended public program at the Captiva Civic Center in February 1969. I explained the work I had accomplished during the first decade of my studies on the islands, announced plans for future work under the auspices of the new all-volunteer organization, and solicited contributions to finance the work.

I presented my idea of a head-start program where hatchling loggerheads would be placed in tanks, maintained in captivity, and released when about a year old. Theoretically, they would then be large enough to cope with predators and have a greater chance of long-term survival. At the time, the State of Florida had a green turtle head-start program in place, and the idea was generally well received by most of the sea turtle biologists around at the time.

I was granted permission to open the head-start facility on Refuge-owned property at Tarpon Bay, on bay-front land the Fish and Wildlife Service leased to those who ran the Tarpon Bay Marina. Construction of the tanks and purchase of related equipment would be financed with money received under a membership subscription plan. A portion of each contribution would underwrite the construction costs, and donors would have their names displayed above a specific tank in recognition of their support.

By April, the program was solidly financed, so I started to build the site and tanks. In June, I began to transplant jeopardized clutches of loggerhead turtle eggs into a protective enclosure in the front yard of our Sanibel Lighthouse quarters. At the same time, I was serving as Scoutmaster of Sanibel and Captiva Troop 88, Boy Scouts of America. So I enlisted several troop members to assist in the construction phase and later in actual operations.

In late 1968, I wrote a booklet entitled *The Marine Turtles of Sanibel and Captiva Islands, Florida*. Roy Bazire of the Sanibel-Captiva Conservation Foundation offered to publish it as a special report for their membership. After the report came out, I entered into an agreement with SCCF, which became the sponsor for Caretta Research. In this way, donated funds earmarked for sea turtle conservation were tax deductible. My turtle program benefitted from this umbrella as substantial contributors responded because of the tax-exempt status. Monies received from my fund-raising efforts were released to Caretta Research as grants from the Sanibel-Captiva Conservation Foundation.

The head-start project was off to a good start. I then arranged with Pine Island resident and commercial fisherman "Tootsie" Barnes to furnish me with frozen catfish. "Tootsie" was a member of the Organized Fishermen of Florida and was very interested in my loggerhead turtle head-start program and sea turtle biology in general. Every week or two, I went to Matlacha to pick up several hundred pounds of fish. They were partly thawed, beheaded, ground whole, and refrozen, to be used as turtle food when needed. Several hundred little loggerheads were housed in the facility, which was open to the public for educational purposes.

Then in late November, the unexpected happened. An early cold front hit the islands. The strong northwest wind created an extremely low tide, and the water intake pipe which circulated bay water through the tanks was exposed and lost its prime during the night. The pump failed and the water temperature in the tanks dropped to the upper forties (°F). Over the next several days, small loggerheads began to perish, mostly from respiratory ailments. I was crushed! I immediately released many of the turtles that were still alive, keeping only the strongest for release in May 1970.

I attempted the program again that year, on a smaller scale, but similar environmental problems proved to be too much. I decided that a large-scale loggerhead turtle head-start program at Tarpon Bay would be unsuccessful, so I shut the operation down.

The objectives of Caretta Research were redirected following the head-start failure. For the next two decades, I concentrated on my field work and applied the principles of wildlife management to sea turtle conservation.

Tagging loggerheads became a major part of my studies, and the scope of this phase of my work intensified and grew. Nesting surveys, egg protection, assessments of hatching success, and public awareness were also key elements. I was able to continue uninterrupted too!

I began to apply Monel metal cattle ear tags to the front flippers of island loggerheads in June 1964, and by August 1967, my original supply was nearly gone. The Sanibel-Captiva Audubon Society had bought the tags when they initially funded my alligator life history studies on the barrier islands, and most of that tag series were now attached to the tails of Sanibel Island alligators. So I called renowned marine turtle biologist Archie Carr, graduate research professor at the University of Florida's Department of Zoology, and asked to borrow some of his tags. He sent me a series to use on the islands in time for the 1968 nesting season. I had met Dr. Carr several years earlier when we both had been named as charter members of the American Alligator Council.

These self-piercing tags were attached by forcing them through the trailing edge of a turtle's front flipper using a special plier-like tool. The outer surface of each tag was factory-stamped with the following information: At one end was a set of numbers identifying the individual turtle, and at the other end, which became the other side of the tag when crimped, was a message offering a reward if the tag and pertinent recapture data were returned to the University of Florida. Caretta Research finally bought its own supply of tags in 1969. These were numerically stamped with a CR prefix, and the reward message requested that Caretta Research be notified directly.

By 1969, recaptures of a sufficient sample of tagged individuals indicated that most Sanibel and Captiva loggerheads returned regularly to the islands every two years for renesting. The remaining adult female population nesting along the coast of the eastern

Gulf of Mexico did so in the interim and also maintained a two-year cycle. In other words, part of the population nests in even years and the others nest in odd years.

The program also documented that like other sea turtles, Sanibel and Captiva loggerheads multiple-nested during their respective nesting summers. Richard Beatty, who had joined me to organize Caretta Research, and I coauthored and published a paper in 1969 on this aspect of loggerhead turtle nesting. The regional scope of tagging operations along the southwest Florida coast increased as the project matured.

Multiple nesting occurs in all the world's eight scientifically recognized species of marine turtles. In loggerheads, one female can deposit eggs in up to seven nests in any one reproductive season. Based on reencounters on the nesting beach, tagging has shown that most local female loggerhead turtles nest three times a season. The internesting interval (the number of days between nestings) averages eleven days between each successive nesting.

On May 24, 1973, I met a unique loggerhead. We tagged her CR-140 during what we decided was her initial nesting that season. She continued to visit the Sanibel beach periodically and deposited another five observed egg complements that summer. Her voluminous egg production totaled 920 eggs! Remarkably, all six nests were dug on Sanibel's eastern end within a four-mile section of beach just to the west of the Sanibel Lighthouse. How this turtle managed to adjust her nest site fidelity so accurately despite the strong influences of tide, current, and drift amazes me still. Someone on the beach patrol team appropriately named CR-140 "Myrtle the fertile turtle."

C-429, a University of Florida tag, was another famous loggerhead. Having completed nesting, she was tagged on Sanibel on May 28, 1968. She was not documented again until June 25, 1972, when she was seen nesting on the other side of the Florida peninsula just south of Melbourne Beach. Another group monitoring that area's sea turtles identified her, and later I published a paper about this unusual nesting relocation. Since this event was documented, a few other such widely separated nestings by specific tagged loggerheads have been reported in the scientific literature.

It is now generally accepted that loggerheads do not remain faithful to a specific beach, as is the case for other species of sea turtles. One of the Western Atlantic's exhaustively studied green turtle populations, for example, nests exclusively on the Caribbean coast of Costa Rica.

Tagging also provided interesting information on the whereabouts of Sanibel and Captiva loggerheads during the two years they are absent from local waters. Without a long-term tagging program, students of marine turtle biology would not have some basic life history data on these unique reptiles.

Over the years, tags were returned to us from all kinds of people and from widely separated geographical locations along the northwestern Atlantic Ocean. Although most tag recoveries came from the Gulf of Mexico, Sanibel-Captiva loggerheads regularly venture beyond its limits. These tag recoveries have established a broad non-nesting distribution for our island loggerheads during their non-reproductive periods.

For example, a specimen tagged on Sanibel in 1969 was caught over a year later near the Chandeleur Islands off the coast of Louisiana. It drowned in a shrimp trawler's net as the crew pulled its bottom-hugging rigs. The shrimper returned the tag and received a $5.00 reward, the going rate for sea turtle tag returns at that time.

A Mexican net fisherman entangled a Sanibel-tagged loggerhead just south of the tip of the Yucatan peninsula at Cabo Catoche. He gave the tag to his village priest who understood English. The priest returned the tag and relevant collection data to Caretta Research.

In 1972, I received a strange, indirectly delivered letter about another Sanibel loggerhead. A Cuban fisherman caught this turtle near Cayo Fragoso off Cuba's northern coast. The letter had been received, apparently via Mexico, by a Miami-based importing company, and its manager forwarded it to Caretta Research.

Several Sanibel-tagged loggerheads have navigated huge distances after nesting here. The record long-distance holder was ensnared and drowned in a pound net 13 miles offshore northeast of Atlantic City, New Jersey. If this turtle paralleled the coast after nesting on Sanibel, she probably reached the vicinity of her demise in a little over 11 months and traveled around 1,500 miles.

In the summer of 1976, a recreational fisherman was enjoying the afternoon angling from a bridge near the headwaters of the York

River in Virginia. Suddenly, he felt a tremendous tug on his line. For several hours, he fought and finally landed a large loggerhead turtle that had taken his bait. He removed the shiny Monel tag, then released the turtle into the river. Along with all the details of the event, he returned the tag to Caretta Research.

Caretta Research received excellent media coverage during its formative period. Interested people in other communities who learned of its work on television, radio talk shows, and in area newspapers came forward to volunteer. As interest developed, the organization became more regional in scope. By early 1973, a complex of 14 units of Caretta Research had developed in coastal communities between Clearwater and Naples. Each unit was under the leadership of a local resident who, after indoctrination and training, carried out Caretta Research's objectives on his or her home beach. In time, this unanticipated growth prompted the administrative committee to dissociate from the Sanibel-Captiva Conservation Foundation. Caretta Research, Inc., became a non-profit, tax-exempt, Title 501(c)3 organization and was officially sanctioned by the Internal Revenue Service in mid-1973.

During the summer, the organization continued to diversify. It established a tagging program on Florida's east coast in the vicinity of Sebastian Inlet State Recreation Area. The purpose was to collect comparable data on Atlantic coast loggerheads to statistically compare to the Gulf coast's nesting population. I appointed Ed Phillips as Caretta's Special Projects Director and asked him to lead the new program.

Because of Ed's reputation as a highly respected school teacher in his hometown of Westfield, Massachusetts, Caretta Research, Inc., received an ongoing annual grant from the Frank Stanley Beveridge Foundation in that town. The money was earmarked to fund the east coast project, with the further understanding that each summer, Ed would select six high school students from Westfield and bring them to Florida to work on his month-long project.

During the 30-day periods he conducted the program, Ed would notify Ross Witham of the Florida Department of Natural Resources if Ed or any member of his group encountered a nesting green turtle. Ross would collect the eggs, hatch them in containers, then use the hatchlings as new recruits in his long-established green turtle head-start program centered at the House of Refuge Museum near Stuart, Florida. A small but growing number of green turtles continued to nest on Florida's east coast. Supposedly, these were what remained of a once-abundant population of these endangered marine turtles.

"Why don't we apply to the State and have our permit amended to allow us to collect green turtle eggs on the east coast, bring them to Sanibel, and rebury them on the beach?" Ed asked. We were discussing his plans for the 1974 summer over the telephone long-distance.

Half seriously, I replied, "We could try this as an attempt to recolonize lower Gulf-coast beaches with green turtles. I saw one green turtle on this beach in '59, and a few years ago I learned that a green turtle was taken on Bonita Beach in '67.

"I can remember conversations I had years ago with Sanibel old-timer Clarence Rutland about sea turtles. He told me in a convincing way that when he was a boy on Sanibel — right after the turn of the century — green turtles were sometimes taken for food on the Sanibel beach and other barrier islands in Lee County."

I was becoming more interested in the concept. "If you really want to try this, we'll work up the details through the mail in hopes of getting an okay before you go over to Sebastian Inlet this summer. We'll have to prepare a formal study plan and make a serious request to get permission. I'll start the paper shuffle next week."

In April 1974, I submitted our written proposal to the Florida Department of Natural Resources. Our plan outlined a simple, straightforward protocol. I asked for authorization to remove up to ten complements of green turtle eggs from Brevard County for rapid transport to and immediate transplantation on Sanibel. A few days later, I received a letter acknowledging receipt of the proposal and advising me that it was being distributed to other sea turtle biologists for peer review. By return mail, I asked to receive copies of these review comments.

Archie Carr and Frank Lund reviewed our proposal, and both shot it down. The State official reviewing our application concurred, and the request was denied.

I found Dr. Carr's reasoning, upon which he based his recommendation for denial, to be illogical, based on what I knew about his tampering with the distribution of the green turtle. For years, he had been importing hatchling green turtles from Tortuguero, Costa Rica, and releasing them in Florida in a well-publicized attempt to reestablish the species in the State. This program had become known as "Operation Green Turtle," and there was no evidence to support the notion that this attempt was ever successful.

Frank Lund was a college student at the time and operated a successful sea turtle conservation and research program on Jupiter Island, Florida. Frank's objections, which I considered to be biologically invalid, had to do with environmental conditions and beach suitability on Sanibel. Any plans for a formal green turtle egg transplantation program were curtailed, and I never raised the issue again — outside of Caretta Research, Inc., and private conversations with Ed Phillips.

I phoned Ed and gave him the disappointing news.

"I expected as much," he told me. Irritated, he continued, "Seems to me it's just a case of professional jealousy on their part, because they didn't come up with the idea first!"

"You're probably right," I responded. "I'll tell you what! When you find more than one green turtle on the beach over there at about the same time and they're nesting close together, within an hour or two of dawn, go ahead and collect their eggs and fly them to Sanibel. Before you collect any eggs, justify doing so if in your view there's evidence, beyond any reasonable doubt, that some survival factor would preclude successful development of the eggs if they remained there."

Two years elapsed before all the elements required in this plan came together. Early in the morning of July 23, 1976, I was awakened by a telephone call from Ed.

He told me excitedly, "I'm at Melbourne Airport arranging to rent a plane. I've got two green turtle clutches that were deposited in a severely eroding section of the beach at John's Island, south of Sebastian Inlet. I'll be landing on Sanibel at the strip within two hours."

Ed, a licensed private pilot, landed a Piper Warrior at the Casa Ybel airstrip with his precious cargo: two clutches of green turtle eggs containing 134 and 146 eggs, respectively. We loaded the containers into our new Caretta Research-owned jeep and drove to a predetermined site on the beach 7.5 miles west of the Sanibel Lighthouse. The transplantation location was ideal because of its high, well-drained profile and because loggerhead turtle eggs deposited here naturally were usually very successful.

When he collected the eggs, Ed had taken accurate measurements of all the nest dimensions. These data included the original egg cavity and body pit depths, singular and combined, and he carefully sketched the intrinsic peculiarities of each turtle's egg cavity. All these measurements were carefully duplicated when we excavated the new cavities. After we carefully cleaned each egg of any adhering Atlantic sand, we buried the two clutches six feet apart. Then we drove wooden stakes to mark each clutch, then we were through with our clandestine operation. Less than five hours had elapsed since Ed had watched the green turtle eggs drop into the Brevard County beach and when the eggs were safely nestled in their new incubation sites on Sanibel Island.

Over the next several weeks, I maintained a special vigil over the developing green turtle eggs. But alas, I was not there to witness the special moment when the first turtles emerged. They were the first of their species in 50 years or more to make the dangerous trek across the dark Sanibel beach. A severe thunder and lightning storm during the night of September 19th caused me to cancel my regular night beach patrol and miss the emergence.

The next night, my coworkers and I observed post-emergent depressions in the beach surface above both nests. These shallow depressions, with ramped or eroded edges on the water side usually caused by scurrying hatchlings heading hell-bent for the water, indicate that neonate turtles had indeed vacated their sandy chamber. Over the years, I have convinced myself that the inclement weather the night before not only kept me off the beach, but hungry raccoons as well. It helps me feel better about missing the event. To this day, Ed Phillips and I insist that all our little green turtles safely reached the surf.

I waited two more nights. Finally, I couldn't stand it anymore and excavated the nests to confirm their success. In the first group, which was the nest that contained 134 eggs, no live or dead hatchlings were found. However, 11 infertile (addled) eggs remained in the cavity. In the second group, which contained 146 eggs, was one live, normal hatchling and 13 unhatched dark eggs. With a great deal of pomp and circumstance, we took the last hatchling to the water's edge and ceremoniously released him (or her) headlong into the surf to join its 255 brothers and sisters.

Our clandestine green turtle egg transplant was a huge success. When I was writing my earlier book, *The Loggerhead Turtle in the Eastern Gulf of Mexico*, I added an appendix which included green turtles. But I did not mention our secret mission or "'fess up" until now.

Years later, in 1995 to be exact, Ed Phillips and I had another conversation about our special green turtle mission. He was on his annual Sanibel visit.

I told him, "I talked to Dave Addison of The Conservancy down in Naples a few weeks ago. He's still heading up their sea turtle program on Key Island, south of Naples. Dave told me there were a few documented nestings by green turtles in Collier County last summer."

Ed was elated. "Fantastic! I'll bet they came from those eggs I flew over from the east coast and we hatched out on Sanibel. Some must have survived, were females, and grew up to nest on the Gulf coast fairly close to Sanibel. I'll be damned, just like I always thought they would, if any made it at all!"

Since Jean had first mentioned to me that night long ago, when we watched our first Sanibel loggerhead, that her father had always heard little sea turtles grew up and returned to nest on the very beaches where they originated, I had rejected the notion. It sounded a little far-fetched, almost make believe. As the years passed, I'd revisit the question from time to time, but I never could accept it as credible. It would take powerful scientific evidence to convince me to change my viewpoint on this hypothesis. Until proven otherwise, I shall continue to look upon this fable as akin to those of Aesop.

The longer I worked with loggerhead turtles, the more I learned. My sea turtle career was a continuous learning experience, and I immersed myself totally in it. Contrary to what many sea turtle students accept, I do not subscribe to the idea that marine turtles return as adults to the same beaches where they hatched.

I prefer a different approach to the unknown factors that control a mature sea turtle's imprinting to a specific beach. It is that key element of their life history, their tenacity to return to nesting beaches, that has resulted in sizeable nesting assemblages for some of the eight species of marine turtles. In most cases, these fundamental behaviors have controlled their destiny and survivability into modern times.

Continuing our conversation, I answered, "Sorry, Big Ed. I just can't completely buy into that concept. It sounds like someone's pipedream to me. I believe that nest-site specificity for most sea turtles is controlled by an established tenacity for a specific beach, but I also believe it is psychologically, or instinctively if you prefer, attained after sexual maturity is reached.

"To be more specific, in my opinion, beach-finding memory is established at the time a turtle makes her first successful emergence to nest. If all goes well at that time, and I don't have any idea what these factors may include, an individual sea turtle — loggerhead or otherwise — will absorb these unknown clues. These rules of nest-site fixity are somehow retained, and when their recall is required, they permit a sexually active sea turtle to navigate and return to her now-favored beach, even after a year or more. Usually but not always, depending on the species, if she does not emerge near the exact site, she'll be very close to the last beach she visited — unless she's a wayward loggerhead or a wandering ridley. To say that the little green turtles, produced by our secret experiment almost 20 years ago, had a level of survivorship that may have allowed a handful to escape the many perils during their development, reach maturity, and return to nest on Gulf coast beaches sure sounds good. Wouldn't it be something if it were true!"

"We'd never get any credit if it were a proven fact, or even if a voice from on high announced it," Ed interjected. "Hell, someone else out there would deny it could happen, based on their preconceived percentages game, don't you know!"

"What do you mean percentages, Ed?" my interest rising.

He continued, "Haven't we always heard that the survival rate of sea turtle hatchlings is extremely low? Of course, this has always been based on the work of 'experts' in population dynamics in a variety of wildlife species. Personally, I have never bought into their bull — the scenarios developed which claim that only one-quarter of one percent, or one out of 10,000 hatchlings or some other invented number, survive to reach sexual maturity."

I made my final comment on the subject. "Wildlife management principles aren't based on cut and dried facts, Eddie. Theory has a lot to do with science. Who's to say that little green turtles entering the Gulf of Mexico don't have a higher rate of survival than hatchlings leaving a beach on the Atlantic coast? The predator base may be entirely different in the waters off Sanibel than off Sebastian Inlet. Hell's bells, I know what you're saying. I'll agree with, you old timer. Our green turtle project had something to do with green turtle nesting recurring in southwest Florida."

Ed Phillips, always wanting to get the last word in, said, "I think we're right, Jasper. Let's drink to that!" He lifted his can of cold beer and tapped mine[1].

Each night I spent on the beach working with loggerheads was a separate adventure, and there were literally thousands of nights. After we received a grant that allowed us to purchase our own jeep in 1973 (a used Wagoneer), I learned that the public's participation in the sea turtle patrols on Sanibel could provide a way to finance these very operations. So, our members and the public were invited to spend a night with us on the Sanibel beach for a contribution. For years, operational costs for fuel, vehicle insurance and maintenance, and related administrative costs were met thanks to this program.

Over the years, scores of very interesting people joined us for an enjoyable night out on the Sanibel beach. I would educate and entertain these visitors and provide them and their families with a very unique learning experience. It made their visit to Sanibel and Captiva very intimate and special. Being out on the night-time summer beach was my great escape, a means to travel back in time. I had discovered my personal fountain of youth and shared it with others.

---

[1] Since this conversation, collection of blood and analysis of DNA from hatchling loggerheads has suggested that loggerheads may return to the beach where they hatched. However, further study is required.

Every night in the field was not a successful mission; we did not encounter a loggerhead during every patrol. Carol Owen from Nashville, Tennessee, was on her third turtle patrol, but she had yet to see her first loggerhead! We were on our way back, headed in the direction of the Lighthouse Point, when I spotted a single turtle crawl crossing the beach far ahead of us. I quickly killed the special filter-fitted headlights, slowed, and crept ahead in the general direction of where the turtle should be. I stopped the vehicle and said, "We have a turtle on the beach. Everyone please stay in the jeep while I check out the situation."

I stepped out of the jeep, crouched, and followed the turtle's crawl track up toward the pioneer vegetation line to have a look. The loggerhead was on an unvegetated section of the beach a few yards above the spring tide line. She had finished digging her nest chamber, and from the way she was curling her rear flippers, I could tell she was depositing eggs.

I hurried back to the jeep and told the group in a loud whisper, "She's laying eggs! Everyone get out and follow me."

Five people, including my assistant Eve Haverfield, eagerly leapt out of the open, top-down jeep. Carol and the other visitors knelt spellbound as they watched the nesting turtle continue to lay eggs.

Systematically, Eve and I recorded the length and width of the turtle's carapace, or upper shell, and her head width. Both front flippers and the rear edges of her shell were examined for tags, either a Monel flipper tag or a special stainless steel shell tag I began to apply in 1983. Neither was found on this loggerhead, so tags and application tools were readied. The moment she began to cover her eggs, I attached a flipper tag. Then, using a rechargeable electric drill to bore a hole through the thick shell, we installed the other tag. Finished!

Carol Owen was truly captured by the moment. Suddenly, in her excitement of finally seeing a nesting loggerhead, she exclaimed, "Oh, my goodness, this is just like being in a *National Geographic* television special!"

But not all trips were so pleasurable or without elements of danger. Apart from flat tires, broken axles, and mechanical problems, there were also scary times. Fierce summer electrical storms could be dangerous, and on very threatening nights, I would cancel the trip. When we were caught out in the elements, we often found refuge in palm-thatched cabanas or in sheltered motel entrances. As a last resort, I would raise the fabric top of the jeep — if it had one. I always disliked covered jeeps, preferring the more adaptable military or CJ models with hinged windshields and collapsible canvas tops. Working with turtles out on the beach was to experience the wind in one's face — along with night insects and tire-thrown sand in your eyes and hair.

One August night, two middle-aged couples from the Mississippi Gulf coast signed up for the turtle patrol. As usual, we met in the parking lot at Bailey's General Store. As the sun was setting, the weather to the east looked threatening. A dark, turbulent squall line with considerable embedded lightning activity had prompted my assistant to call and cancel. But the passengers were eager to participate, so I explained that we'd proceed, but only after I put up the top and connected the doors. The two women climbed into the rear seat and the men joined me up front.

Things started out normally enough. After driving onto the beach at Tarpon Bay Road, we drove westward, watching the final rays of the sun disappear. Things were routine for the first few miles, and the sky was clear ahead of us.

Whenever I found a turtle crawl that hadn't already been driven across, I knew it was unrecorded. I would stop and check the apex of the up and down tracks to see if the disturbed beach was indeed the site of a well-concealed loggerhead nest. Sometimes it would be a clearly defined false crawl — where the female turtle had landed on the beach intending to nest, but due to any number of factors had decided not to lay eggs and returned to the water. In other instances, the crawl could be identified easily as a nest because of certain characteristics of the disturbed sand and shell. I would carefully excavate those sites to verify and document the nest. Next, I would drive a small stake, with coded bands of reflector tape, into the beach at a measured and recorded distance from the nest. The light-reflecting stake would enable us to return later, after the full-term, 56-day incubation period, and ascertain the success of the nest.

By the time we reached Bowman's Beach, we had stopped several times to examine crawls and mark new nests. Each time we stopped, I checked the southeast horizon to see what progress the squall was making. It was clear that the storm was intensifying, was moving in our direction very quickly, and would soon overtake us.

Continuing toward Captiva, I suddenly spied a one-way turtle crawl across the beach. I turned off the lights and asked the passengers to remain inside and wait. Then I stepped out of the jeep to find the turtle.

A few minutes later I was back. Pointing in the general direction of the turtle, I whispered, "There's a loggerhead in those thick sea oats. She's knocking them down and is doing a little exploratory digging, trying to find a spot suitable for an egg cavity. I doubt she'll find the conditions to her liking, and she'll probably do a false crawl."

These words were hardly out of my mouth when gigantic raindrops began to pummel the jeep, and sand and shell fragments began to literally sandblast the jeep as the increasing wind lifted them off the beach. The squall had caught up with us!

Now, I have experienced countless thunderstorms on the Sanibel beach. But even during minimal hurricanes, never have I been exposed to such a powerful wind as that which overtook us at that moment. The sea oats in front of us and the Australian pine saplings beyond them were bending to the ground. The wind screeched and tore at the jeep's fabric top. I thought it would tear into shreds if the jeep wasn't blown over first as it pitched from side to side in the wind. The rain increased, driven sideways by the wind. If things weren't frightening enough by this time, a crescendo of lightning, far mightier than anything I had ever seen while unprotected outdoors, crashed over the beachscape.

Very quietly at first, I began to hear sobbing and then anguished praying coming from the back seat. Scared out of their wits, the two men joined in, and the quartet of seriously frightened people prayed for all they were worth. The more they prayed, the louder they prayed, and the more apprehensive for our safety I became. The wind and lightning began to diminish, but the torrential rain and the prayers persisted.

A bolt of lighting flashed over the beach ahead of us, and for a split second I could see the form of the loggerhead. Foiled by the dense grass and impenetrable roots, she was heading back to the

Gulf. The turtle was about a quarter of the way across the open beach and would escape if I didn't do something. So I drove ahead to block the loggerhead's escape with the front right tire. This confused her a bit, but she slowly turned right to loop around the jeep. I didn't want to get out of the jeep in the intense lightning, so until it ended, I continued to move ahead each time the turtle tried to get by.

Finally, the storm subsided and things began to return to normal. Their prayers answered, courage slowly returned to my passengers. We stepped out of the jeep, and I flipped the loggerhead upside down to prevent her from reaching the water. Then I measured and tagged her. At last we climbed back aboard the jeep, all soaked, spiritually exhausted, and relieved to be heading back.

When Caretta Research, Inc., was originally conceived, I envisioned that the project would have no more than a ten year lifespan. However, it became so successful that we continued operating beyond this self-imposed deadline. By 1977, the heyday had passed and Caretta Research had become an administrative nightmare.

With growing on-the-job responsibilities, I could no longer manage the year-round, day-to-day duties required for the turtle team to function. So I decided to reduce the number of units. In a sense, Caretta Research became "turtle-like" itself, withdrawing into its shell. Many units became autonomous and continue today. For example, the sea turtle conservation and research projects conducted by Mote Marine Laboratory in Sarasota and The Conservancy in Naples evolved from Caretta Research origins.

We continued our work on Sanibel and Captiva into the 1990s, but it was becoming very clear that unwelcome change was coming. Not wanting my efforts to be controlled by the rising breed of young bureaucrats, who were beginning to influence the management of protected and endangered species programs at the State and Federal levels, I passed the torch of sea turtle conservation on the islands to the Sanibel-Captiva Conservation Foundation in September 1991. A few months later, the board of directors dissolved Caretta Research, Inc., at my request.

Ed Phillips, Richard Beatty, and I decided we should leave the field altogether. Before I completely severed my involvement in sea turtle conservation, however, I wanted to ensure that a positive level of communication existed among the region's sea turtle conservation projects. We knew that after Caretta Research abandoned its regional program in 1977, communication between sea turtle people in southwest Florida had quickly disintegrated.

So, for us to leave the scene with a better sense of having completed our mission, Ed invited every non-Governmental sea turtle conservation group on Florida's Gulf coast to send a representative to a meeting on Sanibel. This meeting was aimed at fostering increased communication among the groups. The Florida Gulf Coast Sea Turtle Association was born from that get-together, and it continues today.

After having dedicated over 38 years of my life to sea turtle conservation, 33 of them on Sanibel and Captiva Islands, life's twists and turns convinced me that my plan had come full circle. My wonderful sea turtle career was over.

15

ON A SCALE FROM ONE TO TEN

"I heard on the radio we have a major red tide moving around offshore and to the north of us. It's leaving a monumental trail of dead fish in its wake," I told Bob Barber on a sultry July morning in 1971.

Fresh from the National Bison Range in Montana, Bob had been appointed Refuge Manager and reported for duty on April 19, 1971. He succeeded Tommy Wood, who retired from the U. S. Fish and Wildlife Service on January 9, 1971. The J. N. "Ding" Darling National Wildlife Refuge again became administratively independent from the South Florida National Wildlife Refuges in March, a couple of weeks before Bob arrived on Sanibel.

"What's a red tide?"

I answered, "I started my career with the Service investigating red tide, Bob, so you've asked the right person. I can tell you not only what it is, but also how very little we know about it.

"These biological events in the eastern Gulf of Mexico are caused by a dinoflagellate called *Gymnodinium breve*, which is always present in the Gulf. These organisms rapidly reproduce — some microbiologists call it a bloom — when unknown factors

177

work together to cause the multiplication. A typical static population contains a few dozen of the organisms per liter of water, but severe bloom levels can contain up to 20 million per liter."

I went on. "As individuals, they are short-lived, and as they die, their cell walls rupture and a virulent neurotoxin, known as brevetoxin, is released into the water column. The sheer numbers of these planktonic creatures and the respiratory demand they place on their immediate environment reduce the available dissolved oxygen in the water. Fishes and invertebrates are killed outright by this combination of toxicity and insufficient oxygen. However, filter-feeding organisms like shellfish and tunicates can store lethal levels of the toxin, causing direct mortality to other members in the marine food chain."

A few days after our conversation, the telltale red-tinted, toxic water was lapping at the beaches of Sanibel and Captiva. It entered the passes and reached every bayou and creek connected to Pine Island Sound. Dead fish — first the bottom feeders like catfish, cowfish, puffers, and mullet, and small nondescript minnows and baitfish of all kinds — began to wash ashore in uncountable numbers. Over time, a variety of other species joined the tide-placed windrows of decaying fish along the island shoreline. Giant 600-pound jewfish, 40-pound snook, crabs, and shellfish also washed ashore, adding their decomposing stench to the air. Even the sand fleas and coquina clams living in the intertidal zones succumbed. As we watched in disbelief, it seemed that everything living in the Gulf and Sound had died and washed ashore on our beaches. Dead fish were floating offshore as far as we could see from our customary end-of-the-day sitting place on the Gulfside porch of Quarters 2.

Jean broke the awed silence. "Daddy once told me he heard that red tides are caused by mustard gas. After the First World War, the army dumped a huge stockpile of surplus mustard gas canisters at sea in the northern Gulf. The containers must have corroded, leaked, and released chemicals into the water. Daddy claims that if they really dumped the gas, when a canister ruptures we have a red tide, causing the fish to die by the jillions. This has happened before, just like this."

Then Ed Phillips spoke up. He was visiting for the summer to work in our loggerhead turtle conservation program. "I don't know what causes it, but it sure as hell stinks!"

"From a biological standpoint," I said, "no one knows the environmental conditions that trigger these blooms. It's probably a complex combination of elements, which under the right conditions come together and allow the dinoflagellate to multiply. Water temperature and salinity, the absence of certain chemicals in the seawater, man-made nutrients like fertilizers and pesticides, which are delivered to the estuaries by surface water runoff — all may play a role. Red tides aren't new either; they've been around for centuries and are even mentioned in the Bible. I've not read the passage, but I've been told it's there."

Jean said, "I swear that on a scale from one to ten, this red tide is a ten!"

Loads of dead fish and other sea creatures continued to wash up on the beaches, and the horrendous smell began to drive island visitors away. That's when AAA advised their members to steer clear of the southwest Florida coast, and the Sanibel-Captiva Chamber of Commerce cringed. In 1971, public health, safety, and welfare on Sanibel and Captiva were the immediate responsibility of the Lee County Board of County Commissioners in Fort Myers. In response to valid public health concerns (and a little prodding from our Chamber of Commerce and irate Gulf-front property owners), they dispatched work crews and equipment from the Department of Transportation to Lee County's barrier islands.

County-owned dump trucks, front-end loaders, and motor graders arrived on the islands to begin the cleanup and offset (from a political viewpoint) the public health concerns. The graders scraped the beach, concentrating the dead marine animals into long windrows that paralleled the Gulf shoreline. The front-end loaders heaped the unbelievably foul-smelling rotten flesh into dump trucks for disposal at the county-operated landfill far away on the mainland. The turnaround time for the trucks was soon determined not to be time-efficient or cost-effective, so the county supervisors looked for an on-island disposal site.

The Refuge offered a large expanse of beachfront at the Lighthouse Point, on the Gulf front, a couple of hundred feet west of the lighthouse as a graveyard.

The Lee County heavy equipment operators excavated an enormous trench about 100 yards long, 50 feet wide, and 4 feet deep. It was a mass grave and final resting place for the billions of dead creatures remaining on the beach and for those still floating offshore. These would eventually land if they didn't completely decompose and sink first. It took several days to gather and bury the rotten fish, but in time, that part of our red tide-related problems were behind us.

By the end of July, the odor from the red tide organisms themselves was almost unbearable. As the dinoflagellate dies and releases its peculiar cellular fluids into the water, the toxin enters the seawater and increases the severity of the fishkill. When the contaminated water's surface is agitated by wind, creating waves, the toxin is "aerosoled" into the atmosphere as an airborne contaminant. The droplets of red-tide toxin which are encapsulated and wind-dispersed as a mist become health hazards in their own right.

People with respiratory problems are seriously affected by the toxin and should leave the seacoast right away during a severe red tide bloom. Those who are allergic to the mist suffer a variety of symptoms: burning and watery eyes, nasal congestion, a dry, persistent, hacking cough, and even difficulty breathing. During this red tide, I personally had an extraordinary reaction.

Late one afternoon in July, Jack Rushworth, the manager at the Island Inn, telephoned to say an alligator was in the surf in front of the resort and was frightening the guests. Neither this kind of phone call nor the fact that an alligator was in the Gulf was an unusual event. Our free-roaming alligators frequently enter seawater for short periods of time, especially in the summer when the island's interior is flooded and they can wander. The enormous food supply floating in the Gulf probably resulted in a few more alligators than usual in the surf that summer.

Ed Phillips and I stopped to pick up George Weymouth. George and his family had relocated to Sanibel from Bonita Springs in the mid-60s. We all arrived at the Island Inn to find 50 or more people lined up along the beach watching the frightened alligator. Had they left the reptile alone, it would have returned to its freshwater haunts on its own. So George and I decided we'd have some fun, and also relieve the growing audience's concerns about the alligator being where it was. We would catch the 'gator, measure and mark it, and release it into the Sanibel River system. Catching an alligator in the Gulf of Mexico is no easy task, because the animal has an unlimited area to escape from its pursuer.

Thousands of dead fish floated aside on the reddish, smelly water as George and I waded out toward the 'gator. Air-breathing creatures like alligators and humans are not usually affected by the red tide, other than the maladies I mentioned earlier. However, some marine mammals and reptiles, as a result of ingesting their natural foods which now contain the toxin, can become very sick or even die.

Ed had stayed on the beach, yelling after us, "I may be Polish, but I'm not stupid. I'm not going out there in that rotten water to help you damn fools catch an alligator. I'm a turtle man!"

I laughed. "Okay, you chicken! You stay on shore and try to keep the people back if the 'gator decides to come up on the beach."

George and I continued in the alligator's general direction. As we closed the distance, George said, "Looks to me like a 6-footer. What do you think?"

I looked at the animal's head and in my mind drew an imaginary line laterally across the cranium between its eyes. From that line, I estimated the number of inches to the tip of the nose. This distance in inches would be the alligator's total length in feet. In this case, the distance from the imaginary line between the eyes to the end of the snout was about 6 inches.

I answered, "Looks like a 6-footer to me too."

As we worked our way through the tepid, fish-strewn, waist-deep water, the alligator suddenly submerged and disappeared. We spread out but still moved toward the last spot we had seen the head. By the time we got there, the alligator had not resurfaced.

"Its probably on the bottom sulking," I said. "I bet it's hoping the two of us and everyone else are gone by the time it comes back up. Let's spread out and see if we can find it."

I hadn't gone much more than 40 feet when through the rusty-colored water, I made out the shape of the 'gator. I called to George, "Here it is!"

Alligators have valve-like structures to close their nostrils and flaps to seal their ears to prevent water from entering when they're submerged. Their eyesight is very keen out of the water, but when underwater, they use a well-developed nictitating membrane, some-times called a third eyelid, to completely cover their eyes. The membrane is slightly cloudy, but their vision is not reduced by much.

Apparently satisfied it was hidden from us, the alligator was lying immobile on the bottom. Without telling George, I decided to catch the alligator using a technique I had used literally hundreds of times before on alligators up to eight feet long. Looking down through the chest-deep water, I slowly walked over to the animal from behind and straddled it. My intent was to drop down into the water, grab the 'gator firmly behind the head with both hands, and lock its abdomen between my legs before I resurfaced. Then I would move my right hand to the snout, hold the jaws together, and take the rear left leg in my left hand, using it as a lever to prevent the 'gator from rolling once it began to twist in my grip — and I knew it would.

Down I went on target — at least I thought so. I knew I had miscalculated when I felt the excruciating pain of huge sharp pointed teeth sinking — no, crushing — through both sides of my right hand. Instinctively, I held what little grip I had with my left hand and quickly scissored my legs, clamping myself around the alligator. No way could I allow this powerful animal to begin spin-ning on its body axis as it tried to twist free. I would probably lose fingers or part of my hand if it did.

I leapt up and wanted to scream at the top of my lungs, but then caught myself. That certainly wouldn't be macho in front of all those people watching me from the beach. They didn't even know what had happened.

"George," I called out in as low a voice as I could. "The damn thing's got me by the hand. Please, get over here and help me keep it from rolling!"

George swam over and took hold of the powerful tail and free rear leg. Meanwhile, the 'gator decided to clamp his jaws tighter. There was no way I could free my hand, even when the animal briefly relaxed the pressure now and then.

In agony I said, "I'm going to use eye pressure to see if it'll let go, George. Either it will or we're going to have a blind alligator on our hands."

Now that George had a firm grip on the tail end, I released the rear left leg and placed my left thumb and index finger on the 'gator's eyes. I grunted to George, "Alright Porgy, hold on, don't let him roll."

He replied softly, "I've got him; go for it!"

I pressed down on both of the alligator's eyeballs, forcing them down into its skull. There was no response at first, but as I continued, the 'gator began to exert less pressure on my hand. Soon the powerful jaws began to separate. But I still could not relax and kept pressing, trying to withdraw my hand from the alligator's vise-like grip at the same time. In retrospect, it seemed to take forever, but suddenly my hand was free from the awesome jaws.

I raised my throbbing hand out of the water and examined it. It was beginning to swell. There were very deep punctures and lacerations across my knuckles and palm, and it was bleeding profusely.

I said to George, "It hurts like hell, but I think I can hold the 'gator until you get to the jeep for something to cover my hand. I don't think those people should see all this blood."

Momentarily, he returned and handed me an old towel, which I swapped for the alligator. While George and Ed took the alligator to the jeep I wrapped my hand, then headed hell-bent as fast as I could run for a water faucet at the Island Inn. We would release the alligator later.

George and Ed held the trussed-up subdued alligator in the jeep as I raced home to further clean and bandage my hand. I probably should have had a few stitches but decided to use an antiseptic, butterfly bandage the deeper punctures, and let it go at that. I showered thoroughly to remove the red tide residue from my skin, then with the alligator restrained by Ed and George, we left to turn the alligator loose.

Using a flexible tape, we measured the alligator to be 6 feet 1 inch long. After checking our marking records, I removed a scute keel with a sharp knife from each side of the animal's tail in a coded sequence to permanently mark this particular alligator. George and I then began to coax Ed to join the unofficial Fraternal Order of Alligator Sexers.

I instructed, "All you have to do, Eddie, is take your index finger, insert it into the 'gator's cloaca, and probe to see if you can feel a penis."

Ed declined, telling us in no uncertain terms that he was not a proctologist in training.

Laughing until his sides hurt, George said, "Eddie, I'll show you how it's done." He did ... "It's a male."

Not to be chastised later, Ed gathered up his nerve and repeated George's examination. George was correct.

That night, a strong sea breeze forced us to cancel our beach patrol. None of us could cope with the toxic, red-tide air being blown from offshore. It would be over a week before we could resume our nighttime turtle work. When the team was once able to go out, the jeep had 16 flat tires within one week, all caused by dead catfish spines littering the beach.

After the 'gator-catching expedition, I awoke the next morning, went into the bathroom, turned on the light, looked in the mirror, and nearly passed out from shock. Every square inch of my body was covered with water blisters. I looked as though someone had tapped me all over with a hot fire poker and burned my skin. The blisters were between a half-inch and one inch in diameter. Sobered by what I saw in the mirror, I dashed back into the bedroom and woke Jean.

"Look at my skin! What the heck could have happened to me?" We both looked at my chest and arms in shocked disbelief.

Later, just before I walked next door to the office, we decided I was having an allergic reaction to the red tide. I had never heard of anything like this before, so I telephoned George to see if he was having a problem like mine. But he was blister-free.

To this day, I believe that the wounds caused by the alligator bite allowed the toxin to enter my bloodstream and that the blisters were an allergic reaction to the toxin. I felt fine, so rather than see a doctor, I decided to give my skin condition a few days to see what happened. Slowly the blisters dried, and I completely recovered over the next few days.

That summer, the red tide had a negative impact on the loggerhead turtles too. Usually in the summer, the number of dead turtles that strand on these barrier island beaches is much lower than in the winter and early spring. But from late June until mid-August 1971, 18 loggerheads stranded on the beaches of Sanibel and Captiva Islands. I necropsied most of the carcasses and observed that each specimen I examined had ingested significant numbers of rough pen shells, a common bivalve. Pen shells are filter feeders, so had stored concentrated levels of the red tide toxin. I am convinced that the pen shells were directly responsible for the unusually high mortality rate in loggerhead turtles that summer.

Since the red tide episode of 1971, other outbreaks have plagued southwest Florida. In 1982, a major bloom affected inshore waters and even flowed with the tide a considerable distance up the Caloosahatchee. At the same time, a small species of sea squirt (a tunicate) had over-multiplied, had reached previously undocumented population densities, and had colonized submerged marine grasses and algaes. Turtle grass is one of the region's predominant marine plants and was one variety to which the tunicates adhered.

Turtle grass is also one of the staple foods of the West Indian manatee, an endangered marine mammal. During cold periods, these animals swim upstream along the Caloosahatchee and enter the Orange River east of Fort Myers. Here, warm-water effluent is discharged after cooling the turbines of the electric power plant operated by the Florida Power and Light Company. Several hundred manatees may congregate in this warm water near the plant during the coldest winter months.

In 1982, the very high populations of both red-tide dinoflagellates and sea squirts resulted in an unusual ecological chain of events. Manatees grazed on the turtle grass and therefore secondarily ingested unusually large quantities of the overpopulated sea squirts. Being filter feeders, the sea squirts had accumulated a considerable amount of brevetoxin in their systems. When innocent sea cows ate the combination of turtle grass and sea squirts, the effect was disastrous. The manatees began to die. A total of 37 of these peaceful animals are believed to have succumbed due to the red tide.

In 1996, another mass mortality occurred among the manatees of southwest Florida. Nearly 200 of these endangered marine mammals died, and biologists have implicated the red tide organism as the primary culprit.

16

THE 'GATOR WAR

"Daddy, Daddy," four-year-old Chuck called from the bow of the canoe. "Look at all the buzzards! That's more than I've ever seen in my whole entire life!"

It was Tuesday morning, October 26, 1965, and I was leading a group of Audubon Society birders on a field trip along the Sanibel River. About 30 people were spread among a dozen canoes I had borrowed from the Tarpon Bay Marina. We were about a quarter-mile east of Tarpon Bay Road when scores of the carrion-eating birds frantically flew up out of the dense trees ahead.

"My son and I are going to investigate," I announced. "We'll head up this lateral ditch and see why so many vultures are in there, to find out what the attraction is. You folks please wait here while Chuck and I check it out. We won't be gone long."

I turned the canoe south and paddled into the narrow ditch. "Keep an eye peeled, Chuck. See if you can tell where they're all coming from."

Less than 100 yards from the main Sanibel River mosquito ditch, dozens of black and turkey vultures suddenly crashed through the underbrush trying to avoid us. A small buttonwood strand created a dense canopy on both sides of the ditch, so the birds couldn't get airborne. With stealth in mind, I got out of the canoe and pushed it closer through the shallow water. Along the way, I noticed that the low vegetation and ground cover had been trampled down by the army of vultures.

"These buzzards are having a field day, son. Let's see why there's so many. Whew! Something sure smelly has attracted them here."

We landed on a low bank next to a spoil pile. Chuck, who was first ashore, immediately complained of the stench, holding his nose, making faces, and uttering theatrical gasping sounds.

We were both awestruck! Everywhere were scattered remains of dead alligators — many alligators. Their skulls, pieces of skulls, bone, and entrails had been dragged about by the feasting vultures. I knew right away this was the work of serious poachers; no islander was responsible for this mess.

There are ways to spot poachers. The few island residents who might spend a night out on the river to kill a half-dozen alligators wouldn't have left so much evidence. And they would have taken fewer animals, because hunting and skinning 'gators are difficult tasks. They would also have spread out their hunting trips, lessening the chance of being detected and possibly caught. An islander would have better concealed the remains, making them impossible to find by either vultures or people like me. For example, a skinless carcass would usually be shoved far down inside an alligator cave so the evidence would never be detected.

After a cursory examination of the scene, Chuck and I rejoined the canoeists, described our grisly discovery to them, then continued the interpretive tour.

Later in the day, I returned alone to examine the site, estimate the number of carcasses, and determine their sizes based on skull lengths. After literally driving away the throng of tenacious vultures, I slowly collected the skulls and skull parts in the clearing. Then I wandered into the periphery and discovered more 'gator remains the birds had dragged into the brush. All told, I collected 23 alligator skulls, all from animals four to seven feet in length.

These alligators had been killed by jack-lighting hunters (using head-mounted, battery-powered lamps) from a small boat elsewhere along the Sanibel River. They probably used a small caliber firearm or delivered a silent blow to the head with a hand axe or hammer. The dead alligators were then brought to the site and skinned. After the poachers removed their very valuable hides, they discarded the remains, except perhaps for some of the tail meat. (Alligator meat was not available in restaurants in those days.) For moving and routine storage, hides were heavily salted to preserve them and then rolled up for ease of transportation. Although illegal in Florida, alligator hunting had become a lucrative occupation, and some folks did it full-time.

The 'gator war was at its peak. Battles were going on throughout the southeastern United States, and a few skirmishes were fought on Sanibel. From one end of the Sanibel Slough to the other, dead skinless alligators showed up from time to time, but I believe this was the largest group yet discovered locally. A few days after finding the 23 alligators, I found another six carcasses. These too had been picked clean by vultures, and their bones were scattered all over the banks of the seaplane canal in the Bailey Tract. Brazen poachers right under our noses!

From early 1959 until 1968, my friends and I spent countless hours paddling through the maze of mosquito ditches in the Sanibel Slough. I doubt if any other human has ever spent as much time in these wetlands at night as I have. During the warmer fall, winter, and spring months, I was catching and tagging alligators nearly every night in the island's canals and ponds. It was impractical to hunt them in the summertime mostly due to insects. The instant we turned on our battery-powered headlamps, it was next to impossible to see an alligator's eyes reflecting through the curtain of insects. Tiny bugs would get into our eyes and burn like fire or get trapped inside our ears and painfully serenade us. Sometimes they would be so thick that we literally couldn't breathe without choking. We were tough but not dumb, and we soon learned that a night out in the Slough could be pure misery. So during the summer I preferred to chase loggerheads up and down the beach instead. With the jeep, we could at least leave the bugs temporarily behind.

When the Sanibel Slough channel project began in the late '50s, the land barrier between fresh and salt water was temporarily breached. Marine fish, primarily small tarpon and striped mullet, entered the growing canal system, became landlocked, adjusted to their new environment, and survived. Even today, tarpon and mullet can be found throughout the network of mosquito ditches and man-made lakes.

In late March 1964, George Weymouth and I were out capturing and tagging alligators in the main mosquito control ditch between Casa Ybel and Tarpon Bay Roads. Heading east, we stopped at each lateral ditch and panned our headlights along the canal banks and open water, looking for the fire-like reflection of an alligator eye. As the lights played across the water, small minnows broke the surface and scurried away in fright. Some sizeable mullet were soon leaping helter-skelter around our canoe in a confused frenzy as they tried to escape the beam. So we doused the lights and let our eyes adjust to the dark. When our night vision was adequate to continue, we quietly paddled eastward.

As we moved into a wider section of the canal, I said, "George, I'll check the left bank, you take the right."

George, who was in the stern steering, agreed and switched on his headlight.

Instant pandemonium! A massive pod of mullet erupted in fright. Some beached themselves, some struck the canoe, and several others jumped into the boat. I turned to dumbly regard the clunking fish on the canoe bottom as they thrashed about.

"Owww!" I screamed. Just then, a large mullet, airborne in a confused full-throttle leap, struck me soundly on the right side of my rib cage and fell into the boat.

"George, did you see that?" I yelled, doubled over in pain. "That fish damn near hit me as hard as a man could. I think he broke my ribs!"

Both of us enjoyed eating mullet any way it could be prepared, but experience had taught us that the fish in our boat were not everyday eating mullet. Likely these would have an unsavory muddy flavor and would not make an enjoyable meal. They were big, beautiful fish, but we quickly released them over the side, even the one that had crashed into my chest. I winced every once in a while over the next few days, but I chuckled too whenever I thought of my unusual fish story.

* * *

When I answered the Refuge phone, a voice said, "There's a dead alligator floating in MacIntyre Creek. It's about a hundred yards in from the entrance and hung up in some mangrove roots."

Since I was always on the lookout for one of my tagged alligators, I decided to investigate. I stopped first at Chuck Holloway's repair shop next to the Sanibel Community Church to see if he wanted to come along.

As I suspected, he responded, "Yuh, sure, I'd like to go along. How'r we goin'?"

When we stepped outside, it was obvious how we would travel. I had the Refuge airboat and trailer hitched to the pickup.

At the Tarpon Bay Marina, we launched the powerful airboat from the ramp. The trip across Tarpon Bay was not very fast, since the deep water restricted lift to the boat's hull. We passed through the Cut Off, an opening in the thick mangrove shoreline just west of the long key I knew as the Norberg Tract.

A few years earlier, the Norberg Tract, a tidal mangrove key between the Cut Off and the mouth of Tarpon Bay, nearly fell victim to developers. Adherents of the nearly obsolete dredge and fill mentality, they wanted to construct a bulkhead around the mangroves, fill this with dredge spoil from the grassy bottom of the bay, and build a bridge connecting the proposed subdivision to Woodring Point. Luckily the plan was defeated during county-level zoning hearings. Later, the U. S. Fish and Wildlife Service acquired the parcel.

As the boat cleared the mangrove fringe, I turned a sharp left, floored the accelerator, and sped over the inches-deep shallow water covering the submerged shoal which paralleled the shoreline a few hundred feet offshore. The necessary lift for planing was being provided by the close proximity of the bottom. As we skimmed along, the airboat picked up speed. As we approached Shallow Mouth, we were traveling about 60 mph. I decided to go inside at Shallow Mouth, rather than continue outside all the way to MacIntyre Creek, and turned left into the opening. Chuck, enjoying the exhilarating ride, was seated in the forward seat as we went into the turn. I began to slow, ready to turn a hard right once we were inside the mangrove-lined bayou.

I goosed the six-cylinder Continental aircraft engine to control the turn, but the airboat's rudders refused to respond.

I instinctively killed the engine, but we plowed into the dense mangroves anyway at about 30 mph. A long horizontal limb caught Chuck across his midsection and knocked him and his seat to the rear of the boat. Both landed on the bottom below my seat as the springing mangroves catapulted us back out into open water.

"Chuck, are you okay?" I yelled, fearing he was seriously hurt.

He didn't respond, so I shouted again and jumped down to see how bad off he was. Then he stirred and began to move convulsively. He had the wind knocked out of him and was gasping to regain normal breathing. Soon he came around, looked at me in uncomprehending amazement, and began to check himself out.

"It doesn't feel like anything's broken, and I don't see any blood. I'll be fine in a few minutes," he rasped.

"Let's forget about the damn alligator. I'll clean all these leaves and branches out of the boat later. I'm taking you back to the Marina to be sure you're going to be all right."

The next day, Chuck was bruised and quite sore, but he was soon back to normal. I learned a valuable lesson that day. The technique that allowed an airboat to turn in shallow water did not always apply to tight turns in deeper water.

* * *

During conversations with long-time islanders, I had heard stories about a special place on Sanibel called 'Gator Heaven. Tommy Wood once showed me its exact location when we flew over in the Refuge aircraft. Two mangrove pools, which were not connected to the normal tidal system, he called Government Pond and West Government Pond. These plus a remote unditched extension of the Sanibel Slough immediately to the east were indeed 'Gator Heaven.

Government Pond wasn't exactly easy to reach on foot. Tommy and I had walked there a few times to look for roseate spoonbill nests, but without success. Before spoonbills made their remarkable comeback on Sanibel by the early 1970s, they frequently rested at this secluded pond. On the other hand, West Government Pond was virtually inaccessible. It was surrounded by some of the thickest mature red mangroves on Sanibel. I doubt if many humans ever visited it before 1964.

That year, when the Bureau of Land Management was surveying public domain lands north of State Road 867 (or Captiva Road, now known as Sanibel-Captiva Road), the crew, which included George Weymouth, cut a survey line from the highway right-of-way to West Government Pond. George and I decided we'd drag a canoe to the pond and explore its environs once the water level rose. At the time, it was nothing but cracked, drying mud. I kept an eye on the pond after rainstorms and during routine flyovers. Once the water level was up and 'gators were visible, we began tagging.

It's a dangerous game to tag an alligator. First you have to capture and handle it. Small 'gators can be caught by hand or with snare rigs. The snares were usually made from long Calcutta bamboo poles. A lasso-like looped snare, made from a length of aircraft cable, was securely clamped to the end of the pole. Because we worked at night, we used headlamps so our hands would be free.

Alligators are easy to spot at night with a light — their eyes reflect fire-red, like hot coals. The pole is held out and the noose is slowly moved over the head and down to the neck region, if possible without touching the animal, and jerked tight when in position. Fighting a six- or seven-foot alligator tethered to the end of a 12-foot flexible pole is far more fun than hooking a 150-pound tarpon. Releasing the alligator, however, is not as easy as turning a silver king loose.

We usually worked as a team of three: a pole man, a tail man, and a catcher. And we took turns at the various positions so everyone would have a piece of the action. Once the pole man snared the reptile and it was exhausted after twisting, rolling, jerking, and fighting, it was brought alongside the canoe. The tail man would then grab the lithe, flailing tail and the alligator, suspended between noosed neck and tail, would be stretched out as immobile as possible. Then the catcher would grab the animal by the neck and right rear leg. The alligator was hauled aboard the boat, measured, examined, sexed if mature, and tagged.

In my early alligator marking work in Collier County, I had used a fish tag known as a Peterson tag. This consisted of two identically numbered plastic fiber discs that were attached to each side of the reptile's tail after a thin rigid metal rod had been inserted through the tail.

Later I designed and manufactured my own tags from copper and brass. These also pierced the tail and were self-clamped in place. However, we soon discovered that these and the Peterson tags sometimes fell off and were lost.

In 1956, I developed a new system and began to double-mark individuals using a coded tail scute removal scheme. I continued to use this technique, along with improved manufactured, store-bought Monel metal tags, when I started tagging alligators on Sanibel Island.

All crocodilians have an angular, three-way, divided arrangement of keeled scutes, or scales, on the upper surface of their tails. At a point close to the rear legs and on each side of the tail, the top outer surface of the tail forms two dorsal ridges. These gradually taper together until they join to form a single row of keeled scutes about halfway down the tail. With a sharp instrument, such as a pocketknife, I would carefully remove a few scutes from the single row, or a combination of single and double scutes, from each individual. No two alligators were marked using the same code. Each reptile was now permanently identified even if the more easily seen Monel metal tag was lost.

In 1959, little was known about alligator biology in southwest Florida. Tagging created a means by which I hoped to learn more about their fundamental life history, growth rates, establishment of territories, any seasonal or other territorial adjustments, and population densities.

My first real alligator-related trip into 'Gator Heaven was in early June 1964 with George Weymouth and Hank Chastain. We followed the rough-cut survey line and tried to maneuver a 17-foot aluminum canoe through the very thick mangroves to the edge of West Government Pond. Even though a recent rain had flooded some of the muddy pond, moving the canoe became impossible. Slogging through knee-deep mud, we meandered around the mangrove fringe and found substantial evidence of alligators. We saw no alligators that day, but we did see dozens of flooded and partially flooded entrances to alligator caves around the pond's perimeter.

Most alligator caves on Sanibel are flooded chambers which extend under and away from the banks of canals and ponds. Mature alligators excavate these dens usually near the center of their established territory. The landward end of a den usually terminates under the natural shoring and supporting root systems of large buttonwood or mangrove trees. Seasonally, depending on water levels, an air pocket may exist at the cave's dead end, which is large enough for the resident 'gator to turn around. When alarmed and close enough to its den entrance, an alligator will seek refuge inside. It can also aestivate[1] in its den during the spring dry season or hibernate inside during severe cold spells.

Several cave entrances we observed that day were enormous. In fact, they were large enough for a man to crawl inside, maybe even two people side by side. We could tell the caves were actively being used by examining the ends of the red mangrove roots, which were growing but suspended in midair at the den's mouth, and the amount of vegetative debris present in the opening. We probed into several caves with our long Calcutta noose-pole, but we struck neither resident alligator nor end wall of the cave. We were sure they were home though.

We rotated our tagging areas on Sanibel to avoid constantly intimidating the alligator population. We didn't want them to learn to retreat into hidden caves, where we could not easily capture them, every time they saw a light.

On June 27, 1964, George Weymouth and I made our first of many nighttime visits to 'Gator Heaven. It was mid-afternoon as we approached the pond carrying our equipment, cussing the heat and swatting mosquitos and at the same time trying to be as quiet as possible.

Earlier in the week, Tommy and I had flown a sea turtle nesting crawl survey up to Boca Grande just after dawn. On the way back, I asked him to make a couple of passes over the Government Ponds. Sure enough, the water level was up slightly and a few large alligators were visible, as was a small colony of anhingas on a tiny island in the westernmost pool.

When I told him about the birds, George decided to bring some bands to band any nestling anhingas we might find. The string of bands made him look like a Mexican bandit with a bandoleer of ammunition draped around his neck.

The closer we came to the pond, the fouler the air. "Smells like a red tide, doesn't it George," I remarked as we plodded through the flooded mud along the survey line.

---

[1]   During extremely hot or dry periods crocodilians may become dormant.

Inch by inch, we approached the pond. When we arrived, the reason for the odor was obvious — dead fish were piled up against the far bank. Yet somehow, severely stressed remnants of a once abundant bream population were surviving in the western, deeper section of the pond. Bream were still dying, many feebly flapping at the surface of the rank, muddy waters.

What little wind that could barely reach the pond's surface through the thick trees had windrowed the bream corpses up against the northern shoreline and under the mangrove canopy. I hadn't been able to see them from the air, much less smell their decay from a hundred feet up.

These fish had succumbed due to a combination of natural factors. First of all, bream (or bluegills as they are sometimes called) are a freshwater species, so we collected a water sample which I later tested for salinity. I had no equipment with me to test the water for dissolved oxygen, but I knew the water likely held very little to support the fish. We did have a thermometer, which we later used for reading alligator body temperatures, so we recorded the temperature of the water where most of the fish were still showing signs of life. We knew it was mortally hot for them because, as we waded around, the water actually burned our legs. The temperature reading was 106°F. No wonder there weren't any alligators in the pool! They were waiting back in the shaded mangroves or their caves until the pond cooled after dark.

The next day at the Refuge office, I titrated the water sample I had collected from the surface of West Government Pond. Its salinity was 41 percent that of sea strength. Salinity for North Atlantic seawater is about 35 parts per thousand (ppt) of dissolved chlorides. The water of the mangrove pond was 14.3 ppt. But bream are fresh-water fish! That and the hot water — no wonder they were dying.

Bream and other fresh-water sportfish did not exist on Sanibel until June 1, 1961. Following the Palm Lake excavation just to the north of (West) Gulf Drive near the Island Inn, the developers applied to the U. S. Fish and Wildlife Service to have their new lake stocked with fish.

On the above date, Jim Dillard, from the Fish and Wildlife Service's Welaka National Fish Hatchery in northeast Florida, arrived on Sanibel with a tank truck containing several thousand fingerling copperhead bream and largemouth bass. Jim and I released the fish in Palm Lake and into the Sanibel River system at Casa Ybel and Tarpon Bay Roads. By 1964, both species were well-established in all fresh-water habitats on the island, and fresh-water fishing became a popular new-found sport among residents.

Since West Government Pond had no regular aquatic connection to the island's interior fresh-water wetland system, the fish could not have arrived there on their own. Fish are sometimes distributed by the wildlife species that prey on them. The presence of the small anhinga colony indicated to George and me how the bream first reached the pond. Parenting anhingas probably foraged in the Sanibel River and caught small bream which survived the flight to Government Pond. But occasionally, these small fish managed to escape, perhaps when the adult bird tossed the still-live bream into the air as it was about to feed its offspring. It would take only two bream of opposite sexes to fall into the water and soon create the population. Now it looked as though the bream were doomed. We managed to band a few dozen beige-colored, down-covered anhinga nestlings and then rested, waiting for dark.

Darkness came quickly, since the setting sun was obscured by storm clouds well offshore. But we waited at least an hour after sunset — experience dictated that we would not start until the night was pitch black. We wanted no backlighting, neither natural nor from the other's headlamp, which were our only light sources. Suddenly we heard sounds of flying water to our left, in the direction of the remaining live bream. The strong musky odor of alligator was evident even over the stench of the bloated, rotting fish.

I grabbed the catch pole and carefully made my way to the canoe's bow. George loaded our tagging kit aboard and manned the paddle in the stern, and we began to slowly move across the soupy surface toward the commotion. At the pond's western end, it narrows under the tangled red mangroves, and then a rounded pool extension formed the end of the pond. I turned my headlight on and panned across the steamy surface.

"My God!, George, look!" I exclaimed excitedly. "I haven't seen so many pairs of 'gator eyes in one spot since the time my brother Laban, Warren Boutchia, Ralph Curtis, and I waded out to Mossy Lake east of Bonita back in mid-December of '52 when I was a kid."

"The smell of dead fish must have attracted every 'gator within five miles," George added.

Despite our battery-powered lights shining in their faces, many animals continued their personal feeding frenzy, gorging themselves full of dead and half-dead bream.

"George, how many do you think are here?"

He swung his light slowly around and replied, "I'll bet there's at least 50 out in the open water. And there's no telling how many are back behind the mangrove roots, but I can see a few sets of eyes in there."

Since there were just two of us up against a lot of alligators, we decided that safety should be our chief concern. So we restricted the maximum size of the animals we would catch to eight feet. So began the night's adventure — fast action, near misses, close calls, and substantial data collection. When one of us got tired, we changed positions in the canoe so each of us had our fill of catching alligators.

By 3:00 in the morning, we were exhausted. We had captured, tagged, and recorded 35 alligators. The smallest was 4 feet long, the longest 7 feet 3 inches. A few refused to leave their feasts and were caught more than once. About 20 others were not noosed because they exceeded our self-imposed size limit.

During the arduous slog back to the truck, we talked of nothing but the nights events. I said, "Thank goodness we weren't out there to kill and skin those 'gators, George. Do you realize how much money passed through our hands tonight?"

We returned to West Government Pond from time to time after that to tag more alligators, but we never had a repeat of the total number captured at one site and in the same night. Until now, we always kept our record alligator catch a secret. And through the years, we never found any evidence that the "other side" had found out about our path to 'Gator Heaven.

* * *

On December 28, 1973, the 'gator war ended. The American alligator was officially listed as an endangered species under the

Endangered Species Act of 1973. The hide market quickly dried up, conservation efforts had won, and the lucrative alligator poaching era was finally over.

By this time, I had terminated my serious alligator activities. But it took a real close call to convince me that handling these powerful beasts was impractical, even stupid. Later, many of my cohorts and those who followed them in the alligator handling program would have their time of reckoning too. Some received more serious alligator injuries than I ever did.

In those days, I handled all nuisance alligator complaints on Sanibel. One day a complaint came in on the Refuge telephone: A large alligator had established a basking site too close to a new resident's home, in fact, in his backyard. The caller demanded that the animal be removed. Frankly, I had grown tired and overwhelmed by the number of calls from this particular person. The alligator was innocent of any threatening gestures — it was being persecuted simply because it was there. I advised the caller that if this alligator were relocated, his relief would be short-lived because another alligator would quickly occupy the vacated territory. I suggested that if he were going to live on Sanibel, he'd better adjust. This new Sanibelian did not comprehend this point, so I decided to catch the alligator, collect its pertinent data, tag it, and relocate it on the Refuge.

This obese eight-foot-long bull alligator was very skittish. When approached day or night, he would retreat. Even when I tossed marshmallows[2] (a savored delicacy for alligators) in his direction as a last resort, I couldn't coax the animal to approach close enough to loop its head with my snare pole. However, there were other capture techniques.

A large fish-baited hook could be used, but this sometimes caused a mortal wound in the alligator's gut. An ancient Calusa trick using a baited peg was another option. This is a special carved wooden device secured to a line and sewn into the gut cavity of a fish. Although not lethal, this technique could also cause internal problems for the 'gator, so this alternative was ruled out too.

Another less problematic approach was to rig a snare across the well-worn trail leading from the edge of the water to the alligator's customary basking site. I opted for this method and

---

[2] Before feeding alligators was prohibited, the local grocery stores pushed marshmallows as alligator food. Most of the 'gators in accessible areas on the island were addicted to the sugary treats and would rush toward the purveyor, even leaving the water to grab one.

went about getting the line and suspending it across the trail early one morning. I knew the 'gator would walk within inches of its established path, almost using the same footprints. It would stroll into the open loop, engage it, and continue ahead, tightening the line around its own neck. When the long anchored line became taut, the alligator would struggle to free himself from whatever was holding him and seek refuge in the water. All hell would break loose, so I asked the local residents to telephone me immediately when the 'gator was caught in the snare.

About three hours later, a very excited caller literally screamed into the telephone. "The alligator is caught and has gone back into the lake!"

Dropping everything, I took Bob Sabatino with me. Now a very popular Captiva fishing and shelling guide of high reputation, Bob worked with me as a seasonal employee at the Refuge for several summers in the '60s. He operated his guide business in season and hired on at the Refuge during the summer slow season.

Bob and I had already assembled our 'gator equipment and loaded it into the Refuge truck. We dashed for the site. Both of us thought this would be a simple alligator relocation.

Pulling the alligator up onto the bank and securing it for transport was routine, although we commented on how hefty this particular animal was. It probably outweighed both of us. Because we had the routine down pat, we soon had the angry alligator trussed up and loaded into the pickup. We released the animal near the Alice O'Brien Tower in the Darling Tract. I shooed it toward the impoundment known as the fresh-water side, although it has never been truly fresh. But the reptile lurched and headed for the tidal side.

In retrospect, I should have allowed the beast to follow his own nose. But I wanted him to go the other way, so I dove on top of the moving alligator, planning to drag him across the road. Then he could swim off to do his own thing. My mistake!

Before I knew it, the alligator had twisted completely free from what I thought was a firm grip. He was on top of me and in absolute control. My left arm and hand, with its fingernails torn backward and bleeding, were twisted beneath me and useless. He had me in an agonizing hammerlock and I thought my arm was broken. My right forearm had ended up contorted but was the only barrier between my handsome, youthful face and 84 sharp teeth. He slapped his powerful jaws together earnestly trying to remove the right side of my face. Several times the skin of its outer jaws dragged against my cheek — a few millimeters more and I would need a plastic surgeon.

I grimaced but held a firm scissors hold with my legs across this modern-day dinosaur's abdomen. In fear and pain, I screamed, "Bob, help me, please! He's going to eat my face. Get the damn thing off me!"

In a split second, Bob jumped into the melee and held the jaws closed with one hand and grabbed one of the rear legs with the other. He then unwound the reptile and I managed to crawl out from beneath. Bob saved me from serious facial injury that day.

During the height of the battle, I swore off ever handling large alligators again. As far as I was concerned, the alligators were the victors, at least locally. So a long-term truce went into effect between them and me.

After this bizarre and humbling experience, I withdrew from actively working with the island's alligators — to sort of "save face" if you will.

My role of responding to the growing number of nuisance alligator complaints was picked up by George Weymouth and others on Sanibel Island who were interested in continuing the mission. Foremost was George R. Campbell, author of *The Nature of Things on Sanibel*, the island's wildlife classic, and *Jaws Too!*, an authoritative book on the American alligator's life history.

George organized the Southwest Florida Regional Alligator Association, a group authorized by the Florida Game and Fresh Water Fish Commission to operate the nuisance alligator program on Sanibel. Well-trained island residents who were part of George's program were issued State permits. Thus developed a citizen-based response to alligator complaints. The purpose was not only to relocate alligators, but also to educate new residents who were flocking to Sanibel. They had no idea of how to coexist with alligators.

Another goal of the Alligator Association was to safeguard island alligators from the growing number of state-licensed alligator trappers who operated over on the mainland.

I had long recognized the serious survival problem of the island's alligator population because of the unfortunate interaction between this ancient reptile and man. The major problem seemed to be a dearth of intelligence on man's part. Instead of eating the alligators as our predecessors did, people were feeding *them*. This interaction was becoming a serious problem. If something sensible weren't done, there would be a sad finale, and soon, when some 'gator feeder or child was seriously injured, or worse. So, in 1975, while serving as a member of the Sanibel City Council, I drafted and introduced an ordinance which prohibited the feeding of alligators within the corporate limits of Sanibel. This ordinance, Number 75–29, was adopted by the City Council on May 2.

Later, the Florida Game and Fresh Water Fish Commission adopted the basic concept of our ordinance and prohibited the feeding of alligators under the provisions of a State-wide rule. Conflicts between man and alligator began to wane, but there still have been serious alligator-caused injuries and even loss of human life in Florida. This is due solely to the fact that many once-timid alligators have lost their fear of man — because some irresponsible human fed them!

Statewide as well as locally, many alligators continue to be destroyed after being classified as nuisances and potentially dangerous animals. It's the easy way out for the State, and it increases the bankrolls of those who benefit from the now-commercialized enterprise.

On Sanibel Island and throughout Florida, the American alligator has made a dramatic comeback, virtual testimony to the success of protective legislation and enforcement. But the fact of the matter is, the 'gators won the war.

17

A NEW FATHER — FOUNDING, THAT IS

"**Y**esterday was doomsday for Sanibel and Captiva!" Tommy announced during a mid-morning coffee break.

"Why's that?" I thought I knew what he was talking about, but I was curious and asked him anyway.

He answered, "They drove the first piling for the goddamned bridge yesterday, that's why! When the Causeway is opened, if I ever hear anyone say this place has retained its island ambiance, I'll know for damn sure they just drove across the bridge and think they discovered the place. Our unique lifestyle will be gone forever."

Tommy's mood was usually upbeat. But this time he was upset, even angry.

"You and I and a lot of other people did our share to fight it, Tommy. I just wish Sanibel and Captiva had been a couple of miles further out in the Gulf and the Bay and Sound were several hundred feet deep. That would have slowed down the county politicians and their consulting engineers."

That infamous day was Tuesday, February 6, 1962. The battle over the construction of a causeway and bridges across San

Carlos Bay, from Punta Rassa to Sanibel Island, had been resolved several months earlier. It had been a hard-fought campaign that pitted islander against islander, and sometimes friend against friend, in many community circles on Sanibel and Captiva.

Talk of a link to Punta Rassa or Pine Island had circulated for some time, and although Tommy and I were not in a position to comment publicly and officially either pro or con, we were opposed to it and had fought against it on our own.

Willis Combs spearheaded the opposition and chaired the Sanibel Safety Committee, an activist group which had been formed to combat the encroaching threat. During this time, I was president of the local Audubon chapter, and our Board of Directors unanimously supported Combs' committee. His committee later became the Sanibel-Captiva Taxpayers League and fought Lee County's Sanibel Causeway to the bitter end.

At public hearings before the Lee County Commission, the opinions of individual island residents who opposed the bridge, and the position of the Sanibel-Captiva Taxpayers League, fell on deaf ears. The Lee County Board of County Commissioners were determined and proceeded with plans for the design and construction of a bridge and causeway to connect the islands to the mainland — supposedly to improve our lives.

In the early '60s, the permitting process for such public purposes was easy compared to today's bureaucratic nightmare. The Lee County Commissioners directed that planning should proceed, so the responsible county officials applied for a Department of the Army permit to construct a causeway and three bridges across the Bay.

By Federal regulations, the U. S. Fish and Wildlife Service was required to assess the environmental impacts of the proposed project and submit these in a report to the District Engineer, U. S. Army Corps of Engineers, in Jacksonville, Florida. This document, jointly executed by the Bureau of Sport Fisheries and Wildlife and the Bureau of Commercial Fisheries, was submitted to the Corps of Engineers on July 22, 1960. At this time, I worked for the Bureau of Sport Fisheries and Wildlife. The Fish and Wildlife Service would soon be reorganized again, and my employer would become the Division of Wildlife Refuges.

The report covered many aspects of the project and found that if built as designed, the construction would indeed seriously affect the natural resources in the vicinity of the Causeway, primarily because of the dredging and filling operations. Secondly, the dam-like effect of the dredge-created spoil islands would inhibit tidal flow and cause salinity reductions in lower Pine Island Sound. Reduced salinities would eliminate the scallop beds in the lower Sound, because fresh water entering the sea from an estuary tends to sheet-flow over the denser and heavier salt water. As a result, the shallow flats would be covered with fresher water due to the Caloosahatchee's discharge characteristics. Those fishes and invertebrates intolerant of reduced salinity ranges would soon leave the area or die, unable to repopulate their once-productive niche in the shallow marine habitat which dominated the estuary.

The Fish and Wildlife Service did not openly oppose a bridge to Sanibel. Because of grave ecological concerns, however, it did suggest design alternatives that would not result in damage to the county's fisheries. It recommended that the project be redesigned — the Causeway, or dredge-filled sections, should be eliminated and only a bridge be built completely supported by pilings. The Florida State Board of Conservation and the Florida Game and Fresh Water Fish Commission both concurred with these recommendations.

A few days after the report was released, Fish and Wildlife Service staff members met in Jacksonville with representatives of the Corps and the Lee County Commission. The Service's position opposing the design was presented. Lee County representatives admitted that some impacts to the local fisheries would result, but it was the county's position that the advantages of the project would outweigh any environmental losses. Lee County admitted that their budget for the construction was already at its limit, and the suggested modifications to provide better tidal flushing would exceed their self-imposed monetary ceiling. Upon reviewing all public and agency input, the Corps eventually sided with Lee County, and the permit for construction of the Sanibel Causeway, as designed, was issued on September 29, 1960.

Anti-bridge islanders, however, threw a few more monkey wrenches into Lee County's well-lubricated political gears. The confrontations continued, with more public hearings, and before the controversy quieted, the final insult came down to the question of the validity of a $3.9 million bond issue to finance the Causeway's construction and Sanibel's destruction. This was ultimately tested before the Florida Supreme Court, which upheld the Circuit Court's bond validation. The sale of the bonds was unsuccessfully challenged in the courts by the Sanibel-Captiva Taxpayers League.

Eager to begin, the Lee County Commission approved a series of construction-related contracts on October 19, 1960, pending sale of the bonds. A final public hearing held on November 15, 1961, resulted in the Florida Attorney General's office making a recommendation to the Trustees of the Internal Improvement Trust Fund that the right-of-way across the biologically productive bottom of San Carlos Bay be granted to the Lee County Board of County Commissioners. The Trustees at that time were the Florida Governor and Cabinet — seven elected officials. They had sided with Lee County and accepted the county concept of opening up Sanibel and Captiva Islands to major development. Soon thereafter, heavy marine construction equipment began to assemble at the site, ready to begin the link.

The engineers who had designed the alignment of the Causeway and bridge system had assumed that the southernmost bridge, which would connect the Causeway to Sanibel, could land at the northern end of Bailey Road a few hundred feet to the east of Bailey's General Store. Francis Bailey, who opposed the Causeway, did not want to convey a right-of-way easement for a Sanibel-side bridgehead to Lee County. The Causeway and bridge were then realigned to meet Sanibel Island further east on a broad Bay-to-Gulf parcel of land owned by Hugo Lindgren. A Swedish-born New York entrepreneur, Hugo Lindgren was the chief private-sector advocate of the Causeway. Like many of the pro-bridge property owners, he saw only dollar signs.

The Sanibel Causeway officially opened to traffic, with county-generated grand-opening fanfare, on Sunday, May 26, 1963. Jean, Leslie, Chuck, and I took advantage of the one-time-only opening day free passage that afternoon and drove to Bonita Springs to visit Jean's family. Change was already obvious — soon after the ribbon-cutting ceremony, traffic onto the lighthouse grounds and use of the beach parking lot suddenly quadrupled.

I was on my porch, fascinated by the dramatic increase in public use, and Tommy was relaxing on the Gulf-side porch of Quarters 1. He shouted over and said, "Charles, I'll bet Mr. Darling rolled over in his grave today."

Quietly, I nodded in agreement.

At first, changes to the islands were subtle. Prior to the Causeway, there had been four real estate sales offices and about a dozen real estate agents on both islands. But large parcels of Gulf- and Bay-front property on the eastern end of Sanibel were soon scraped clean, excavated, developed, and marketed as select resort and subdivision properties. New real estate offices sprouted, land sales increased tenfold, and property values began to skyrocket. Sanibel was becoming the island of the Golden Fleece.

When the Island Water Association began to distribute reliable potable water in late 1966, Sanibel and Captiva were ripe for this land boom. In 1967, the Lee County Commission hired an Atlanta-based planning firm to create a comprehensive plan for Lee County. This plan proposed extremely high dwelling unit densities and high-rise building development for Sanibel and Captiva. Under the planner's assumptions, the islands would support a population of nearly 100,000 people.

The five politicians, mostly inept thinkers, elected to the Lee County Commission changed in individual composition and politics a few times in the decade after the Causeway was opened, but they have never functioned well as planners. In the early 1970s, several commissioners seemed to develop personal vendettas and enjoyed doing a variety of disservices to the people of Sanibel and Captiva and to the delicate environment of both islands. The ruling clique on the mainland still regarded the voters and residents of Sanibel and Captiva as second-class citizens. To the majority of the commissioners and many of their hired lackeys, Lee County's barrier islands were going to be developed to their full potential — come hell or high water. Their incompetent maneuvers and meddling succeeded in spoiling what limited character was left on both fragile islands.

The concept of taking control of their own destiny and becoming a municipality had briefly stirred the islanders in 1958. But this idea did not become a popular rallying point at that time, due to the limited number of permanent residents and voters.

On February 12, 1960, I registered to vote at Bailey's General Store. However, I had to register as a Democrat — Florida was a one-party state. Francis Bailey, who served as island voter registrar for the Lee County Supervisor of Elections, did the honors. I became the 155th registered voter in Precinct 16, the only precinct on Sanibel Island at the time.

In early 1973, a poll was conducted by the Sanibel-Captiva Planning Board, a non-profit citizen's group that had formed after the Causeway was built, to foster planned growth on the two barrier islands. The poll was designed to ascertain the level of interest within both communities to the notion of becoming incorporated. Results indicated that the residents of Captiva were not interested. A break in attitude, barely noticed and hardly talked about, had actually occurred between the two islands in the early '60s but did not manifest itself until the idea of incorporation was tested. The poll's outcome was also clear: There was enough interest among the Sanibel people to explore self-determination.

On a Saturday night in late Fall 1973, during our quiet time on the porch of lighthouse Quarters 2, I said to Jean, "Porter Goss stopped by today and asked me if I would be interested in serving on the Home Rule Study Group. He thought that since I've been around here forever, as he put it, I would bring my experience to the group. I thought the proposition over for a few minutes and declined. I supported the role of the group, but I was already wearing too many hats. Anyway, it was nice to be asked."

The arguments over incorporation reminded me of the clashes over the Causeway, and like that emotional issue, the issue fueled debates whenever two or more people got together. I was personally convinced that the only way we could preserve a genuine part of the real Sanibel and its environment, already being stressed and challenged, was to become self-governing and in control of our own destiny.

In August 1974, I hosted the annual post-nesting season cookout for the volunteers of Caretta Research, Inc., at the lighthouse. During the awards ceremony, I announced that if the vote in favor of incorporation was successful, I would become a candidate for the new City Council. But my announcement was premature. Since I was a Federal employee, I would have to take several extra steps to qualify as a candidate before I could publicly announce it.

After Bob Barber's departure on October 28th, Glen Bond became the Refuge Manager at the J. N. "Ding" Darling National Wildlife Refuge on December 13, 1973. Bob had been active in a Lee County Commission committee charged with drafting a land use plan for Sanibel and Captiva. Glen wasn't interested in the incorporation debate, or any non-Refuge issue related to the possible birth of a new city government. On the other hand, I was convinced that the proponents of incorporation would win.

As time for the vote approached (and after I had done my homework on my possible future political activity), I told Glen of my intent to become a candidate for City Council. I asked that he contact the Regional Refuge Supervisor, inform him of my decision to run for the office, and request that my participation in the local government as a private citizen be approved. Further, I requested that if I were elected, I be granted an irregularly scheduled tour of duty which would permit me to attend meetings. Perhaps my supervisors felt I would never succeed because all gave their approval that I could become a candidate.

The debate intensified, and on November 5, 1974, the voters of Sanibel approved incorporation. Over 63 percent of the eligible voters had cast their votes in favor of Sanibel becoming a city.

Fifteen other candidates and I qualified for the City Council election. Of these, the voters would choose five council members on December 3, 1974. I knew or had met most of those on the ballot — a few were pre-Causeway islanders. Campaigning consisted of a debate during Candidate's Night at the Sanibel Community House and a few gatherings over morning coffee at residents' homes. I enlisted a rock-solid campaign committee and was convinced I would be among the top five and be seated on the Council.

By 11:30 the night of December 3rd, the votes were tallied and the results announced. Elected to the new City Council were Porter Goss, Vernon MacKenzie, Zelda (Zee) Butler, Charles LeBuff, and Francis Bailey — in that order — with Porter receiving 60 percent of the vote.

The organizational meeting of the first City Council was held on December 11th at the Sanibel Community House. Sanibel's Founding Fathers, as we five had been dubbed, were sworn in. Jean stood with me during my part of the ceremony, and our children were in the audience. While I took the oath of office, Jean held my 1904 edition of the *Standard Bible,* issued to lightkeepers by the U. S. Lighthouse Service, for my left hand.

Next, we drew lots to determine which seat number each member would receive. This drawing also determined the length of each Councilperson's term. Francis drew seat one, I seat two, and Porter seat three — these seats were two-year terms. Vernon drew seat four and Zee seat five — both four-year terms.

Getting down to business right away, we unanimously elected Porter Goss Sanibel's first Mayor. The first meeting lasted about eight hours, a harbinger of things to come. Over time, the length and frequency of meetings would exact a toll from most of us.

As the end of my term approached, I felt a sense of incompletion. We had developed and passed a Comprehensive Land Use Plan on July 19, 1976, and the workload slowed slightly, but there were further objectives and programs to pursue. I didn't want to see my seat claimed by someone else, at least not yet, and certainly not after just two years. So I announced that I would seek reelection. Although one businessman threatened to run against me, to my great surprise, I was unopposed at the close of the qualifying period. I was automatically reelected and served Sanibel until November 1980.

Eventually, I was elected Vice-Mayor for a year, but I never served as Mayor during my six years as a Council member because I could not commit the time necessary. Personally, I was pleased with my reasonably good attendance record, at least until the end of my tenure when I was winding down my political career.

During the year I served as Vice-Mayor, Francis Bailey was Mayor. He was unmarried at the time, so Jean would tell her friends that she was Sanibel's First Lady. But I already knew that!

All was not easy for the members of the two Councils on which I served. Neither was it easy for the elected members of our community who came after the first five. The position is truly a thankless job, one in which an incumbent does not befriend the opposition. The time I spent conducting my share of City business was incomprehensible and perplexing to some members of the defeated and angry anti-incorporation segment of the business community. Unbeknown to me, some of these business people were conspiring against me.

It came out of the blue. Glen Bond called me aside in late June 1976 and said, "I just had a phone call from Rudy." (Rudy Rudolph was Glen's supervisor in the Service's Atlanta Regional Office.) "Someone here on the island is trying to cause a problem for you. Rudy received a telephone call from a very irrational individual who demanded to know how you could sit on the Sanibel City Council. He insisted on finding out where you got all the free time to attend the hearings and meetings being held concerning the Land Use Plan."

I'm not sure Glen wanted to tell me more, but I pressed the issue. "Who called, Glen?"

"Herb Purdy."

Astonished, I blurted, "Herb Purdy!? It sure took him long enough to try and get even with me. I knew he wasn't one of my fans because of a run-in he and I had back in '69. I intercepted him one evening, after I received a complaint, when he was illegally operating his jeep on the beach. I don't think we've spoken to each other since."

The basic question — where did my personal time during which I functioned as a councilman come from? — required a simple review of my annual leave records. My approved irregular tour of duty more than adequately allowed for my participation at the regular Tuesday City Council meetings. I had used 74 hours of annual leave (accrued vacation time) to attend 16 special Council meetings between January 1 and June 25, 1976. This information was provided by memorandum to the Regional Office and I was never informed of any further discussions between Glen, the Regional Office, or Herb Purdy. The personal attack, launched by Purdy and any cronies who may have been in agreement with him, had failed.

The main issue, one that probably confounded my political opposition the most, was how, as a Federal employee, I could physically sit on the Council. Simply put, the public didn't understand how the system worked. I became aware of this fact very suddenly one night just prior to election day 1976.

Jean had been working at Scotty's Pub for about six years, and as events would have it, I had the car this particular night and would pick her up when she was through. I arrived early and decided to go into the lounge and have a beer. One lone seat was available at the bar. I sat next to an individual whom I recognized as a Sanibel postal worker, but I did not know him nor had ever spoken to him. He was enjoying himself, that is, until he noticed I had taken the next seat. The bartender probably should have cut him off two or three drinks ago.

Within minutes, he began his attack. "LeBuff, haven't you ever heard of the Hatch Act?"

In an overload of anger, he launched a tirade against the City and those who served on the Council, particularly me. He accused me of serving on the Council illegally, yelling, "I know the Hatch Act, and there's no way you can serve in an elective office!"

My first reaction was to get up and leave, but then I had a better idea. For a fleeting moment, I thought I'd just knock him across the side of his face with my fist. But I returned to my senses and cooled down, considering the source sitting next to me.

"You don't know what the hell you're talking about!" I retorted. "If you know the Hatch Act so well, I suggest you read it and become enlightened, if you can comprehend what you read."

The Hatch Act of the time regulated the political activity of Federal employees, and contrary to my antagonist's opinion, it unequivocally sanctioned my involvement in local politics. The Act clearly allowed a Federal employee to become active in local political matters and to seek political office in nonpartisan elections. The Sanibel City Council was nonpartisan. The squabble ended and he sat silent, mulling over what I said. I got up and left.

Not only did I sacrifice most of my free time, I also lost a lot of money (on paper anyway) during the six years I served my community as an unpaid Council member. In 1965, I had formed my sign company, Sanibel Sign Services, the island's first commercial sign shop. Jean and I ran the business on a part-time basis. After I was elected, we suspended the business to avoid any accusations of conflict of interest. Had I continued my sign manufacturing operations, there would have been allegations of conflicts — the Council developed the City's first graphics ordinance, and we heard countless requests for sign variances. I reopened the business in 1981, again part time, and in 1990, Jean and I began to operate the business full time.

Serving on the first City Council was an historically significant and unique experience, and I shared the honor with some very remarkable people. Sitting in Council meetings was not easy — it was extremely hard work and only occasionally enjoyable. Legal wrangling, lawyer's interpretations, and meetings *ad nauseam* took the fun out of it, but there were times and important issues that I found satisfying.

In the early summer of 1976, with completion and adoption of the Comprehensive Land Use Plan fast approaching, the debate, personal attacks, and even serious threats against some Council members intensified. Personality conflicts between councilmen and members of the business community, accusations and false-hoods related to the intent of certain Council members, and charges of conflict of interest abounded. Members of the Planning Commission and certain members of the City administration were subjected to nearly the same level of harassment.

These were difficult days, but the results demanded by the majority of Sanibel's voters were soon to come to fruition. Knowing this is what kept me on a steady course. But this is not to say I didn't have my own detractors and character assassins.

* * *

In May 1976, Caretta Research, Inc., received a grant from a New York-based foundation. This provided cash with which to purchase a new vehicle for use in our sea turtle conservation and field research efforts. We bought a 1976 CJ–5 jeep and equipped it for patrol operations. I no longer had to rely on the Refuge jeep. Now other members of the organization could drive, and I could take a night off now and then.

After we bought the jeep, we launched a membership drive. For a contribution, residents and island visitors were encouraged to make reservations to inspect Sanibel's "red light district." If we were lucky, maybe they'd see a nesting loggerhead. Later on the beach, we explained that the island's red light district was nothing more that a growing multitude of stakes, driven into the beach, which had been marked with red reflector tape. These coded stakes identified the locations of loggerhead turtle nests we were monitoring through their incubation periods. We certainly didn't intend to raise more than eyebrows when we suggested such an illicit activity existed on Sanibel.

In late June 1976, I received a phone call from someone who claimed to be a visitor staying in a local timeshare condominium. This male caller asked to be booked for a sea turtle patrol on a night when we could accommodate two couples. I checked the calendar and reserved space for four people the next Saturday night, July 3rd. By this time in my life, I could no longer stay in the field all night on worknights, but I did usually stay out until the early morning hours on both Friday and Saturday nights. After I had their names and phone number, I instructed the group to meet me at the foot of the lighthouse at 9:00 Saturday night.

It was customary during the July 4th weekend for Sanibel, Captiva, and the Causeway islands to be crowded with people. Local resorts were nearly at capacity. To make life more pleasant for the taxpayers and their guests when the Memorial Day, Independence Day, and Labor Day holidays approached, the Lee County Mosquito Control District would swing into full action. Their skilled pilots and crews, mustered by Director Wayne Miller, aerially sprayed Sanibel and Captiva at the crack of dawn on the 3rd. As usual, they used a squadron of ancient but well-maintained DC-3s (known as C–47s during World War II). Cruising full throttle at treetop level, these twin-engine aircraft flew multiple side-by-side patterns along the length of both islands, spreading a foggy mixture of diesel fuel and Baytex or Malathion. These two adulticide formulations were sometimes used alternately to avoid development of any chemical tolerance or resistance among our salt marsh mosquito population.

I planned my Saturday to include installing a citizen's band radio in the new jeep. We used these inexpensive radios to communicate at night with our other turtle patrols on other barrier island beaches up and down the coast of southwest Florida. So, after sundown, I was working in the Refuge shop at the lighthouse with the door wide open, trying to finish installing the radio before it was time for the people to arrive. The mosquitos were hardly noticeable, a far cry from what it was like 17 summers before.

A ferocious squall had passed a few hours before dusk. The rain and wind had almost died, and a pungent, earthy smell permeated the humid atmosphere. I had already mounted the antenna at the rear of the jeep. Now I was bent over, my head under the hood, trying to fish the cable through the firewall and into the frame to connect the radio to the antenna. On a puff of wind, I suddenly got a whiff of something more pleasing and aromatic than rotting mangrove and buttonwood leaves.

"Nice perfume!" I thought, neither thinking nor questioning where it was coming from. I was intent on my work.

Seconds later, out of the near darkness, came a faint feminine voice. "Mr. LeBuff?" It was barely audible. Then louder, "Hello. Are you Mr. LeBuff?"

Looking up, I saw a beautiful, tall woman gracefully striding across the lighthouse cul-de-sac coming toward the shop. She was now just steps from the doorway.

"Yes, I'm Charles LeBuff. Can I help you?"

Now smiling broadly, she said, "Hi, I'm Carmen. My friend called you earlier in the week to make reservations for us to go out with you tonight on your turtle patrol. But everyone else changed their plans, so it'll just be me."

She was very attractive, with shoulder-length raven hair, dressed in tight white slacks and a very close-fitting white T–shirt. I couldn't help but notice her voluptuousness and that she was bra-less and bare-footed. I thought I detected an ever-so-slight Spanish accent and assumed she was Cuban, probably in her mid-to-late twenties.

Her words seemed to hang in the air, and I thought, "It'll just be her? Damnation!"

I continued to watch her graceful gyrations and body language as she approached ever closer to where I was. The elegant perfume, not overpowering, permeated my every breath. I noticed too she had been making unwavering eye contact with me from the outset.

Nervously, I swallowed and stammered, "You're uh ... uh ... alone? How did you get here?"

"I parked in the parking lot on the beach." She pointed toward the Gulf lot.

Suddenly, a gut-wrenching feeling came over me and I was scared to death. I just knew something wasn't quite right. So I lied, "I tried to call the number your friend gave me several times in the past few hours, but I never got an answer." I lied again, "As you can see, I'm having jeep trouble and won't be able to make the beach patrol tonight." At least this looked plausible because the jeep's hood was up. I continued, "I'm sorry I couldn't reach you or anyone in your party to let someone know what happened. It would have saved you the trip."

She seemed more than a little irritated. "Oh, no! I'm very disappointed. I just know it would have been a pleasure-filled night. I was so looking forward to seeing a sea turtle. We'll just have to call again and reschedule. Good night."

Waving, she turned and pranced off into the darkness. Neither she nor her friend ever called back.

Why was I so nervous? Years before, I promised Jean I would never allow myself to be alone with another woman at night on the beach. I always had a group of people with me to counter any embarrassing accusations. Some nights were all women, but I made sure I was never alone on the beach with someone from the opposite sex — unless it was Jean herself. This time, that old promise was tested again, but the experience with lovely Carmen was an extreme case — a close encounter of the best kind!

The next day, I couldn't wait to tell my friend Jim Anholt about it. Jim had worked in the turtle project for several years. When I told him the story in detail, he agreed without question that someone was trying to set me up, probably for political reasons.

It would have been easy to fall under Carmen's spell and patrol the beach alone with her. But soon, at a preplanned location, the beach would have suddenly lit up with strobe lights and camera flashes, and another politician would have bitten the dust.

18

THE UNHOLY TRINITY

When Sanibel and Captiva entered the 20th Century nearly a hundred years ago, the islands looked much different than they do today. I'm referring to their vegetation, not their commercial or residential development. Farm fields and citrus groves dominated the upland ridges which, except for the Wulfert area, roughly paralleled seasonally flooded swales, the fringes of the Sanibel Slough, and scattered minor sloughs throughout the island's interior. The tallest trees were strangler figs, sea grapes, cabbage palms, and slash pines — all long-established native species. Other than those on or near homesteads, the large trees that remained after general deforestation for crop and fruit cultivation were confined mostly to the more isolated, inaccessible ridges. I can't resist chuckling to myself whenever I hear someone, even a highly respected environmentalist, talk about the "virgin" and "pristine" vegetation of Sanibel Island. In reality, almost everything native that grows here, except mangroves, is second-growth or younger.

When island farming was destroyed by a series of hurricanes in the first half of the 20th Century, the land was abandoned and generally became fallow. Financially strapped farmers sold out and moved away. Here and there on Sanibel, on what appears to be

untouched land, we can still observe prominent furrows at the surface of once highly productive farm fields. There are several long-
abandoned homesites within the "Ding" Darling Refuge where the
scarred earth from early vegetable farming operations is clearly discernable.   To the uninformed, these areas look like a dense
untouched subtropical landscape.

Over time, native vegetation reestablished itself on the once-
cleared sites. But due to several factors, the islands took on a
totally different appearance than before. As you drive down
Periwinkle Way, Sanibel-Captiva Road, and interconnected side
roads, you are not looking at the "genuine" Sanibel Island.

Before modern mankind settled these islands, two natural elements controlled the diversity of the vegetation and wildlife.
Periodically, fire and hurricane-caused salt-water inundation maintained the natural ecosystems in a finely tuned balance. Savage
hurricanes, more powerful than those documented in recent
history, occasionally pummeled primitive Sanibel and Captiva
Islands. Extremely high storm surges produced tides over 20 feet
above sea level. Sanibel and Captiva were completely submerged,
only the tallest trees showing above water. Today, meteorologists
and insurance companies call such hurricanes "500-year storms,"
even though they do not occur, of course, at exactly this interval. If
weather conditions are favorable, several storms of this magnitude
could occur in any given year. We have indeed been lucky.

After an intense hurricane, the inundating waters caused by the
storm surge would drain away by breaking through the island's
perimeter ridges or gradually percolate down to the underlying salt-
water aquifer. Despite slow evaporation, the Sanibel Slough basin
would retain a flooded reservoir of seawater for months. It would
then take many years of precipitation and seasonal flushing to bring
the Slough back to its optimum fresh-water and savannah ecosystem. Simply put, the occasional sea-water flooding maintained the
integrity of Sanibel's and Captiva's vegetative ecology.

During the dry season, lightning strikes would ignite the
Slough's tinder-dry marshes and adjacent uplands. Raging and
unchecked, these wildfires would race from one end of the island to
the other. Fire helped maintain what Nature intended the environment of Sanibel Island to be. After people began to occupy the
island, they feared these fires because of the danger they presented

to their homes and material possessions. Every wildfire, whether ignited by accident or by natural forces, was battled and extinguished. By 1950, large expanses of the Slough and adjacent uplands seldom burned anymore, and the vegetative communities began a long-term and ongoing transition.

In 1955, the Sanibel Fire Control District was established. Since then, all wildfires have been quickly and effectively extinguished. Since no growth inhibitor or any kind of natural control now existed, the demise of the Sanibel Slough began.

With growing conditions now to their liking, three exotic plants became well-established on Sanibel and Captiva. I call them the "unholy trinity": cajeput (*Melaleuca*), Brazilian pepper, and Australian pine. In addition, other less-known exotic plants are becoming major problems for land managers and wildlife populations on these islands. Some have already spread into our natural ecosystems and are establishing strong footholds. Their presence has been basically ignored outside the J. N. "Ding" Darling National Wildlife Refuge. The fast-growing ear leaf acacia, for example is springing up along the margins of the Slough. If unchecked, it will soon invade the wetlands.

By the mid-1970s, the presence of the "unholy trinity" had dramatically changed our landscape and began to directly reduce the populations of resident wildlife species. For example, the fast-growing Brazilian pepper quickly moved into disturbed-earth sites such as subdivisions, ditch banks, and roadway drainage ditches. More slowly they invaded the well-vegetated ridges and periphery of seasonally flooded wetlands. Their dense, fast-growing canopy quickly rose above the native plants, which included many food plants and grasses upon which animal life foraged. These soon died due to lack of sunlight. To add insult to injury, the naturally-produced chemicals released by the shrub's ground-covering leaf litter prevented the highly desirable native vegetation any chance of recovery.

The invasion of Brazilian pepper has had a particularly severe impact on two resident creatures: the gopher tortoise and its ecological associate, the eastern indigo snake. These two harmless reptiles were once very common on both islands. Due to road kills, commercial collection for the pet trade, development of their prime habitat, and exotic plant invasion, both species are now seriously threatened. It seems that the high ground, so important to their survival in viable populations, also offers the best building sites for humans.

Today, the most environmentally damaging member of my "unholy trinity" to affect Sanibel's unique interior wetlands system is the Brazilian pepper. Over the years, I've made significant contributions to the battle to recover our islands from this weed tree and the other two plants. But I must confess, I bear some responsibility, however innocent, for the spread of Brazilian pepper. Here's how it happened.

It was Thursday, January 14, 1960, and Tommy and I were done! We had finally completed the seaplane dolly at our new aircraft base in the Bailey Tract. Looking over the results with an air of satisfaction, Tommy said, "Now we need to do a little landscaping around here to dress up the place and give us a little shade and protection from the wind later on. We'll stop at Clarence's on the way back to the office and see what he might have in pots that he'll give us."

Clarence Rutland operated a small-scale plant nursery in his backyard on Periwinkle Way. He grew native and exotic plants, some of which he sold, but he was kind-hearted and gave many varieties to islanders to plant in their yards. He was proud of his small coconut grove that he had planted at the rear of his property; he was field-growing the palms for a cash crop.

After bringing Clarence up to speed on what was going on in the Refuge, we listened to his latest tidbits of island gossip. This was customary, but I never heard him say anything bad about anyone. In those days, islanders knew everyone else's business. In fact, it was often said that if a sandfly passed gas at the lighthouse, someone would hear about it at Redfish Pass within half an hour.

Tommy directed the conversation to the reason for our visit. "Clarence, we need some plants so we can spruce up our seaplane base. We've already planted some rye grass, but we need some shrubs and trees to really dress it up. Do you have anything that will do the trick?"

Clarence thought about it for a second, then replied, "I do have some small gumbo limbos and mastic trees in gallon cans you can have. They should do all right there. Oh! I can spare a couple of cajeput trees and maybe about a half-dozen Florida hollies too. The hollies originated in South America, and I'm selling them fairly fast because the few that are already growing on the islands were so pretty when their fruit ripened around Christmas, now everyone wants one so they can make wreaths. The Florida holly is an attractive plant with its tight clusters of bright red berries. Y'all probably already know they're a great wild bird food too. The robins love 'em."

We walked among the plants with Clarence while he picked out the specimens he wanted to give us. I carried them to a spot near his back steps.

When we were ready to leave, Tommy said, "Thanks Clarence. Charles will pick up everything in the morning."

Clarence replied, "There's one catch, Tom. You can have the plants as a gift, but only on one condition."

Tommy smiled and said, What's that?"

Now grinning himself, Clarence replied, "The next time you fly down to the Keys, I want to go along so I can fill up on lobster."

Laughing, Tommy said, "You've got a reservation!"

As Clarence had told us, Florida hollies, also called Christmas berries and Brazilian peppers, were already being sparsely cultivated on Sanibel and Captiva and were generally well managed by the property owners. They were being put in as hedge plants, although a few homeowners planted them as individual ornamentals in their landscape schemes. Clarence Rutland was playing the role of "Clarence Pepperseed" and was having a great deal of fun doing it.

The next morning, I picked up the plants and met Tommy at the seaplane canal. At his direction, I planted the six Brazilian peppers and two cajeput (*Melaleuca*) saplings around the periphery of our seaplane base. I also placed a false mastic and two gumbo limbos nearby.

On my own, I planted a coconut just to the northwest of the electric winch we used to pull the seaplane dolly out of the water. I had found the mature seed that morning near the lighthouse.

Many years have passed since that Friday, and my coconut palm became a tall sentinel overlooking the overgrown and long-abandoned seaplane base. But unfortunately, my coconut now appears to have become a victim of an insect-borne virus known as Lethal Yellowing. This fatal palm disease is sweeping these barrier islands and is systematically killing our original strain of coconuts, the Jamaica Tall.

Over the next decade, Brazilian peppers invaded all habitats on Sanibel Island, even some locations in the mangrove forest. Their spread occurred very quickly — the mosquito control ditching program underway at the same time improved the growing conditions for Brazilian pepper. Seeds were dispersed by the thousands, and later by the millions, as more trees matured and fruited. Migratory birds, primarily robins, and raccoons were the chief dispersers. After gorging themselves with ripe pepper fruit, the robins flew unrestricted everywhere around the islands. The indigestible seed at the center of the fruit passed through their gastrointestinal tracts, and the birds aerially sowed these viable seeds more efficiently than a farmer could. The freshly cleared ditch banks and spoil piles created by the mosquito ditching machines were bombarded as millions of pepper seeds fell out of the sky.

These berries also affected the robins. As digestion proceeds, the skin and fleshy portion of the fruit capsule breaks down, and a chemical is released that can result in acute intoxication. It is common to see pepper seed-stuffed robins arrive at a bird bath, drink, and soon literally stagger about the basin. When completely drunk, they can even pass out and fall to the ground.

In 1965, Tommy and I again innocently became Brazilian pepper growers. Recurring rain-caused erosion along the dike at the Darling Tract had become a problem, so Tommy decided to try to stabilize the dike's shoulders and berm with Brazilian pepper along those areas that were prone to serious washout. We had collected several buckets of mature fruit, and as Tommy drove slowly along the dike, I stood in the bed of the jeep pickup and hand-sowed the seeds on the bare earth. Many of these seeds germinated successfully, but they really didn't prevent or stop the erosion. Instead, they did in time create a barrier that made it difficult for Refuge visitors to view the wildlife. And the complaints came in.

By 1972, I realized we had helped create a true environmental monster. As the peppers thrived, grew, and multiplied, they began to choke out the native and more desirable vegetation. Still considered beautiful by some residents, these trees had virtually turned the interior wetlands into a monotypic forest.

We soon learned that our involvement in the invasion by this damnable plant was minor. There were other seed sources just across the Bay on the mainland and other nearby infested islands. And the engorged robin seed bombers flew across the water in great flocks back in those days.

The upgrading of wildlife diversity, which Tommy and I assumed we were doing, had soon run amok. Native wildlife food-producing plants, which created a real and dependable biological diversity, were being choked out, shaded to death by the thick and quick-growing canopy of the Brazilian peppers. My opinion of this plant changed overnight; it was as though I had been struck by lightning. It was only a matter of time until I became the island's first "Pepper Buster."

There is another downside to this plant. It is related to poison ivy, and some people who come in contact with the leaves or the sap have allergic skin reactions similar to poison ivy dermatitis. A few years ago, some creative entrepreneurs harvested the fruit of this plant, dried the berries, and marketed them as red peppercorns. They were shipped to food purveyors who supplied the northern restaurant industry. At the swanky restaurants that featured red peppercorns, more than a few customers were taken seriously ill, and the practice, I'm told, was investigated and stopped by various health department agencies.

* * *

Tommy and I were nearly responsible for what could have been another devastating impact on Sanibel's environment. For a fleeting moment, we both thought we had inadvertently introduced another foreign noxious plant to the island's fresh-water wetlands.

On February 20, 1962, we had flown to South Florida Refuge Headquarters at Loxahatchee National Wildlife Refuge to spend the day in Federal court in West Palm Beach. We were involved in separate cases at Loxahatchee, so this court date was long-standing for both of us. Tommy had helped apprehend a notorious and habitual alligator hunter who was brazen enough to actually live out in the Loxahatchee marshes for a week at a time.

His floating, makeshift, portable campsite was in a dense willow head. His jungle hammock was suspended just above the water level. His equipment, water jugs, canned foods, and salted and rolled 'gator hides were stored in several floating, galvanized wash-tubs. After dark, he poled his plywood pirogue through the flooded open marsh and around the scattered tree islands. He spent the night checking his baited hook sets, looking for alligators they may have caught, and skinning those that had been hooked.

This habitual violator was out in the Refuge doing his thing again, and his presence was completely unknown to the Refuge staff. During day and night patrols, Refuge officers had not noticed him or his dim light. Nor had any of them heard a tell-tale gunshot, since this character seldom used a firearm. But one day, Tommy and the Refuge Biologist happened to spot his well-concealed campsite from the air during a waterfowl survey.

Directed to the site by Tommy's radio communications, two Refuge officers driving airboats converged to find the man asleep in his hammock. The officers made the arrest, seized a tubfull of alligator hides, and destroyed the camp. So today, this case was being heard before the United States Magistrate the same day that several fishing license-related violation notices that I had issued, while on temporary law enforcement duty at Loxahatchee several months earlier, were scheduled to be adjudicated.

Loxahatchee's airboat landing near the Headquarters was also used as a tie-up for our floatplane. This was located on the eastern side of the rim canal, which as usual was festooned with large float-ing mats of very healthy water hyacinths along both canal banks. The water hyacinth had been introduced to Florida from South America, via Louisiana, not long after the turn of the century. This floating plant soon became naturalized and was classified as an aquatic pest plant because of the way it dominates fresh surface waters. It had adapted well and like my "unholy trinity," the hyacinths soon escaped into the general environment.

In one of many previous conversations with Tommy about Sanibel's interior fresh-water wetlands system, I asked him why water hyacinths were not found on Sanibel. Why had they not pro-liferated in the mosquito ditches being dug through the Slough?

Tommy explained what he knew about the situation. "Sadie Hiers once tried to get them to grow in a small pool at Hiers By-the-Sea Cottages on Gulf Drive. But for some reason they didn't make it. I don't know why, unless it has something to do with our water quality. Maybe there was an upper stratification between the surface water and the deeper saltier water in the canals at the time of year she tried. On the other hand, the banana water lilies that I brought over from Loxahatchee seem to be doing well in the Bailey Tract."

After the court sessions ended late in the afternoon, we said goodbye to our coworkers at Loxahatchee and took off for Sanibel in the seaplane.

Above the Caloosahatchee, about halfway between Fort Myers and Sanibel, Tommy exclaimed, "Charles, we've got a mat of hyacinths hung up in the water rudder on the left float. I've been watching them for awhile and thought they would have fallen off by now. It's nearly dark, so I don't want to take the time to land and pull them off. We'll need all the daylight we have left just to set down safely."

After we landed and secured the plane to the dolly, Tommy operated the winch to pull the plane and its cradle out of the water. I checked both floats for the stowaway hyacinths but found none.

"I don't see the hyacinths, Tommy. They must have fallen off."

He replied, "They were there as we came around for our approach. They could have broken loose when I lowered the rudders. Tomorrow first thing, I want you to take the canoe and check this whole canal to see if you can find them."

"Damn!" I swore to myself. "Talk about a needle in a haystack!"

The next day I slowly paddled twice down each side of the wide canal, carefully inspecting the wet marginal bank, the adjacent dry bank, and the breadth of the canal. I found no hyacinths. If they fell off just before we started our descent, they did so off the Refuge and hopefully in a dry upland area. In those days, to avoid damaging the airplane's wings during any turns, I routinely kept all the woody vegetation close-cropped several yards away from the edge of the water along the seaplane canal's margins. The cattails which lined parts of the canal were periodically sprayed with an herbicide to prevent their spread into the landing and taxiing zones.

* * *

Thank goodness the two cajeput trees I planted in 1960 did not survive. I do not want to be remembered as a cultivator of this noxious pest. Deliberately planting Florida hollies has been embarrassing enough.

Today, this tree's earlier common name, cajeput, is being replaced by its scientific generic name. Scientists and laymen alike now refer to this extremely invasive tree by the first of its two-part technical name, *Melaleuca*. Other common names, still used in some circles for this man-introduced Australian tree, include paperbark tree and punk tree.

The *Melaleuca*'s Florida origins are unclear, but it is believed they were first imported to this hemisphere in Miami in 1908. The Koreshan Unity, a religious and social group, headquartered in Estero since the turn of the century, had acquired seed and cultivated a few of these trees in 1912. When I arrived on the local scene in 1952, southwest Florida was nearly free of *Melaleuca*.

I roamed the area on foot and on horseback during my high school years, and later into the late '50s, by jeep or cut-down Model A Ford. I knew the region and its ecosystems well. I knew of only three *Melaleuca* groves. These trees had "escaped" from the Koreshan cultivation in Estero. At that time, one stand was on the south bank of the Estero River behind the post office. From there it ran across the narrow highway in a southeasterly direction. Another stand grew east of the Tamiami Trail north of the Estero River. The third group of *Melaleuca* was several miles away immediately north of the Ten Mile Canal. I doubt if the three plots totalled more than ten acres of these trees.

Single trees and small orderly groups of *Melaleuca* were common as landscape plants in yards throughout the area between Fort Myers and Naples. But the tree had not seriously affected the environment when I first observed the species in 1952.

I found the *Melaleuca* to be remarkable because of the way they grew so densely. In some thickets, it was impossible to walk between the trees. Don McKeown and I would remove handfuls of *Melaleuca* leaves, crush them in our palms, and vigorously wipe our exposed skin, using the oily residue as a makeshift mosquito repellent. But the juice wasn't very successful in helping us cope with the hordes of insects so commonplace in those days.

Melaleuca seeds are contained in small compact capsules, each containing up to 250 seeds. When the whole plant or a section of the tree is stressed, the mature seeds are released to drift in the atmosphere. One tree can contain 20 million dormant but viable seeds waiting for the right environmental conditions for release.

Natural pruning (the dying and sloughing of lower branches) and fire are two major factors that regulate seed release. The seed is tiny, ranging between one-half and one millimeter in diameter. Wind can disperse viable seeds many miles from their source of origin. The sheer number of seeds makes the tree prolific, and seedlings germinate in a carpet-like fashion. One strong gust of wind can cover several acres of distant land with enough seeds to begin another grove.

This species does exceptionally well in wet areas but is also very successful in dry upland habitats. The seeds are nearly inde-structible. In the late 1930s, land developers tried to sow *Melaleuca* aerially in the eastern Everglades on the assumption that the tree's appetite for water would help dry out the vast marsh. Back then, the water regimen in the great grassy river was at a high-er elevation than it is now, so the seeding attempt failed. Due to mankind's more recent manipulation of the waterflow into the 'Glades, the ecosystem has been damaged. Its optimum high water level, which earlier had prevented the aerially-sown *Melaleuca* seeds from germinating, is a thing of the past.

Now years later, the trees that were growing in communities adjacent to the Everglades are marching dramatically into the wilderness. Growing in optimum soil, temperature, and moisture conditions, a *Melaleuca* can grow six feet per year and produce seed in less than four years. As established groves mature, their staggering total seed production is causing these ultra-aggressive trees to spread like wildfire throughout the wetlands in south Florida.

Sanibel Island is no exception. In 1958, there were very few *Melaleuca* trees on the island. Those that were here were widely separated individual trees, most at homesites where they had been affectionately planted. As the island began to develop, more *Melaleuca* were planted in new subdivisions as buffers and visual screening along property lines. They were readily available and, if purchased, inexpensive. However, most islanders simply drove down to Estero and dug up what trees they wanted from the highway right-of-way.

In May 1979, during Brazilian pepper spraying operations in the Bailey Tract, I discovered the first volunteer *Melaleuca* sapling on the Refuge. It was a healthy 8-footer, and over the next few weeks, I found several others of similar size in the same vicinity. They had escaped! All I had was the chemical used to kill Brazilian pepper, so I applied it to the foliage of the trees. But I found this particular product was unable to kill *Melaleuca* completely.

In other parts of the State, land and wildlife managers were finally recognizing the dilemma they were facing: The vast and complex wetland systems of southern Florida were succumbing to the steady invasion of this tree. Chemical companies began to reprogram research and development efforts, and new herbicides were brought online to combat the invasion. These new products made killing cajeput trees expensive but feasible.

By 1982, resident ecologists on Sanibel Island had become cognizant of the severe threat these despicable trees posed for the ecological health and integrity of the island's interior wetlands. These environmentally wise individuals convinced local officials that a City program should be launched to combat the menace, before these trees established a foothold in the Sanibel Slough.

The City hired Charles Pounds as their Noxious Plant Control Officer. He launched the program by first mapping known *Melaleuca* trees already well established on developed lands. Even the Lee County Electric Cooperative, which provides electric power to the islands, assisted many times by lifting Pounds (no pun intended) in their tall bucket trucks. He could then peer from his observation point above the vegetative canopy and locate and plot any *Melaleuca* trees in view. This way, he accurately developed his maps to document the location of the tree's infestation centers. However, in some locations where even this high vantage point wasn't adequate, the Lee County Mosquito Control District made one of their helicopters available to carry him aloft. Charles Pounds' *Melaleuca* search and destroy mission had gained wide support.

It wasn't long before the City Council was appropriating up to $20,000 per year to fund the Sanibel noxious plant control program. Property owners who had *Melaleuca* on their lands were encouraged to join with the City in eliminating the trees from their properties. Most citizens were convinced of the threat and openly cooperated with the program. But a few hard-line *Melaleuca* lovers refused, even after the City agreed to pay for removing the trees and replacing them with native vegetation. Over time, these holdouts acquiesced and the program was completed.

Charles Pounds' technique was labor-intensive but simple. If the tree was in someone's yard, it would be cut down, hauled away, and the stump treated with an approved herbicide.

Later, the program was redirected into the interior wetlands. But because vehicles could not penetrate the island's wetlands to haul away the trees, the technique was modified. The seed-producing, mature trees were sawed down, the seed capsule-bearing branches were removed and carefully stacked nearby, and the trunks were bucked up into four-foot-long sections and placed on top of the limbs. This process was used to consolidate the seed source to prevent any possible seed dispersal beyond the immediate vicinity. Seedlings were pulled out of the soil and saplings were chopped down at their bases. Then in a *coup de grace*, the stumps of all sizes were chemically treated. Thousands of *Melaleuca* were killed in this way, with a 90-percent success rate. Obviously, everyone involved with the program knew that some retreatment was necessary to kill the survivors.

According to City officials at the time, the last known residential *Melaleuca* tree on Sanibel was ceremoniously removed on September 18, 1989. Soon after this well-publicized but inaccurate event, Pounds' position became an unfunded activity at the next round of budget hearings. His job was eliminated in Sanibel's 1990–91 budget — prematurely — by a Council mostly unfamiliar with the big picture!

Contrary to popular belief, *Melaleuca* has not been eradicated from Sanibel Island, nor has the last residential tree been removed. In late 1996, Roger Zocki and I paddled several miles along the main mosquito ditch on Sanibel Island, between Rabbit Road and the Gulf Pines subdivision. We passed hundreds of healthy *Melaleuca* trees on both sides of the waterway.

One *Melaleuca* tree, growing in a previously uninfested area, can produce a monotypic grove with over ten thousand trees in as little as ten years. This species has the potential of so altering the Sanibel Slough that it will no longer function as a viable, biologically productive ecosystem.

Island land managers must now get out into the Slough and become aware of the ecological seriousness of this ongoing problem. Those responsible should move quickly to establish priorities germane to the local pest plant control program. It is essential that *Melaleuca* be controlled before the recently proclaimed total war against Brazilian pepper is launched.

* * *

Australian pines (*Casuarina* ssp.) are not related to true pines. They came to North America by ship, for man's commercial intentions and landscape purposes, in the late 1800s. Three of the 45 species are known to have been introduced in southwest Florida. A small number of what is now the most abundant Australian pine on Sanibel arrived here around 1920. They were planted as cultivated specimen trees. On Sanibel, the Botany Bay oak (*Casuarina equisetifolia*), was first used as an ornamental and was planted to grace present-day Periwinkle Way and the long-gone Gulf beach road that once connected the Casa Ybel with the Island Inn.

Around the same time, a few dozen of these trees were planted at the Sanibel Island Light Station as ornamental topiary trees. They lined a concrete walk which led from each quarters, around the oil house, and to the bayside pier. Also at this time, farmers planted another Australian pine, the Brazilian beefwood (*C. glauca*), in the Wulfert area, where it is still common. These trees were used primarily as hedgerows to protect produce and citrus crops from damaging winds. The third form, Cunningham's beefwood (*C. cunninghamiana*), is common in the inland sections of the south Florida peninsula and is more cold-tolerant than the previous species. This tree is not known on Sanibel or Captiva, but it does occur around some of the older farm fields in the Iona-MacGregor area and can be seen along parts of Gladiolus Drive.

In its native Australia, the Botany Bay oak was harvested and exploited by British lumber interests, shipped to England, and used as a cabinet wood during the early 19th Century. Some exquisitely crafted pieces of antique English furniture were produced from its lumber. Today, finer cabinet woods have replaced the Botany Bay oak in the furniture industry, but it continues to be used in one way or another on its native continent and in many parts of the subtropical and tropical zones of the Earth where it has been introduced.

Apparently in the northern hemisphere, this fast-growing tree has some major growth problems. When it attains what in its native environment would be a harvestable mature size for commercial use, here in Florida the heartwood is typically found to be severely rotted and unusable as a dependable quality wood product. Most of Sanibel's "majestic" Australian pines — the old originals, a few of which still grow along Periwinkle Way — and younger mature trees which line public parking lots and other roadways suffer from this condition. They are like sitting ducks, just waiting for the right wind direction and intensity to bring them crashing down.

The two Australian pines on Sanibel and Captiva Islands propagate by two dissimilar strategies. In other parts of the world, the Brazilian beefwood develops conelike seed-bearing fruits, but not so in Florida. Here, the tree multiplies by producing a vast number of suckers from its roots. These spread into an ever-enlarging group which slowly marches across the landscape.

The much more abundant Botany Bay oak produces small conelike fruit capsules which contain many seeds. The seeds can be transported by wind and insects while the cones are still attached to the branches, or by water after the cone drops to the ground. When high water levels occur (due to heavy precipitation or storm surge), the seed-laden cones can be carried about by floating on the water.

Hurricanes and tropical storms have been the most significant causes of the Botany Bay oak spreading along our coastlines. If one simply walks along the Gulf beach a couple of weeks after a major storm, one which produced a surge above the normal spring tide line, the number of germinating Botany Bay oaks erupting from the sand at the high water mark is staggering — in the millions! In 1960, Hurricane Donna was responsible for the dense mature Australian pine forestation which today is so abundant on every Gulf-front barrier island beach south of Anclote Key near Tarpon Springs.

I completely detest Australian pines! In fact, I doubt if there is anyone who dislikes them more than I. This hatred actually surfaced during the aftermath of hurricane Donna. At that time, I held this tree generally responsible for the hardships which had been imposed on those of us who lived on the islands during Donna's aftermath. The damage extended beyond mere inconvenience. Earlier, I described the damage these trees inflicted on our electrical distribution system. Time-consuming and labor-intensive work was required to remove the fallen trees from our roads and power lines. These trees caused considerable harm to structures when they toppled and broke apart on nearby buildings which were literally in the trees' shadows. Woe to those property owners who unwittingly allow these weed trees to grow to maturity next to their investments and priceless, irreplaceable possessions!

I am well aware that the island's Australian pines, like other tall, well-foliated trees, do create excellent shade. And the wind rushing through their dense, specialized, needlelike leaves makes delightful and soothing music. I also recognize that they have been naturalized and will forever be linked to coastal southern Florida, because like other noxious trees, these cannot be permanently eliminated from Sanibel Island either. Therefore, I grant that their shade has value near the open beach, and perhaps this factor and their secondary use as firewood are their only redeeming qualities. Without the shade provided by the Botany Bay oaks, a summer beach outing on these barrier islands would be a trip into an inferno. But these trees should not be allowed to remain on our shorelines at the very edge of the high-tide line. A well-managed natural beach is an area of open space essential not only to man's quality of life, but also to the survival of wildlife species with which we share that ecosystem, including habitat which should be dominated by native beach vegetation.

The Sanibel city government continues to support a policy of beach naturalness, at least for the present. City ordinances prohibit mechanized raking of our beaches, or other types of mechanical cleaning. The City fully recognizes that a marine organism-cluttered beach is essential for the health and stability of this unique ecosystem. However, some not-so-savvy newcomers to these barrier islands, apparently fresh out of urbanized America who have adopted Sanibel and Captiva as their personal Utopia, don't have the background by which they can understand the reasoning behind this doctrine. They are vocally belligerent toward the leave-it-natural attitude. But then again, some residents exhibit the same mindset when they object to control programs launched against ecologically undesirable plant species — Australian pines out on the frontal beach. Whatever the City's long-term beach management policy — and unfortunately over time it will change — those of us who care for Sanibel (and Captiva) must continue to insist that the survival of Australian pines out on the open dynamic beach system be prevented — in perpetuity.

My hatred for the Australian pine continued to develop over time. It slowly grew as I witnessed this tree's subtle negative impacts on the island's environment, vegetation, and wildlife.

Like the other members of my "unholy trinity," Australian pines develop into monocultures. This is especially true on the dune systems of barrier island beaches after the upper nontidal dry beach has been freshly "tilled" by storm surge washover. The disturbed condition of the beach surface readily supports seed germination. Their specialized leaves, incorrectly called needles, drop and blanket the ground, and over time, these can build up into voluminous amounts of vegetative litter up to several feet deep. Combined with the shade created by thick stands of these trees, chemicals that leach out of the leaf duff absolutely prevent the growth of native plants. The native vegetation, which has evolved to accommodate wildlife populations by providing food and cover and stabilize surface soils, cannot survive. Without the quality ground cover and its food producing plants, migratory and native birds and other forms of resident wildlife are seriously impacted.

Contrary to the views expressed by a handful of old-school beach geologists, by outcompeting our native flora, stands of shallow-rooted Australian pines which have invaded the frontal beaches have subjected our marvelous beaches to erosion. Eventually, the erosion causes these weakly supported trees themselves to topple into the surf in a tangled mess. The downed trees then form a nearly impassable barrier to anything, man or beast, trying to use the beach. It has been documented that fallen Australian pines lying near or in the intertidal zone impede wave wash to alter surf characteristics and accelerate the effects of erosion. The once widely held concept that these trees protect beaches from erosion is now an internationally recognized absurdity.

This is not to say that some wildlife species don't take advantage of Australian pine-dominated areas. The trees, or the stands they develop into, are not completely undesirable to resident and migratory wildlife. Woodpeckers and their like nest in the trees, as do larger birds like owls and American eagles.

Out of sight, seldom venturing from beneath the Australian pine leaf litter, live three native reptiles. The ground skink, a small brown lizard, and the diminutive and harmless southern ring-necked snake occur in sizeable populations. Another species frequenting the same habitat is their chief predator, the eastern coral snake. In fact, of all our island's native snakes, the very common and highly venomous coral snake is abundant in the peculiar ecosystem created by the mix of scattered mature Botany Bay oaks and typical upland subtropical vegetation known as West Indian hardwoods. Before the introduction and naturalization of Australian pines, these colorful snakes did very well in the upland hardwood habitat, and they will continue to thrive even after the Botany Bay oaks and beefwoods are removed. These trees have already been eliminated from lands within the J. N. "Ding" Darling National Wildlife Refuge.

The most severe impact this tree can inflict on wildlife diversity — a grove can become almost a total biological desert — is the impact they have on nesting sea turtles. For example, there are documented instances in southern Florida and around the world where female marine turtles have landed on beaches to nest and have crawled into extremely dense stands of Australian pines. These endangered and threatened reptiles are not agile on dry land. They can become totally lost, unable to turn around in a maze of Australian pine tree trunks. If undiscovered in these circumstances and not rescued, they slowly perish, a tortured death even within view of their ocean home.

Many, many times, I have watched loggerhead turtles, after laboriously ascending an island beach, strike densely matted and radiating roots of these undesirable trees during excavation of their egg chambers. Because the rear flippers of sea turtles cannot penetrate the shallow underlying root systems, a beach lined with these trees in the turtle's primary nesting zone creates a unified line of obstacles. Forced to abort the site and return to the water, a turtle later has to expend considerable energy again to climb the beach in a more hospitable site elsewhere along the coast. This is the reason that land managers in south Florida's barrier island park systems, at all levels of government, have recognized the severity of the competition between the needs of jeopardized creatures and Australian pines. They have therefore taken the necessary action to remove these weed trees.

Management and control of the "unholy trinity" and other exotic plants on these islands will always demand a well-financed and persistent program of followup retreatment. This is the key! But even with the best environmental ethics, complete eradication of undesirable, exotic, and noxious pest plants on Sanibel and Captiva is not realistic — it approaches a true impossibility. I hope that the new generation of local environmental champions, community leaders, and public servants learn to use the word "control" more frequently in their vocabulary whenever they speak of these demons.

19

PERILS IN PARADISE

"**M**ommy! Daddy! Come outside, quick! See what's coming across the bay!" Leslie exclaimed as she dashed into the house, sliding across the slick, varnished livingroom floor.

Jean, Chuck, and I followed her outside to the porch of Quarters 2. I could see a dark squall line coming; it was about halfway across the mouth of San Carlos Bay. Fort Myers Beach was already obliterated. The lightning and thunder increased as turbulent air moved steadily toward Point Ybel.

"Look, see what I'm talking about, Daddy," six-year-old Leslie excitedly continued. She pointed out several funnel clouds and long waterspouts descending all the way down to the water. These had developed along the leading edge of the squall line that was racing toward us. We counted five waterspout systems before the rain reached us and cut off our visibility.

As the storm enveloped us, the sky darkened, and the wind drove the torrential rain sideways. Our dwelling actually lurched when the extra-strong gusts hit.

A year or two before, Ross Leffler, then Assistant Secretary of the Interior, and his family had vacationed in Quarters 3, the cottage at the lighthouse. At that time, he gave me a hand-held wind meter. As the screaming wind and lightning intensified, I took the plastic instrument outside and braced myself against the porch railing to record the wind speed. The maximum speed I recorded that evening was 78 mph — 4 mph above minimal hurricane force — just from an ordinary late summer squall.

As the lightning increased, I stood on the Bay-side porch and counted those lightning strikes that I knew hit the tall wrought-iron, well-grounded lighthouse tower. I counted 22 strikes in all. Each flash reminded me of a fluorescent light trying to start. How frightening it must have been for the old-time lightkeepers whose job required them to remain up in the watchroom on such a turbulent night.

I have long appreciated the threat of lightning to one's health and safety, especially near tall trees and open areas. South Florida is the lightning capitol of the nation, and I tried to teach my children to respect this natural phenomenon at an early age. "When you hear thunder, its time to get inside. Lightning can develop far ahead of an approaching storm, and only fools stay in the water swimming or out on the open beach shelling when a thunderstorm is imminent."

Waterspouts are tornadoes that develop over water and usually dissipate quickly when they reach land. Occasionally, boaters get caught in these violent systems, and sometimes small vessels are damaged or are capsized.

On October 1, 1960, Leslie was attending a children's party at the old Bailey homestead on Periwinkle Way. Jean had dropped Leslie off and returned home. After she pulled the car under our quarters, she dashed up the steps yelling for me to come outside. To our west was either an impressive tornado or an immense waterspout — we couldn't tell at the time if it was over water or not. Hearing the excitement, Tommy and Louise Wood came outside and we joined them on their porch. We were spellbound as the twisting mass of air disappeared in a mixture of rain and dark storm clouds over the Bay.

Bounding every third tread down the stairs, Jean hollered behind, "I'm going back to the Bailey's house to see if Leslie and everyone else is all right!"

Everyone at the party was fine. But later in the day, we learned through the island grapevine that the storm had struck the main building of the then-new Sanibel Marina and killed an island resident. Marina employee Freddie Purnell was taking cover from the storm when the twister suddenly picked up the building. Eyewitnesses said it looked as though the structure had exploded before it and Freddie's body dropped into the nearby canal.

* * *

Most of us who live on Sanibel and Captiva Islands feel relatively secure from the high crime rates that are prevalent in urbanized societies. However, there are other kinds of perils on these barrier islands, other than lightning and violent weather events, that usually don't come to mind and are certainly not advertised.

Especially to those newcomers who spend considerable time on our beaches searching for shells, I offer a few words of advice and caution: Tread softly and carefully. Embedded in our beach sand are a multitude of sharp objects. For example, the sharp-pointed, partly buried tails of horseshoe crabs, catfish spines, and razor-sharp pen shells can cause extremely painful, bacteria-laden puncture wounds. Everyone should wear beach shoes.

Probably the most agonizing injury one can receive here is a stingray strike in the foot.

Stingrays are generally harmless cartilaginous, flat-bodied fish. With graceful winglike pectoral fins, they seem to fly through the water with birdlike grace. But at the base of their long, whiplike tail is a spine which is usually held flat inside a fold of mucous-coated flesh. They often partly conceal themselves in the sandy inshore bottom, within a few feet of the dry beach, waiting for a hapless crab to come along. Their protective coloration makes them almost impossible to see when they are partly covered with sand. If you accidently step on this creature or otherwise put it on the defensive, it instantly whips up the tail, bringing the spine into position to pierce your foot.

Stingray puncture wounds are very painful and can result in long-term damage to your foot, especially if any tendons are severed by the spine. Because a protein-based toxin coats the spine and invades the wound when your foot is stuck, prompt medical attention is required. The first thing to do is immerse your foot in the hottest water you can stand to prevent the toxin from moving upward into the body. Then seek professional medical attention.

No one in my immediate family has ever been jabbed by a stingray — at least not yet — because we practice what is locally termed the "Sanibel Shuffle." To do this maneuver, plant your feet firmly on the bottom and shuffle or push them through the sand. Should you contact a buried stingray, your foot will first touch the ray under or along the trailing edge of a pectoral fin. Most likely, the fish will then abandon its hiding place and race away. Of course, the best way to avoid a spine strike is to wear sneakers or some other appropriate footwear.

During late spring and early summer, stingrays congregate along our beaches for their annual breeding activities. When wading or swimming, if you are suddenly surrounded by a group of jumping stingrays, do not panic. Unless stepped on, they are harmless during this activity, so just calmly shuffle yourself to shore.

Another group of marine creatures common to our waters are jellyfish. These come in assorted shapes and sizes, but they all have a few things in common. They are not fish, and most are venomous. They can deliver painful stings when a wader or swimmer comes in contact with their stinging cells. Some stings are very painful, and this time I'm speaking from personal experience.

For years, I have used the time-tested soda water regimen for treating jellyfish stings. When swimming in the Gulf or Bay, I usually take an unopened, fresh bottle of club soda in an ice-filled cooler. If I or someone in my party is stung, we head to shore and liberally douse the affected flesh with the club soda. The stinging sensation begins to go away immediately. If the victim is an adult, the prescription is somewhat modified: The club soda is mixed with a liberal portion of Scotch, ice is added, and in conjunction with the external application, this concoction is taken internally. Seriously, the external treatment does work, and the internal follow-up helps, but if the victim is susceptible to any allergic reaction, then medical attention is recommended.

* * *

Another common peril, a nuisance that most beachgoers experience, are our sandburs, or sandspurs as they are known locally. These very sharp, spine-covered grass seeds are abundant in the foredune system and in the open, dry, sandy areas along the beaches. Barefooted people, usually children, are most likely to know if they step on them, ruining a fun day at the shore. It is almost as painful for the person removing the sandspur as it is to the individual who stepped on it.

For the person removing the sandspur, I recommend the following method. Firmly hold the victim's foot with one hand, and wet your other thumb and forefinger with your spittle. Then grasp the sharp seed with those well-moistened digits and suddenly yank it from the victim's flesh with a quick jerk. The spit softens the sharp spines so they won't embed themselves in your thumb or finger.

During our years at the Sanibel Island Light Station, when our children were young, Jean and I welcomed the lush growth of sandspurs between the light station compound and the water's edge. They were like a natural fence and kept our usually barefooted children playing in the yard. Once they each learned to swim, our fears faded away and we let them wear shoes.

* * *

The beach ridge system and the Mid-Island Ridge — actually any upland system on our barrier islands — are home to a more potentially dangerous wildlife species. The venomous and secretive coral snake is abundant on Sanibel in these habitats. Florida's most dangerous snake, the eastern diamondback rattlesnake, also lives here, but fortunately from some viewpoints in limited numbers. The change in habitat caused by invading pest plants, represented by members of my "unholy trinity," has reduced the habitat available for gopher tortoises and indigo snakes, both harmless creatures. However, the change has also reduced the preferred home of our widespread but small population of diamondbacks. So, if we improve habitat for gopher tortoises and indigo and coachwhip snakes, we do so for diamondback rattlesnakes as well. Personally, I don't have a problem with that.

Shortly after our arrival on the island, our neighbors James and Snooky Williams summoned me to their Gulf-front cottage. A large rattlesnake was sunning itself on their path leading to the beach. This was a beautifully marked snake, a 4-footer. I caught it and later took it to Lester Piper in Bonita Springs. This was the first and last rattler I removed from Sanibel, although a couple of years later, I killed one at the lighthouse.

My next rattlesnake experience occurred in the early spring of 1960. I had been up to Stewart Pond doing a waterfowl survey and decided to head for the Bailey Tract by way of Rabbit Road. Rabbit Road was a soft sand and shell road in those days. As the jeep bounced along the rutted washboard track, I heard a series of gunshots ahead of me near Gulf Drive. I could make out the color of the island school bus as I drew closer. When I reached the bus, I found its driver, Al Fortiner, outside the vehicle busy reloading his revolver. He was standing near, yet safely beyond the striking range of, a giant eastern diamondback rattlesnake. I could tell the snake was injured but still alive as it writhed on the road, rattling and desperately trying to reach cover beyond the nearby road shoulder.

Al was a part-time Lee County Deputy Sheriff, a school bus driver for white Sanibel and Captiva children, and a dragline operator for the Lee County Mosquito Control District — but not a very good shot. With one of his first six shots, he had managed only to wound the snake. After reloading, he fired again a few times. Finally, his eighth round mortally wounded the rattlesnake.

I tossed the dead rattler in the jeep and drove to the lighthouse, where I properly stretched, then relaxed the specimen to measure it. You don't stretch a snake out taut to accurately measure it. From the tip of its nose to the base of the rattle, this snake measured 7 feet 3 inches. This was the largest wild eastern diamondback rattlesnake I had ever seen, before or since. It has been documented that this species can attain a maximum length of 8 feet.

On October 14, 1961, Jean's brother and I were canoeing in the Gulf a few yards off of Point Ybel. Jean, her mother, and Leslie were on the Bay side, just west of the pier, heading for a favorite spot to find lady's ears, an attractive collectible local seashell. Jean was nearly eight months pregnant with Chuck at the time.

All eyes were glued to the beach at their feet as they moved ever so slowly, examining each shell and looking for a "keeper." Jean's mother, Louise Williams, suddenly blurted out, "Jean, Jean, a rattlesnake! Don't take another step!" She grabbed her daughter by the back of her maternity top and pulled her backward out of harm's way.

Just a few feet in front of them, a 5-foot-long diamondback was stretched out on the wet beach. This specimen was likely a newcomer to Sanibel Island; it probably swam across San Carlos Bay after floating down the Caloosahatchee from some distant place. All snakes can swim, and doomed rattlers, caught by tide and wind, have been documented floating 25 miles offshore in the Gulf of Mexico.

Jean's mother, frightened and over-excited, recalled an old wive's tale and proclaimed, "Dear God in heaven! It's going to mark the baby!"

"Hush, Mama! Hold Leslie and stay away from it!" Jean scolded. I'm going to get Charles!" She turned and ran to find me.

"Charles, there's a rattlesnake by the pier. Hurry, come kill it!" she yelled from the beach.

Quickly, I was on the shore heading pell-mell for the Bay, a paddle in hand. Jean brought up the rear, running just as fast as she could in her condition.

The snake had inched ahead a few feet but hadn't reached the vegetation by the time we arrived. My first inclination was to capture this handsome specimen, but the excited family members urged, "Kill it, Charles! Kill it!"

For some reason, and very unlike me, I raised the paddle and killed the snake — the first and last diamondback rattlesnake I would kill on Sanibel Island. Over the years since, whenever I came upon a rattler or responded to a phone call about one, I always collected it alive and released it uninjured on the limited habitat available for such upland species in the J. N. "Ding" Darling National Wildlife Refuge. I have no personal knowledge of anyone on Sanibel or Captiva ever having been bitten by a venomous snake.

Contrary to my mother-in-law's warning, the rattlesnake did not "mark" Chuck, but Jean's running apparently did move things ahead a bit, and he was born a month early. Then again, I think like me he has a little snake in his soul, because he too respects and enjoys them and their kin.

* * *

"Can you believe the size of that thing?!" I remarked as my father, my father-in-law, Duke Williams, and I looked down at an immense fish as it slowly made its way past the old Coast Guard pier at the lighthouse. The structure had been severely damaged by hurricane Donna over a year earlier, and we were in the process of rebuilding it.

The fish was a huge hammerhead shark, at least 12 feet long. These awesome creatures are a common species in the Gulf of Mexico. While aloft in the seaplane with Tommy, I had often observed hundreds of these and other shark species during cold weather. They congregate in the shallow, warmer water above the large sandbar south of Point Ybel and in similar places along the coast. In fact, this early sighting of so many sharks close to where I liked to swim gave me a new perspective on my relationship with sharks.

In various parts of the world, some of the same species that occur along the southwest Florida coast are documented maneaters. Great white sharks are known to occur in the Gulf and have been caught off the Sarasota County coast. I had heard about a shark bite on Captiva some years ago, but I was told that the culprit had been a hooked shark and not one which voluntarily took bites out of people. Nevertheless, I adopted a new swimming policy for my family: Do not swim at night, nor when the water is cloudy or murky.

Over the years, while on my nightly turtle patrols, I sometimes saw swimmers, even a few skinny-dippers, out in the pitch-black Gulf waters. As they swam and frolicked, they would agitate microscopic marine organisms in the water around them. Their activity would produce huge amounts of bioluminescence, or phosphorous as the glowing water is commonly called. I'd say to myself, "If anything would attract a nearby hungry shark, it would be all the cold light those people are generating. A shark could easily interpret all the bright water to be a group of feeding prey fish and move in for the kill."

. I'd often stop and tell swimmers (especially the female skinny-dippers, hoping they would run out of the water) that I certainly wouldn't be out in that water, and that they were acting like bait, generating all that phosphorous. Some would listen and heed my suggestion, but others would make a wisecrack and ignore my words of caution. Then a few minutes and miles later, when I reached "The Rocks," shark sports fishermen would have huge lemon and bull sharks hauled out on the beach. I'd shudder and get goosebumps thinking about the swimmers I had warned earlier.

Then the movie *Jaws* was released. The movie caused some apprehension among a few of us on the islands, knowing what was out there in the Gulf of Mexico and being aware of the real potential threat.

Then in October 1986, the inevitable happened! It was a scenario I had envisioned many times. In the turbid Gulf of Mexico, in front of a resort complex on Sanibel's midsection, a man holding a seven-year-old girl was wading just over waist deep. Everyone in the water was having a great time and enjoying their Sanibel visit. Without any warning, the child screamed as she was being pulled from the man's arms by some unseen, submerged force. Then he glimpsed a horrifying sight: A shark had grabbed the youngster by the upper part of one leg. His reaction was instinctive and proper: He tugged and kicked at the frenzied fish until it finally loosened its grip and released the terrified girl. Prompt medical aid and good followup care resulted in saving the child's life and leg. The species of shark was never accurately identified.

In the future, the next victim may not be so fortunate.

20

LIGHTHOUSE LIFE

Living at a United States Lighthouse Establishment (the name the Lighthouse Board gave to the agency controlling American light stations until 1910) was not as romantic and relaxing as some historians and novelists have suggested. Most stations were remote, the keepers and their families were subject to dangerous and harsh elements, boredom ran rampant at times, and salaries were low. In its early years, the Sanibel Island Light Station met all these criteria. The mosquito problem alone must have been nerve-racking. Only the hardiest of people, or strong-willed persons who were paid or otherwise financially compensated to live in such conditions, could have stood it. I was paid to relocate here and to live and work on a more primitive Sanibel Island compared to today's standards. But there's no way I would have traded places with anyone.

Generally, lighthouse life was a great adventure for my family and me. Each day brought new experiences that made Sanibel, especially Sanibel B.C. (Before Causeway), an extraordinary place to live, work, and raise children. I am certain that others who lived on the islands at the same time as well as those before me experienced similar, if not worse, living conditions. However, none of the light keepers and only a few of the long-time residents of either island ever took the time to write down their experiences. To my knowledge, none has shared these times and values with others.

* * *

From the very beginning, Jean took to the island and to light-house living much better than I did. After all, as a youngster she had lived on Marco Island for 12 years. There too, her drinking water fell from the heavens to collect in cisterns. She never had to depend on electricity or indoor plumbing, because the home where she was raised did not have these amenities. On the other hand, I had grown up with these conveniences and had to learn to cope with many aspects of island living.

Every summer during the first four years of my lighthouse tenure, I had to clean the outside fresh-water cisterns. Due to past hurricane damage to the gutter and downspout system, the diverting butterfly fixture was no longer working on Quarters 1, so to ensure relatively clean water, the cistern had to be hand scrubbed.

Once the rainy season started and thunderstorms occurred nearly every afternoon, I would unscrew the drain plug on the cistern and allow its contents to escape out onto the ground. I would then set a ladder against the tank, climb to the top, hoist another ladder up onto the cistern, open the lid on the tank's cover, install the second ladder to reach the cistern's bottom, and climb down inside the nearly dark tank with scrub brushes and buckets.

My first trip inside the round wooden tank revealed that our potable water supply was by no means clean or for that matter safe. I found a fearsome assortment of live and dead particles in the dregs of the tank: live and floating cockroaches, dead tree frogs, southeastern five-lined skinks (a native lizard), and even the skeletal remains of rats. Despite the screens covering the openings around the cistern's top, various creatures somehow managed to get inside. Some could have flowed off the roof in the cascading rainwater, along with a substantial amount of bird excrement. I had to overlook this unhealthy condition and resolved that as long as I lived there and had to depend on this water supply, I would keep my discovery of the contaminants to Tommy and myself. Besides, the steady summer rains would soon refill the cistern and maintain the topped-off level of the tank, and the drinking water supply for the two residences was assured for months to come. Until now, I have never revealed, to my family or anyone else, what biological remnants I found during my inadequate seasonal sanitizing process.

At lunch on October 2, 1963, I had just filled a glass pitcher from the kitchen spigot for Jean to make another batch of iced tea. As I lifted the pitcher, something floating in it suddenly caught my eye. I took the container out to the porch to examine its contents in better light. The water was full of tiny rodlike, clear crystals.

"Jean, come see the water in this tea pitcher! I want you to see what we've been drinking. I'm taking this over to the office to show Tommy and see if he's aware of this."

After briefly examining the water in the pitcher, Tommy remarked, "Damn, Charles! I don't know what this is. I've never noticed anything like it before."

I had already purged the cistern of last year's water, and fresh rainfall had refilled it over the summer. So whatever had invaded our water supply had done so since my last cleaning. It suddenly dawned on both of us that the quarters' roof shingles were made of asbestos, and our water supply was likely being contaminated by asbestos fibers. This was several years before asbestos was identified as a major public health hazard.

Tommy then made a wise decision. "To be on the safe side," he said, "I think we had better stop using the water for drinking right away and use it only for non-potable purposes."

So, Jean and I personally contracted with a Fort Myers company to rent a water cooler and have bottled water delivery service. We drank bottled water for the remaining years of our stay at the Sanibel Island Light Station, even long after the Island Water Association first piped fresh water to Lighthouse Point.

From time to time, I think of how my family and I drank the cistern water daily for nearly five years before my discovery. I sometimes wonder if there are any documented health problems, which may be linked to ingesting asbestos fibers, awaiting any of us in the future. Then again, scores of healthy people, some of whom I know reached advanced ages, consumed the same roof runoff long before we did. Only time will tell.

* * *

When Jean, Leslie, and I arrived on the islands, the black and white races were segregated, as they were in all southern communities. Such signs as "White Only" and "Colored Restrooms" were typical and were prominently posted at both commercial establishments and government centers, such as the Lee County Courthouse. As a teenager in Naples, where I practiced the art of sign making, I was often called upon to hand-letter racially oriented signs bearing similar copy. Public schools, hospitals, restaurants, and even cemeteries were segregated. But on the islands, the races managed to coexist. Even though the segregation attitude was certainly present, it existed more so in some households than in others.

Back in the heyday of the island's farming era, long before I became a resident, there were two public schools on Sanibel. One served the children of black farmers and sharecroppers, and the other educated the children of the white population, many of whom were similarly employed. After the collapse of this economic base following the total tidal inundation of Sanibel and Captiva during the 1926 hurricane, farming was no longer a profitable enterprise on either island. The black population dwindled to a few families, and their school was closed. Black youngsters from the islands who attended grades one to twelve were then required to travel to Fort Myers for their education — separate, don't you know, but supposedly equal.

The white school prospered, and by the time we arrived on Sanibel, the white children were being educated in the building which today is the Old Schoolhouse Theater on Periwinkle Way. (Hopefully someday this structure will be relocated to Sanibel's Historical Village.) As Leslie approached the age at which we could register her as a first grade student in the one-room Sanibel School, the Causeway was nearing completion. This altered the scope and future of education on Sanibel and Captiva. The Lee County School Board started planning and constructing a new Sanibel Elementary School on Sanibel-Captiva Road in 1962.

Jean's niece Debra, the oldest daughter of Ed and Floy Phillips, was the only close family member to attend the old Sanibel white-only school. Debbie came to stay with Jean, Leslie, and me at the lighthouse for a few months in 1961, so she completed part of her second-grade education at the Sanibel School.

Black children were shuttled to the ferry landing in a station wagon contracted by the Lee County School Board. Carl Jordan[1], a black man, owned and operated the shuttle. I met Carl not long after my arrival on Sanibel — he was and still is one of the friendliest islanders I have ever known.

Black students were not allowed to take the first ferry. This was reserved for the older white students headed for school on the mainland and for regular paying passengers and their cars. If for some reason the white school bus was late and missed the first ferry, the black students had to wait for the third ferry.

The black school children were bussed from the Punta Rassa ferry landing to the various schools in the Dunbar area east of downtown Fort Myers. These youngsters often arrived at school as much as 45 minutes late, after the school day had already started, on those occasional mornings they had to wait for the third ferry. Because of this protocol, Sanibel's black children were hard-pressed scholastically and had a difficult time catching up with their classmates.

When I grew up, I was insulated from the racial segregation issue. I never knew it existed. Because there were no blacks on Marco Island, Jean had never seen one until she began to ride the school bus from Marco to Naples to attend Junior High School. When I arrived in the area in late 1952, my classmates and new friends told me how the segregation system worked. But at that age, I never really noticed or addressed the issue either pro or con. Back in the mid- to late '50s, my father would always comment on the segregation issue during the many annual Naples Swamp Buggy Parades that we watched or in which some of the family participated.

After my family arrived in Naples, my brother Laban soon began to build hunting and racing swamp buggies. For years, he entered the annual Mile 'O Mud races and the associated parades in Naples, and we all usually turned out to support him. Jean once raced as a copilot with Brenda Hunter in one of her husband Joe's buggies in the Powder Puff Derby, a race for the ladies. In 1976, Laban and his buggy-building partner, Terry Metzger, built a small air-cooled racing buggy for Chuck, my 15-year-old son. Chuck successfully raced in the under-18 competition for several years.

[1] Carl and Mozella Jordan are the first black people to own land on Sanibel Island.

My father almost sounded like a broken record at these parades. He'd always say, "No one around here wants to go to school with them or sit down and eat with the Negroes. But look at how the white people turn out to watch and applaud the marching band from Dunbar High School in Fort Myers."

My father was absolutely right! Those bands from that small segregated high school were fantastic to listen to and watch as they proudly paraded and played their special rhythmic marching music. The spectators' recognition of their excellent performance was always overwhelming as the band marched along Fifth Avenue South and strutted their stuff in Cambier Park.

I wouldn't be honest if I didn't admit how irked I later became with the segregation system. I used to watch the young Gavin children, whose Sanibel roots went back close to the beginning of the 20th Century, face that ferry ride each morning and return to the island late each afternoon, having had to wait yet again for the white children to cross San Carlos Bay first. When school wasn't in session, black and white youngsters would often be seen playing together, but they weren't allowed to ride on a ferryboat together or much less attend the same school as classmates. Because there were no Kindergarten or pre-school programs on either island, my daughter Leslie started first grade in September 1963. Segregation had finally been knocked down by the courts, and the first year that the modern multi-room Sanibel Elementary School opened, segregation in the public school system, and in general, had come to an end. Three years later, my son Chuck entered the local school system, and according to his former teacher Mrs. Daniels, the Sanibel School would never be the same.

* * *

A few years after the Sanibel Causeway opened, the national demand for illegal dope and drugs began to be felt on the islands. Dope-dealing and drug-smuggling became a lucrative enterprise for some individuals. Marijuana was the predominant controlled substance being landed here — it came to the islands by watercraft to secluded shores and on the mainland by light aircraft on isolated roads and private airstrips. It's likely that some even arrived on

Sanibel and Captiva at each of their airstrips, before these fields were replaced by real estate and resort developments, respectively.

During the heyday of pot smuggling in the late '70s and early '80s, small boats would covertly leave shore to meet larger sea-going vessels. These may have transported tons of the drug directly from its centers of origin in Central America, South America, or the West Indies. Middle-sized craft, like shrimp boats, would sometimes transfer the illicit cargo off the mother ships far at sea, or the load might be directly transferred onto fast, shallow-draft runboats. These vessels were usually piloted by wily and highly skilled operators who knew the coast and its waterways far better than most of those trying to intercept them. These craft were pushed full-throttle into the protective maze of our mangrove coasts, where their cargo was disbursed into the well-organized network of smugglers and dealers for nationwide distribution.

Everyone entangled in this risky business made considerable amounts of money, but eventually, most were apprehended, convicted, and punished. However, very few individuals were actually caught in the act of drug-running. Most were caught because they made the big mistake of evading income taxes and living far beyond their usual means, and the long arm of the Internal Revenue Service reached out and caught them.

Sanibel, Captiva, and the neighboring islands continue to host smuggling activities. Drug-laden shrimp boats are often stopped and boarded by authorities offshore or after reaching port. Sometimes these boats are filled to their gunnels with tightly compressed bales of dried marijuana. Commonly known as square grouper, these bales of contraband cargo are then seized by law enforcement officials. In February 1980, such an event started a comical, almost unreal, chain of events.

On July 20, 1970, during one of the many times I functioned as acting Refuge Manager, I hired Ede Stokes, long-time Office Assistant at the J. N. "Ding" Darling National Wildlife Refuge. One day she came to my desk and said, "Charles, George Zajicek is on the telephone and wants to speak with you."

George and his wife, Betty, owned and operated Surf n' Sand Cottages, a small Gulf-front complex on Sanibel's eastern end. We had become good friends after their two sons, Paul and David, had

joined Boy Scout Troop 88, which I helped organize in 1969. I
served as the troop's Scoutmaster for about three years.

"Hey, Big George!" It was my customary greeting.

"Hi, Charles. You won't believe what's happening out in the
Gulf in front of my place!"

"What's going on?"

George continued, "The Coast Guard is throwing overboard
what looks to me like bales of marijuana from their cutter and is
trying to chop them up with their boat's propellers."

I was astonished at the revelation. "I thought they always
brought the bales in for evidence, and after a trial, they destroy the
grass by incineration! They must have come across an abandoned
load, or maybe some smugglers threw the weed overboard in a
hurry when the Coast Guard began to close in on them."

George continued, "Not this time. I don't know how many
bales they've chopped up, but through my binoculars, I can see
pieces of the stuff floating around their boat — and not much of it
is sinking."

Thus began what to me was the great local comedy of the
decade.

A day later, I noticed that scores of islanders, from teenagers to
gray-hairs, strangely began to converge at the Point Ybel beach.
They arrived singly and in small groups — not normal activity at
all. Many were doing the famous "Sanibel stoop," a term usually
associated with shellers — people bending over to pick up
seashells. Others were sitting on the beach and closely fingering
through shells and marine plants, almost as if they were searching
for tiny shells. On the second day, as we kept watch on what was
going on from the office or porch, I noticed the arrival of a few of
Sanibel's finest on the scene. At the time, I had no idea what was
happening. I just thought the whole unfolding scenario was
strange.

At dinner that evening, I asked my daughter, "Leslie, what's
with all the kids suddenly showing up on the Point Ybel beach and
acting like they're shelling?"

She blushed, broke eye contact, and giggled, "It's pot, Dad. It's
almost like red tide has hit the square grouper." She burst out in
full laughter, then regained her composure and continued. "The
word's out that pot's washing in on the beach, and practically

everyone I know has been out there collecting it. It's almost like a gold strike, Dad, and the rush is on!"

I told both of my children, "I don't want to see or hear about either of you getting involved in what's going on at the lighthouse!"

The reply from both was, "Okay, Dad." But I somehow knew that my fatherly instructions had probably fallen on deaf ears.

Del Pierce had transferred from Idaho and had replaced Glen Bond as Manager of the J. N. "Ding" Darling National Wildlife Refuge on November 21, 1977. Del was a very modern, progressive, but laid-back person in his own western way. He let those of us on the Refuge staff with law enforcement authority know he didn't want us to become pot cops. When he learned of the situation, he preferred to let the local authorities handle the problem, even though the situation on the Point Ybel beach was clearly under our Federal jurisdiction.

According to the book *Policing Paradise*, written by Sanibel's first Police Chief, the Sanibel Police Department recovered and destroyed an estimated 50 pounds altogether of salt-water-soaked marijuana at Point Ybel. But many times that amount had reportedly been found and carried off the beach under the noses of the police. So now, more than 16 years later, I rehashed the event with a few who have reasonable personal knowledge of what really happened that cold February week.

In 1980, a bale of pot — and I'm told they come in assorted sizes — had a bulk value of around $300 per pound. An 80-pound bale was therefore worth about $24,000. When distributed and sold on the street, a one-ounce bag would bring up to $25. So, a good-sized bale had a final street value of somewhere around $32,000. Yes, indeed, it was a lucrative enterprise!

On-the-scene Sanibel police officers repeatedly announced that anyone apprehended with the illegal drug on their person would be forced to help rake up the beach and remove the unwanted substance. Small piles of marijuana were being torched as they were gathered by regular police and auxiliary officers, but each change of tide left another continuous row of mixed marijuana and sea plants stranded on the point.

Under cover of darkness, the pot-hunting public — now arriving from far and wide armed with flashlights, lanterns, plastic bags, and empty tackle boxes — descended on the Point Ybel beach.

Beneath the rhythmic flash of the now 100-year-old Sanibel Lighthouse, they eventually found and surreptitiously removed far more marijuana than the Sanibel Police Department ever suspected. I learned that the largest chunk, appropriated from the lapping Gulf waters by a young lady from Sanibel, weighed 35 pounds.

The pot was saturated with seawater by the time it reached the beach. The "criminals," mostly teenagers, flushed their find with ample amounts of tap water, but it was impossible to remove all the absorbed salt. Placing the grass in a microwave or a standard oven for a short period made it smokeable but not very palatable.

When left to their own devices, Sanibel and Captiva teenagers have always had to be somewhat ingenious. So, not to be outdone, most of the kids mixed amounts of their free stash with packaged brownie mix for another pass through the oven. It went into their tummies, not their lungs, but produced the same effect.

Occasionally, whole square grouper, which had probably been tossed over the side by some about-to-be-caught smuggler, would float in on our beaches or into our mangroves, be discovered, and be reported to responsible officials. I had personal knowledge about a few times bales were found by respected islanders ... and not reported but never wasted. It was burned, of course, but only after it was rolled up in cigarette papers first.

During summer turtle patrols, I often fancied finding a bale or two that had just landed on the beach. I'd pick it up and "dispose" of it at top dollar to finance new equipment for our sea turtle operations. But such was never the case. I would often joke with my coworkers that if we did fish out a square grouper or two, with our luck it would be a setup. The gendarmerie of southwest Florida are masters at entrapment.

I am in no way condoning what happened, but I just can't keep from laughing when I think about the incident. Had the Coast Guard retrieved the floating marijuana and taken the bales to their Fort Myers Beach station, which I always understood was their normal procedure, I would have missed what I will always think of as Sanibel's paramount comedic escapade of the eighth decade of the 20th Century. And then too, for an extra chuckle, I could have eaten some of the sea's unusual bounty which floated in that February, and not known it.

* * *

During our years at the Sanibel Island Light Station, Jean, the children, and I would leisurely look for shells on the Point Ybel beach a few times a week. We searched for both living and dead specimen shells, which were then added to our growing collection. From our own experience and talking with longtime resident shellers, like James and Snooky Williams, Jean and I soon learned that the best shelling occurred just after the weather was at its very worst. After powerful and chilling cold fronts dashed across the Gulf of Mexico with bitterly raw and incessant northwest winds, shelling was at its best. If the wind didn't blow long or strong enough, we never reaped the shelling bonanza that the worst weather provided. Summertime's south and southeasterly winds tend to clean the beaches, returning millions of sun-bleached shells and other organic residues to the Gulf bottom with each ebbing tide. James and Snooky, our neighbors, made a living by tediously hand-collecting and selling huge numbers of long-dead ark shells from the Sanibel beaches. The fruits of their labors were packed in burlap sacks and periodically shipped north to supply the aquarium industry. These decorative and visually-pleasing products were used to cover bottom filters in pet-store and household tanks.

The quality of Gulf beach shelling is thus directly tied to climatological events. If the weather-produced wave agitation at the water surface does not last long enough for its energy to be transferred to the bottom, organisms are not dislodged by the scour-like action of the bottom currents. Once loosened, shells and other benthic organisms roll along the Gulf bottom in the direction the wind is blowing. Wind, and its submerged current counterpart, soon cast the marine debris at the surfline and leave still-alive shells hopelessly stranded as the tide recedes. These powerful winter storms, and only those of long duration, dump quantities of even deep-water species of uncommon shells like junonias, lion's paws, and sometimes spiny oysters onto our beaches.

Many of the people who seek these gifts from the sea live permanently on Sanibel and Captiva Islands, and at first, like me, probably spent many hours collecting seashells. Today, most of the shellers, other than those active at the crack of dawn or the fall of dusk, or when the tide is just right, are more than likely new residents or visitors. Residents, especially the serious collectors, complain to one another about the intense competition.

Shelling, especially live shelling, has become a controversial and sometimes confrontational topic of discussion on Sanibel Island. Today, live shelling within the city's limits is prohibited. This total prohibition followed an assortment of ill-conceived bureaucratic regulations in my view. To take a live seashell from nearby beaches or mudflats, or anywhere in Florida, an adult non-resident, unless accompanied by a properly licensed guide, must carry a valid Florida fishing license.

The over-collecting issue became a highly charged emotional debate soon after Sanibel incorporated. A Live Shelling Committee, appointed by the City Council, was charged to study the issue. This committee eventually selected a graduate student from the University of South Florida in St. Petersburg to lead a scientific study to determine the real effects of live shell collecting. Over time, the proposed study stumbled and died due to inaction and lack of financial support. Although I represented the City Council on this committee, I never publicly supported any program that would completely prohibit the traditional collection of live shells from these beaches.

The recently enacted State and local legislative reaction to the live shelling question was founded on a purely anecdotal set of data, and in no way was this concept based on scientific reasoning. In fact, some leading marine scientists felt that Sanibel's reigning politicians — those elected to their offices after the sensible years ended — gave in to the vocal demands of what was really a minority of layman shell collectors, a new breed of self-proclaimed, want-to-be conservationists. In the scientific community, Sanibel's credibility suffered because of the political response to a still unanswered and pressing question.

However, while total prohibition of live shelling is absurd and nearly unenforceable, on its own merit, the rule has created a sound conservation element, the necessity of which can be argued *ad infinitum*. On the other hand, unless their environments perish, seashells will always adorn the tidal zones and Gulf beaches of these seashell islands, protected on the beaches and in the shallows or not.

Marine invertebrates are some of the most prolific life forms on the planet. The reproductive potential of the lowliest bivalve boggles the mind. For example, one large quahog clam can produce about 25 million eggs in a spawning season. If a healthy ecological niche exists for the offspring produced, the optimum population level will be maintained at a sustainable level, for wildlife and human food as well as for our enjoyment. Collecting stranded, soon-to-die shells from the Gulf wavewash will in no way deplete the general population of these organisms.

During the height of the live shelling debate, when the City Council first approached the issue, I had a lively conversation on this topic with Jean's father. While living on Marco, he had worked on the Doxsee Company's clam dredge off and on for about five years, until the cannery was closed in 1947. When not toiling on the dredge, he was a commercial gill-net fisherman, now a vanished breed.

Hardshell clamming flourished for over a half-century in the waters below Cape Romano. The Cape is located a few miles south of Marco Island and borders the upper reaches of the Ten Thousand Islands. Up until the early '60s, many of the old-timers claimed there were just as many clams as there were a hundred years ago.

When the clams, technically known as southern quahogs, were discovered there in sufficient quantities to support commercial exploitation, clam harvesting became a year-round enterprise. Beginning in the late 1890s, they were dug by hand at low tide with two-pronged clam hooks. A good clam digger could collect 30 bushels during the six hours the tide was low enough to allow a wading man to dig. In 1914, the clam dredge was invented, which allowed full-scale mechanical digging of clams. However, hand digging still continued for many years thereafter.

During one of his very interesting discourses, Duke Williams related, "When I worked on Doxsee's clam dredge, they had their cannery at Marco. The other cannery, owned by the Burnham Company, operated until about 1930 at Caxambas. It shut down long before we moved to Marco. About 25 of us worked onboard to operate the dredge and handle the clams, and about that many more folks worked at the cannery or ran the boats that hauled the clams between the dredge and the cannery. The dredge could dig 500 bushels of clams on a 12-hour shift, a long day's work. We could operate as long as the water wasn't over 12 feet deep. There were plenty of clams farther out too, but they were too deep for us to reach. Over time, those we couldn't reach would reseed the dredged bottoms."

He continued, "The Doxsee cannery at Marco once steamed and canned 1800 bushels of clams in just one day. Clams did get a little scarce by 1944, but the railroad pulled out of Marco at about that time too. I believe it was because of the wartime economy and transportation more than lack of clams that they shut down. Hell, if the Indians and the Doxsees couldn't completely wipe out all them clams, a whole slew of bent-over Yankees on the Sanible beach picking up shells ain't going to kill off all the other kinds of shells either! 'Specially the shells that live on the bottom in deeper waters where folks cain't wade. I don't know if the clams down in them waters south of Caxambas are as thick as they used to be. If they ain't, it's not because we dug them for someone to eat. It's because of all the building and dredging and canal digging and drainage and all the other changes to the water flow and man-groves that's been allowed to go on down in that country!"

I think I agreed with my father-in-law's common sense.

* * *

Through our lighthouse years, when the shelling was at its peak, the weather would deteriorate quickly, and plummeting air and water temperatures would impact terrestrial and marine crea-tures from man to manatee. On December 10, 1962, forecasters alerted us that the subtropical atmosphere of Sanibel and Captiva Islands was about to undergo a temporary seasonal change. A major cold front was about to pass through the area and bring with it the season's first possibility of frost. Indeed by mid-morning, the wind began to shift around, first to the southwest and then increasingly from the northwest.

Although both lighthouse quarters had what originally was a coal-burning cast-iron fireplace in each of the four rooms in the main part of the building, they were not functional as such. In fact, the top of the four-flue main chimney of Quarters 2 had a weather-beaten strangler fig growing from it. So I knocked a hole through the plaster-coated antique bricks on the chimney's surface in the room we used as a livingroom at the time, then I broke into the opening beyond the inner firebrick lining. To prepare for the coming winter, we purchased a two-burner kerosene space heater in hopes of heating some of the house. An electric blanket helped, but body warmth worked best. I installed a length of metal stovepipe from the heater into the drafty flue to discharge the carbon monoxide. Earlier we had used unvented fuel oil heaters — it's a wonder the poisonous gas didn't do us all in.

Even though we had no vented heater our first year or two, it seemed that the structure itself handled the exhaust job fairly well. The lighthouse quarters were built when high ceilings functioned to help cool the buildings. There was no insulation except for dead air spaces between the tongue-and-groove interior wall covering and the outer combination of sheeting and clapboard siding. As the wind speed increased, any heated air, or cooled air for that matter, within the building was forced outside through any tiny cracks or openings around poorly fitted doors and windows. If there was any kind of breeze outside, it was next to impossible to heat or cool the quarters.

The morning of December 11, 1962, I awoke on time, quickly dressed into warm work clothes, and shuffled across the icy wooden floor in sock-covered feet to the kitchen to start the coffee. The house was freezing, and the wind just at daybreak was blowing gale-force outside. I could hear it shrieking through the skeletal members of the light tower, and a variety of loosely secured things outside were banging about in the semidarkness.

Like any other day, I began my morning regimen by placing a pitcher beneath the cistern spigot to draw water for the coffee. But nothing happened — not even a drop fell into the pot — because the pipe was frozen solid. After I told Jean what was going on, I retrieved both children from their warm and cozy beds and put them in bed with their mother. Then I dashed outside in the moaning wind to discuss the situation with Tommy.

"It's too damn cold outside to work or do anything in the office," Tommy griped.

His cistern faucet was much closer to our common water source than mine, so his water flowed and he was able to make coffee. Like Jean, Louise was still tucked in bed trying to keep warm. The office had only a small, dilapidated electric space heater that could not overcome this much cold.

He continued, "My thermometer on the porch says it's 22°F out there. Earlier I heard on the radio they had snow flurries in downtown Fort Myers last night. Go on home, Charles, and crawl back into bed with your family. I've decided that we'll both be given administrative leave today because of the severe weather!"

Of course, I did what I was told.

The below-freezing temperatures lasted for several days, and even after the warming trend began, the unrelenting northwest wind blew for another few days. Shelling at the Point Ybel beach was indeed prime, the best we had ever seen before or since. Up until this storm, I had found three beach-worn junonias, then added another, the best, a few days after the storm petered out. Leslie was the first in our family to find a lion's paw that same winter.

* * *

More than seashells were stressed and perished because of the strong wind, low tides, and below-normal temperatures. Over the next few weeks, the vegetation at Point Ybel and throughout the islands took on a much different appearance.

We were proud of our many tall coconut palms that graced the landscape of the light station compound. Those that had been planted along the walkway, which led from the quarters to the boat railway on the Bay, had been planted by light keepers in the 1930s and had since matured. I planted several near the quarters myself. These had sprouted and were doing very well. Many years ago, before the severe hurricanes of the '40s washed them and the beach away, the Gulf side of the station had been the site of a well-established and graceful grove of stately coconut palms, some deliberately planted, some volunteers.

Within a few days after the freeze, the leaflets on the fronds of 90 percent of our coconuts had turned a tell-tale burned-brown color indicating severe cold stress. In a week, the hearts of the palms were beginning to droop, and we knew these beautiful trees would soon die. We lost 32 coconut palms at Point Ybel that winter. Elsewhere on Sanibel and Captiva, more coconuts suffered from the hard freeze and many died. Years later, a lethal yellowing blight would reach the islands to decimate our coconuts.

It didn't become obvious for a few days after the storm, but the most seriously impacted wildlife species was the West Indian manatee. The first casualty we found was an 8-foot female that stranded on the Bay beach just west of the Coast Guard dock (now turned into a public fishing pier by the U. S. Fish and Wildlife Service) at Point Ybel. Then over the next several days, whole, bloated, and odiforous manatees and parts of manatees began to land on Sanibel between the lighthouse and Woodring Point. At the lighthouse end alone, to the east of the ferry landing, the remains of five manatees came ashore, and another three came to rest on the Bay side between there and Woodring Point. It's anybody's guess how many others succumbed to this severe freeze and came to rest and sink unobserved in our mangrove estuary.

Florida's manatees are members of the same species that is distributed throughout the West Indies, Central America, and northeastern South America. In Florida, the manatee is at the northern periphery of its natural geographic range. As water temperatures begin to drop in the late fall and early winter, its range becomes very restricted. Because of their intolerance to cold, manatees gather in warmer population centers in rivers and near industrial water discharge outlets.

At about the time the Sanibel Island Light Station's lantern was lit for the first time, manatees were distributed in Florida but subject to major mortalities due to cold weather. In terms of total numbers, their statewide population was completely unknown, and no agency was concerned about their failure or success. They were sometimes hunted for their edible flesh or oil.

These migratory marine mammals seasonally move up and down both coasts of Florida. As their environment cools as winter approaches, they slowly move into fresh-water, spring-fed rivers. The river systems originating from springs that flow into the Gulf are located north of Tampa Bay. On the State's opposite coast, many discharge into the Atlantic via the St. John's River. The headwaters of these spring-fed rivers were created long ago, when deep-water artesian aquifers were geologically diverted over time and came welling to the surface. The water temperature of this subterranean outflow seldom dropped below 70°F even during the coldest winter.

As Florida's southern counties grew and electrification raised the standard of living for an increasing human population, manatees became more dependant on human technology. I have been long convinced that their statewide population began to grow and become more successful each time a water-cooled electric generating turbine came online. Soon, many manatees in southwest Florida no longer had to migrate north in the fall to reach the life-saving warmth of the spring-fed waters in the central Florida peninsula. The alternative — to remain here and face the elements, become cold-stressed, develop respiratory diseases, and die — was no longer necessary. The survival outlook is very grim for those that opt to remain in the chilled estuarine waters around Sanibel and Captiva after the first winter cold front reduces water temperatures. After a severe cold snap like that of December 10–15, 1962, they begin to die *en masse*.

In November 1958, the local manatees were given a new lease on life. To keep pace with regional development, the Florida Power and Light Company constructed an oil-burning, water-cooled electric power plant near Tice, east of Fort Myers, on the banks of the Caloosahatchee. Water is circulated through the electric generating apparatus by pumps which draw water from the Caloosahatchee and force it through the plant's cooling system. In the process, excessive heat is transferred to the water, which is then discharged into an outflow canal leading to the Orange River, a beautiful subtropical river which meanders into the Caloosahatchee west of the power plant.

By 1962, the manatee population in southwest Florida still had not discovered this cold-weather refuge along the Caloosahatchee. Over time, however, through a communication system known only to manatees, individuals and family groups began to find this warm-water haven.

Cold-stressed mortality among manatees was still occurring into the early '60s. In July 1969, the power company's second generating unit at the Caloosahatchee site went online. But by then, southwest Florida's manatees had learned to congregate around the warm-water effluent coming from the plant, and cold-weather mortality among manatees in our region has since become rare.

Over the next decade or so, most local manatees discovered the warm-water effluent discharged from the plant's turbines, and by the 1980s, they would congregate there by the hundreds every winter to escape the cold weather. Their association with man was complete.

However, our relationship with manatees can never be considered a harmonious one. Electric power plants indeed improved the survival of this ungainly marine mammal, but man's recreational pursuits have negated these benefits. Manatee deaths due to boat propeller collisions continue to increase, and other human activities account for far more sea cow deaths per year than cold weather ever did.

The manatee situation can be viewed from another aspect. For decades, marine and wildlife biologists were convinced that Florida waters supported approximately 2,000 manatees. Reproduction and mortality levels were thought to be in sustained balance. Then in the mid-'90s (supposedly because of improved census techniques), a statewide manatee survey determined that there were closer to 3,000 of these endangered animals in Florida waters.

When electric plants were providing additional winter habitat conducive to their long-term survival, manatee numbers may have exceeded their pre-Columbian (before Columbus visited this hemisphere) population levels in the United States just before the 1990s. They were never abundant in Florida, and their presence here is likely no more than a strong foothold. The massive manatee dieoff in southwest Florida in early 1996, mentioned earlier, suggests to me that the population had reached its peak, so the dieoff may have actually been a mechanism to bring the species back to its environment's historical holding capacity.

* * *

By 1969, we had entered a world of modernization and high technology, for we now had both a Refuge phone and a remote two-way radio transmitter/receiver in Quarters 2. Jean had involuntarily become an unpaid Refuge employee, handling most of the after-hours communications.

Our family began a unique manatee bonding experience on June 3, 1969, when Jean routinely answered the Refuge telephone extension in our home. As usual, I was glued to the TV newscast.

Charles!" she hollered. "It's Hervey Roberts from Captiva!"

Hervey and I had served together in the local Audubon Society and later the Sanibel-Captiva Conservation Foundation.

Answering the phone, I heard an excited Hervey exclaim, "Charles, there's a live baby manatee floating around out in front of our house, and the chop is beating it up against our seawall!"

"Is the mother with it, Hervey?"

"No. Hazel and I have been watching it for about half an hour, and there's no adult in sight."

"I'm on my way!" I hung up the phone and dashed to tell Jean what was going on.

The Roberts lived just a few houses south of the popular island watering hole and social center of Captiva B.C. — Andy's Dock — owned and operated by Andy and Dessa Rosse. I made the trip in the Refuge station wagon in record time. I found Hervey and Hazel and a few neighbors in their backyard keeping tabs on the young manatee.

"It's over near those mangroves and still at the whims of the wind," Hervey said, pointing.

I followed the direction of his raised hand, saw the manatee's tiny nose break the surface as it caught a breath, and said, "You told me it was little, Hervey. You didn't say it was an infant! It must have been born just a few days ago. Still no sign of the mother?"

Hervey said, "We've been scanning the cove continuously, and there's absolutely no sign of an adult. She was probably done in by a boat!"

I waded out, reached down, and lifted the totally black neonate manatee in my arms. The orphaned baby sea cow probably weighed no more than 50 pounds, but it was an exact duplicate of a giant adult — except for the still-attached umbilical cord. I had never seen a newborn manatee before.

I quickly thanked the Roberts for calling me and gently placed the little guy on the back seat of the Rambler wagon, then dashed back to Sanibel.

"KIE 6–28, Unit 2 to Base," I spoke into the car's mobile radio microphone.

A moment later, I heard Jean reply, "This is 6–2–8 Base. Go ahead Unit 2."

"I've got a baby manatee. He's not beaten up too bad at all; he's really cute. Would you please fill the bathtub about half-full of water so I'll have some place to put it when I get there?"

Jean replied, "Ten-four! It'll be ready."

She was used to having unusual creatures in the bathtub by now, but this would be our very first manatee. At other times, our bathtub had temporarily harbored a variety of world-wide fresh-water turtles, a juvenile American crocodile, and alligators of assorted sizes. A little later that same summer, she would have three clutches of loggerhead hatchlings (about 300 tiny turtles) in the tub because they emerged earlier from my hatchery compound than expected. At the time, both Tommy and I were detailed to Loxahatchee National Wildlife Refuge for a few days.

My plan was simple. I'd house the sea cow overnight in the tub, get on the telephone the next morning, and begin calling around to find a foster home for the orphan.

First thing Wednesday morning, I telephoned our veterinarian for a source of suitable nursing supplies and a recommendation for a formula to feed our cute little houseguest. Jean and the children then raced to Fort Myers to purchase nursing supplies and a formula of dried bitches' milk from the vet. Next, I began to look for a more suitable residence for the little manatee.

I called every public and privately owned marine laboratory and tourist attraction in Florida that Jean, Tommy, and I could think of, including the Miami Seaquarium and Marineland of Florida. But the answer from each was basically the same: "I'm so sorry, but we can't take it. We aren't equipped to handle an orphan manatee, especially one so tiny. It'll just die, anyway."

Totally frustrated, I made one more effort and called the leading California marine-oriented exhibit. But once again I met with the same response.

I was completely upset and angry. "What the hell am I supposed to do, knock it in the head because no one will help?"

Concerned for the manatee's welfare and supportive in my frustration, Jean said, "No! We'll give it our best shot and try to keep it alive until we're able to find it a proper home."

Early each morning, after it had a tummy-filling bottle feeding, I lifted the manatee out of the bathtub, carried it outside, and placed it in a small pond located along the road between the lighthouse and the pier. We had recently rerouted the Gulf-side entrance to the lighthouse to the Bay side of the point, and the pool had been created during the project. It was perfect for a little manatee: It had partial shade, was about 3 feet deep, had good water quality, and best of all, no one who didn't know it was there would notice and harass the orphan.

Several times each day, if I was working at Headquarters, I would stop what I was doing and check on or bottle-feed my new buddy, as did everyone else in the family. The manatee required several feedings each day, so Jean and the children cared for it while I was working elsewhere. In the evening after we had all bathed, I would retrieve the manatee so it could spend the night protected inside the house. Because it was much easier to feed it in the tub, we all would feed it a few more times before retiring.

We were proud of the way the manatee progressed. It was actually growing and seemed to have adapted well to our tender loving care.

After two months of searching, I was still unable to find it a permanent home. My old boss, Lester Piper, offered to house it at his Everglades Wonder Gardens, but he made it clear he would do so only after it had started taking solid food, like Romaine lettuce. Neither he nor I had any idea when that would be, and he convinced me that my family and I were doing an excellent job. "Just the fact that it's still alive after all these weeks tells me you're doing as good a job as anyone could."

The little manatee was getting heavy. It was becoming a chore to retrieve it from the pond each night, carry it to the house, and climb the stairs precariously holding it in my arms. Going to and from the pond, I often thought, "What if I dropped it?"

I was becoming more concerned about this possibility, so when it reached a weight of around 70 pounds, I decided to leave it outside 'round the clock. It fared well, continued to grow, and consumed an increasing amount of formula ... that is, until Thursday, August 7th, when I discovered it had died during the night.

We were all heartbroken and in tears as we ceremoniously buried the little manatee in our private little wildlife cemetery on a spot at the very tip of Point Ybel. We had done the best we could and kept it alive for 64 days. But I had learned a sobering lesson.

I vowed that never again would I attempt to maintain an injured or orphaned animal if I could not find a care-giving wildlife agency who would accept responsibility.

I was delighted when Care and Rehabilitation of Wildlife was founded on Sanibel by Jesse Dugger and Shirley Walters. C.R.O.W. was incorporated as a non-profit organization in 1972 and has been financially supported by island residents as well as visitors ever since. Its objective is to assist injured wildlife, so they took a great deal of responsibility off my shoulders.

* * *

Earlier, I explained my intense dislike for raccoons. Considered obsessive by some of my coworkers, this attitude was formed early in my career because this marauding mammal disrupts loggerhead turtle nests on island beaches. Like human poachers, raccoons thwarted my sea turtle conservation efforts.

When the environment is in natural balance, raccoons rely on a host of natural foods, including sea turtle eggs. I am well aware of this, so if they were in a human-free environment, I would accept a valid predator-prey relationship between incubating sea turtle eggs and their age-old predators. But when the raccoon's population level rises as it usually does on every barrier island this mammal shares with mankind, they serve no biological role that's good for wildlife or humans, including and especially themselves. Most raccoons that exist in very dense populations usually carry some disease. Periodically running rampant through raccoon populations are such infectious maladies as distemper and rabies.

Before the proliferation of garbage dumpsters in our commercial and multifamily districts, raccoons depended on the island's natural resources alone, and they fared very well. Today, most dumpsters have become rubbish-strewn communal feeding sites. Upset household trash containers have also fostered a dislike for raccoons among many residents. But a few misguided people can't seem to understand what is best for a raccoon's well being. They continue to generously and regularly, even secretly, feed these wild animals, and in so doing, they unwittingly foster human dependency, close contact, and thus the spread of fatal infectious diseases among the crowds of raccoons that gather at the feeding stations.

My worst experience with raccoons occurred on the evening of August 18, 1962. Being on a biweekly pay status meant that we made a regular family shopping trip into Fort Myers every other week. Our trips were usually consolidated and included filling such needs as haircuts, purchase of bulk supplies, and if time permitted, a matinee movie. Otherwise, like most other islanders, we shopped for staples and dependable high-quality meats at Bailey's General Store, then on the shore of San Carlos Bay. Trips into town had to be carefully timed so that we were back at Punta Rassa before the last ferry departed for Sanibel. Heaven forbid if we had car trouble!

On this particular Saturday, Jean and I had unloaded the children and had carried several bags of supplies up the stairs. Those items requiring refrigeration were unbagged first and put away. We decided to leave the other foods on the counter tops and kitchen table while we relaxed and had a well-deserved break for iced tea in the family room. This room was the breeziest part of the house — the original kitchen — in the east wing of the quarters. Here we rested and discussed the events of the day, comfortable because the four large windows provided excellent cross-ventilation from the cooling seabreeze.

(We didn't have the luxury of air conditioning until May 1968, when we purchased a small window unit and moved our bedroom into the former kitchen wing. This isolated the cool to one room. In 1969, after I went through a lengthy justification process, the Fish and Wildlife Service furnished two massive wall units to air-condition all of Quarters 2. Our comfort improved, but our monthly electric bill soared.)

I decided to get more tea before we continued to put away the rest of our supplies. Walking into the living room, I heard some serious ruckus going on in the kitchen. It sounded as though things were crashing to the floor, some breaking, and this noise was intermixed with savage snarling. As I looked through the doorway into the kitchen, I was horrified. A white raccoon darted between my legs and dashed out the still-closed screen door through a huge hole in the screen. In disbelief, I counted another eight 'coons of assorted sizes scampering about the war zone that used to be our kitchen. They dashed past me out the door, across the porch, and down the stairs to join their white comrade.

"Jean, you won't believe what's happened!" I hollered as I walked back into the family room. "I always believed raccoons had it in for me, and now they're trying to get even!"

"What are you talking about?" she asked, looking at me bewildered before following me back into the kitchen. "Good grief, I'll say they certainly got even!" she mumbled in a shocked tone. She panned the crime scene and began to assess the damage the furry masked bandits had visited upon us.

A large bag of flour had been knocked onto the floor, torn open, and dragged around the room. White footprints covered the dark varnish-stained wooden floor. Slowly I realized it was flour that adorned the pelt of the white raccoon who was the first to flee the scene of the crime.

The cleanup was a monumental task. Only those canned and bottled goods that weren't smashed to bits on the floor could be salvaged. Boxes and bags of rice, flour, sugar, noodles, and the like had been torn open and scattered helter-skelter. We cussed and cleaned up into the wee hours. The next morning, the humor of the incident began to set in.

Late in the day on Sunday, after I told Tommy about the event, he laughed and commented, "You know how smart 'coons are, Charles. I think Jean may be right: They just got even with you for spraying and masking turtle nests so they can't find the eggs so easy. Paybacks are hell. I think we'd better get some quarter-inch hardware cloth and cover all the screen doors on both quarters. They're intelligent enough to come back and try again."

On his next official buying trip to downtown Fort Myers, Tommy bought enough wire at Franklin Hardware for me to do the job.

* * *

For many years, the lone telephone for both Sanibel and Captiva was located at the Sanibel Island Light Station. The early telephone service provider to southwest Florida was the Inter-County Telephone and Telegraph Company, but exactly when its overhead open-wire circuit lines reached Punta Rassa is unclear.

Once commercial telephone service reached Punta Rassa, the U. S. Coast Guard connected to a vacant cable pair within the long-existing submerged international telegraph cable that left Punta Rassa, traveled across Sanibel, and then overseas. The cable left the mainland from a tiny concrete terminal building at Punta Rassa, then ran underwater along the bottom of San Carlos Bay to a junction on Sanibel. After crossing Point Ybel underground, the cable ran underwater again, its next terminal at Havana, Cuba.

The small cable hut is still intact at Punta Rassa. After traveling north along the cable, crossing the Sanibel Island Light Station, a telegraph-transmitted message was received at this hut announcing to the nation the battleship *Maine* had exploded and sunk in Havana harbor on February 15, 1898.

Other than for genuine life-threatening emergencies, the Coast Guard's telephone was off limits to the public. Islanders and visitors wanting to use a telephone to reach the outside world had to cross the Bay on the ferry, or by some other water vessel, and use the commercial telephone at Punta Rassa.

Many years earlier, Western Union ran a connection from the Sanibel cable hut terminal, then continued the line westward along the Bay to Bailey's General Store which housed a voice-line terminal for the Western Union Company. Later, this line would be abandoned.

Sometime between 1905 and 1910 (the exact year is unclear), Frank Bailey purchased telephones and equipment to give Sanibel its first telephone system. His workmen strung galvanized aerial wires from his store on the Bay to the Island Inn. These wires followed existing shell-surfaced roads, which today are known as Bailey Road, Periwinkle Way, Tarpon Bay Road, and the original Gulf Drive (between the Casa Ybel and the Island Inn). A few drop lines were installed at residences along the way. Thus Sanibel's pioneer phone system, albeit limited, was created.

In the mid-'50s, the InterCounty Telephone and Telegraph Company met with Francis Bailey and other community leaders, and both parties entered into an agreement that islanders would not seek a franchise for an islander-owned telephone system.

The InterCounty Telephone and Telegraph Company was eliminating any future competition.

When Jean, Leslie, and I arrived at the Sanibel Lighthouse in 1958, private telephones were not available. By 1961, rumor had it that the InterCounty Telephone and Telegraph Company would soon be accepting applications for general telephone service on the islands, so Jean applied. In late 1961, a new six-pair telephone cable was laid across the bottom of San Carlos Bay from Punta Rassa to the old cable hut's location, about 200 feet east of the ferry landing, to accommodate the anticipated increase in subscribers. On April 10, 1962, our own telephone was finally installed in our quarters, right beside the Refuge extension that the Fish and Wildlife Service had installed for official purposes in 1961.

Our number was MOhawk 3–4100, and we were on a party line. The telephone system continued to be upgraded, and on June 1, 1965, the island exchange was changed and our number, a private line, became GReenleaf 2–4001. When the 472 exchange came online, with its microwave transmission technology combined with improved and larger cable, it replaced GReenleaf. Nothing really changed — it simply became a numerical prefix — but some islanders complained to the phone company anyway. (Some people always gripe about simple, elemental issues.) The disenchanted island residents were irked and felt shunned by big business. They wanted the new telephone exchange to be prefixed SEashell, not 472.

* * *

We brought our new son, Chuck, home to the Sanibel Lighthouse from Naples, where he was born, at two days of age. He grew up a typical island child: He loved the outdoors, fishing, shelling, swimming, boating, and getting into mischief, especially fishing.

One of Chuck's favorite pastimes was playing on the lighthouse tower. He considered it to be his personal jungle gym. My son became very proficient at doing a variety of acrobatic-like maneuvers on the iron lighthouse. As he proceeded with his moves, small groups of tourists would often gather to watch him do his dramatic routine — that is, until Tommy noticed him one day high on the angle braces and well above the lowest horizontal crosspiece. He was so amazed at Chuck's ability, he didn't say anything to him. Chuck hadn't started grammar school, yet he was already aspiring to reach lofty heights.

Soon thereafter, at our next two-person safety meeting which we were required to hold monthly, Tommy brought up the subject. "Chuckie's climbing too high on the lighthouse. I saw him up close to the second horizontal member a few days ago. I'm afraid he's going to show off a little too much one of these days and slip, fall, and seriously injure himself, if not worse."

That evening, I told Chuck there were new rules on how high he could climb on the light tower. "Tommy told me he doesn't want you to climb any higher than where the lower braces cross. Now, son, be sure you do what he wants. Don't get me in trouble." The don't-get-me-in-trouble part usually worked.

Chuck replied, "Okay, Dad. I'll keep low."

Our entire family occasionally climbed the light tower as a group, but *inside*. I think every relative that ever visited us — and there were some we had never met before — just had to climb to the top at least once. One of Jean's nieces, Floy's daughter Lisa, had to climb it at least once a day. (Her father, Ed, would bring the family to spend most of each summer with us so he could work with sea turtles.) I don't think one day or evening passed when Lisa wouldn't ask — as she rubbed my head, conning me and pleading — "Uncle Charles, can I go up in the lighthouse? Pleeease?" Soon, up the spiral stairs some of us would go to enjoy the view.

During the latter part of the '60s, weather permitting, the entire family and some of our close friends would climb the tower, open the double door in the watchroom, and go outside on the platform to watch the brilliant nighttime Saturn V rocket launches. When visibility permitted, we excitedly watched all the night Apollo shots up high on our vantage point.

Unknown to me, Chuck had secretly continued his lighthouse exercises, both on and inside the lighthouse, well into his teen years. During most of this period in his life, the entrance door to the light tower was unlocked, because the Coast Guard had cut the lock and never replaced it. I don't know how Chuck learned of this, but when Refuge employees, Jean, or I weren't around, he'd climb up inside the tower for his own enjoyment. At least that was safe.

Over the years, we frequently intercepted people who had started to climb up the stairway tube. We had to tell them the lighthouse was off limits to the public. I wish I could have advertised and charged admission. I'd be rich today.

* * *

In 1969, the Coast Guard authorized the Refuge to install a whip antenna on top of the light tower for our two-way radio communications system. Then in 1976, the Coast Guard granted me permission to install my television antenna on top of the light tower. This was shortly after the television cable system came to the island and the company would not, at first, connect us at the lighthouse.

On November 14, 1977, the Refuge received a letter from the Chief of the Coast Guard's Aids to Navigation Branch, Seventh Coast Guard District headquarters in Miami. The letter reviewed the various Refuge-oriented equipment installations on the lighthouse that the Coast Guard had approved through the years. The letter said they had never authorized installation of a radio in the lighthouse. Neither manager Glen Bond nor I knew what they were talking about; we were completely mystified. The letter did inform us that the radio would be returned by the St. Petersburg Aids to Navigation Team, but we should not install it in the lighthouse.

Several weeks later, on their routine trip to check the light's bulbs, batteries, and charging system, two young "Coasties" brought the radio along with them. I recognized it immediately: It was mine! It was an old battery-powered AM/FM radio that I had fitted with a piece of wire clotheshanger to improve reception.

I immediately launched an investigation into this very serious breach of lighthouse security to determine just how the Coast Guard acquired my radio. Before they left to return to their St. Petersburg base, the two Coast Guardsmen securely affixed another padlock in the long-vacant hasp at the base of the tower's stairway tube. Then they handed me another key — in case we had to work on the Refuge's radio antenna.

During the light tender's previous inspection trip, the radio had been discovered inside an antique wooden storage cabinet that was still in place in the light's watchroom. The Coast Guardsmen had taken it with them to St. Pete and dutifully turned the radio over to their superiors.

Months before, 16-year-old Chuck and some of his buddies — which probably included, at one time or another, Francis Bailey's son, Patrick, Joe Gault, and John Costanzo, now owner of Sanibel's famous Johnny's Pizza — had taken the radio up in the lighthouse to enjoy the improved reception that the altitude afforded. In fact, the sound quality was so good that Chuck decided to leave the radio up there and enjoy it from time to time — until the Coast Guard discovered it in their cabinet.

At about this same time, I learned Chuck was still climbing the exterior of the lighthouse but not limiting himself to the first level of crossed braces. A winter resident who had witnessed him doing his acrobatics was concerned for his safety, visited the office, and ratted on him. When the man and his wife walked through the light station compound heading toward the fishing pier, he said he had looked up at the lighthouse, as every visitor does, and saw a red-headed youngster climbing high up in the cross-members.

The man told me, "My wife and I watched horrified as the young man slid all the way down the metal on his way back to Earth."

Chuck and I had a long discussion that night. I terminated his high-climbing act then and there.

Recently, now years later, I asked him, "Chuck, just how high did you ever climb on the lighthouse when you were a kid?"

He paused, then said, "Dad, you don't really want to know. In those days, I could have climbed up one side of the lighthouse and down the other if I had wanted to, but I didn't. A few times I almost decided to climb up over the railing and onto the lower landing, but that would have been kind of hairy, so I didn't."

In a fatherly tone, I added, "I knew you were climbing higher than you were supposed to, but I could never catch you at it."

Surprised, he said, "How did you know?"

Smiling, I answered, "Hells, bells, Chuck! We could see your handprints all over the lighthouse, even on the stair tube, up at the very top just under the I–beams."

* * *

Once tight, close-knit communities, Sanibel and Captiva Islands changed forever on May 26, 1963, with the completion and opening of the Sanibel Causeway. A life-altering stigma enveloped the seashell islands, and at that instant in our history, when the first vehicle drove over the bridge, the island ambiance was snuffed out. Since then, Sanibel, and to a lesser extent Captiva, have become affluent bedroom communities of sprawling Fort Myers. From other points of view, Sanibel and Captiva are among Florida's better resort destinations, places known far and wide for their now-commercialized, parking fee-required natural attractions.

Following the opening of the Sanibel Causeway, long-time islanders began an almost indiscernible exodus from the islands. It was barely noticed because those who moved away were replaced with a growing number of new residents. These post-Causeway citizens were assimilated into our population and began the subtle alteration of our island culture and long-held traditions.

After the City incorporated in 1974, people began to move away in greater numbers. Some did so to escape the new city government which they had opposed. Others simply fled the congestion caused by spiraling numbers of visitors, mostly the "day-trippers," as they had been dubbed by the newer residents. Many of the people who threw up their hands in despair at what had happened to Sanibel and Captiva and had sold out and moved away were the very individuals who had eagerly supported construction of the Causeway.

* * *

As completion of this book approached, Jean, our 12-year-old granddaughter Amber Young (Leslie's and our son-in-law Tim's child), and I were walking along the Point Ybel beach. Jean and I were reminiscing, telling Amber old stories of what life had been like for her mother, uncle, and grandparents while we lived in the shadow of this historical landmark. These particular stories make up the anecdotes in this chapter.

Jean and I talked about the family-like closeness and friendliness of the island people who accepted us into their community nearly 40 years before.

"Those were real special times, weren't they?" I said to Jean. She responded, "I enjoyed every minute, and I would go back in time to live that way again. I realize that one of these days, we'll have to, temporarily, when another hurricane like Donna hits us, or worse. We'll have to do without some of the amenities we take for granted now and get out the Aladdin lamp again."

I added, "All we'll hear, though, is complaining from most of the new people, because they won't be able to cope without their lighting and air conditioning."

Amber spoke up, "Why would people complain about not having air conditioning, Grandma?"

Amused, Jean said, "Everyone who has air conditioning, including Granddad and me, takes it for granted, Sweetbaby. When I was a little girl, about your age, we didn't even have a fan in our house on Marco to cool us. We had to sleep under mosquito bars in the summertime. They were like what they have on display in Clarence Rutland's house at the Sanibel Historical Village. Remember when Granddad and I took you there a while back?"

Amber thought for a moment and said, "I remember, Grandma. We went into that old store too, and Granddad told me that he worked in that store sometimes at night, helping to stock the shelves with groceries, so it would help with your grocery bill."

Awed by Amber's memory, Jean replied, "That's right! Mr. Bailey would let people charge groceries to help them out. He sure helped us lots of times. Charles and Jane Rhodes were our first friends who lived on Sanibel. Charles worked at Bailey's, and your Granddad sometimes helped him stock the store's shelves at night to make extra money to help pay our grocery bill."

Hungry for more information, Amber continued, "People must have been different in those days. Right, Granddad?"

"They sure were, Amber." Everyone on Sanibel knew just about everyone else who was a permanent resident. We would help one another out when necessary, we didn't depend much on the local county government to do things for us, and we would greet each other with a wave when we passed on our not-as-crowded roads. In fact, remember the house that had the mosquito netting over the bed at the museum that we just talked about? Well, that was once the home of my old friend Clarence Rutland. Almost everyone on Sanibel and Captiva who knew him, and most did, called him Uncle Clarence. I can remember other people who lived here who were called aunt or uncle too. Let's see, some that come to mind are Uncle Arthur Gibson, Uncle Jake, and Aunt Pearl Stokes."

Amber asked, "If those people weren't related to you, why did you call them aunt or uncle?"

Jean spoke up, "Here in the south, when you called someone who wasn't a relative aunt or uncle, it was a term of endearment that we gave to our elders to show our respect. The aunts and uncles were considered by most who knew them to be good people who had made cultural or other contributions to our communities."

Amber quickly responded, "Granddad, can I ask you a question?"

"Sure," I said.

"Where have all the uncles gone?"

21

EVERYONE'S STORY HAS AN ENDING

Ⅰn September 1974, the U. S. Coast Guard notified the Bureau of Land Management that it would modify the Executive Order of December 19, 1883. This Order originally had withdrawn public domain land and established the Sanibel Island Light Station. Most of the remaining 53 acres of the Sanibel Island Lighthouse Reservation would be returned to the public domain. The U. S. Fish and Wildlife Service responded immediately. They requested the withdrawal of the Point Ybel land as a permanent addition to the J. N. "Ding" Darling National Wildlife Refuge.

On April 7, 1976, the Coast Guard submitted a Notice of Relinquishment to the Bureau of Land Management covering 48 acres of land and improvements at Point Ybel. The notice excluded 6.32 acres of their Point Ybel property. That which they were to retain included the 50 x 50-foot plot of land on which the light tower stood, plus a 5-acre lot in the interior of the property. The larger of the parcels was for a series of towers, part of a radio communication and aids to navigation system the Coast Guard was planning.

The wheels turned slowly, but the process had started. Eventually, most of the lighthouse point would be transferred to the U. S. Fish and Wildlife Service for wildlife refuge purposes. The Service published their proposal for withdrawal of the property in the *Federal Register* on August 26, 1976.

A year later, in October 1977, the Fish and Wildlife Service reversed its decision. It decided that the property on Point Ybel was incompatible with the Refuge's objectives, and the high level of public use which existed on the lighthouse property should not be promoted.

During this time in the Service's history, the agency had again been reorganized. This redirected the line of supervision, from the Refuge Manager to the Regional Office support staff, to a new level of control. The revised chain of command included an Area Manager, which was a new intermediate-level supervisor. The Refuge Manager was responsible to the Area Manager, who was then responsible to the Regional Office in Atlanta. For major decisions, the Regional Office was supervised by the Central Office in Washington, D.C.

Unlike the former Regional Refuge Supervisor in Atlanta, who had worked closely with the people of Sanibel and Captiva, the Area Manager, headquartered in Jacksonville, Florida, could not comprehend the close cooperation that had been established between the islanders and the Service. Earlier, supervisory officials at the Regional Office had strived to bring the memorial Refuge and land acquisition program to fruition.

That the lighthouse property would no longer be essential to the mission of the Fish and Wildlife Service, once a new headquarters was built on Refuge property, was primarily the Area Manager's decision. He determined that the process by which most of Point Ybel would be transferred to the Service should be canceled. He recommended this to the Regional Director, who concurred and took action to nullify the transfer.

Those of us at the J. N. "Ding" Darling National Wildlife Refuge now knew that once new administrative and maintenance facilities were constructed in the Refuge, the Fish and Wildlife Service would abandon their lease agreement with the Coast Guard and vacate the light station property. During this period, I was offered another rental unit at the Government's residential complex at Tarpon Bay. Jean and I knew we would probably be forced out of Quarters 2 at some future time, so we elected to leave the lighthouse point. With mixed emotions, we moved out of the Sanibel Island Light Station on July 30, 1979.

As soon as I learned the effective date of the Service's move, I quietly notified the Sanibel City Manager of the pending situation. I was still a member of the City Council and wanted the City involved early in determining the future of the lighthouse point. The Coast Guard had approved the Service's continued use and management of the land until the new Refuge office was completed. In my opinion, the City would be the best entity to negotiate some kind of agreement with the Coast Guard for the tract's management — to be sure the property remained open to the public. A few private individuals had already made application to use the buildings. But I didn't want to see land use at the lighthouse head in that direction.

In early 1982, the City of Sanibel successfully negotiated an agreement with the U. S. Coast Guard and took over management of the land. They actually hammered out a much better deal than the Service ever had.

After abandoning the two keepers' quarters in 1949, the Coast Guard never had any intention of financially supporting maintenance or improvement on either structure. To this day, the Coast Guard never cared if the historic quarters blew or burned down. The City negotiated with the Coast Guard and received $50,000 in Federal funding to repair and upgrade the two major buildings. The lighthouse quarters were reroofed for the first time since the 1920s, electrical service was upgraded to meet code, and central air conditioning was installed.

Today, City of Sanibel employees reside in the two lighthouse quarters. Tenants are selected through an application process and are rotated every two years. The present occupants of Quarters 1 and 2 pay a fair market rental rate, which is then reduced for an established amount of annual community service they are required to accomplish at the lighthouse point. Today's residents are not required to work on the light tower or its light, nor do they have any responsibility for its care.

* * *

My story nearly came to a premature end on December 17, 1979. At a staff meeting earlier in the month, Refuge Manager Del Pierce said, "The Wildlife Drive needs to be mowed before anyone takes off on Christmas leave."

The shoulders of Wildlife Drive had grown up over the summer, and the vegetation would obscure the view for the hordes of visitors who would arrive at the Refuge during the holidays.

My schedule wasn't overloaded, so I spoke up. "I'll mow."

I had already started the process on the 12th with the Refuge's tandem-wheeled tractor. It was fitted with a side-mounted bush-hog style mower. Everything was proceeding well. I was nearly done by the end of the week but would have to mow a few hours the next week to finish a section west of where the powerline crosses Wildlife Drive. I left the mower on the dike in the evenings and used the Refuge-owned motorcycle to travel back and forth from the Refuge office to the dike.

Monday the 17th was a cool day. I arrived early to put the finishing touches on the project. I parked the motorcycle at the Cross Dike, near the Alice O'Brien Observation Tower, and climbed aboard the tractor.

It was around 11:30. I was finished and heading back to the motorcycle. Traveling against traffic about a half-mile west of Colon's Point, I suddenly felt something very hot on the back of my neck, burning me. I braked and stopped the tractor. I put the transmission low-high range selector gearshift into neutral and stepped off the machine to see what was spraying and burning me.

As I stepped off the tractor, I saw hydraulic oil spewing from the mower controls. A millisecond later, as my feet touched the ground, the tractor's rear left double tires rolled against my body, knocked me to the ground, then ran over me. The inside tire crossed the thigh of my left leg, and the outside tire crossed the left side of my chest. The wheels had knocked me down with such force that my body was slammed to the ground — it was as if my body was dropped horizontally from a height of three or four feet.

At the instant the tires were about to cross my torso, I realized what was happening. I tensed every muscle in my body, ready to accept the punishing, deadly crush. I thought this was the end. That spontaneous reaction probably saved my life!

I couldn't believe it. I was still alive! But as I ever so slowly got to my feet, I didn't think I would last long. Because of the blood that was pouring out of my mouth, I assumed I was mortally injured internally and would probably die soon.

I told myself, "You can sit here and wait for help, but if you do, you'll probably go into shock and die."

Despite the rising pain, I decided to walk to the motorcycle and get help. I started staggering in that direction.

Its diesel engine idling, the tractor was moving straight ahead 100 yards in front of me. I must have missed the neutral position and shoved the gear selector full-ahead and engaged low range when I tried to escape the hot oil and abandoned the tractor.

The machine was approaching a curve on Wildlife Drive. I paused for a moment and watched as the machine continued straight ahead, left the top of the dike, angled across the berm, and plunged into the deep canal.

I had to walk $1^1/_2$ miles to reach the cycle. I wanted to collapse a few times during the agonizing hike but was determined to go on. A few cars passed me, but I sought no help. I was determined to keep walking and not sit down. At the end of the agonizing walk, I reached the motorcycle, climbed on, and headed for my home — the closest telephone — at Tarpon Bay.

Workmen were installing the first permanent water control structure in the dike. I stopped to tell them what had happened. "I've had an accident. My tractor's in the canal out on the left, almost as far as the overhead powerlines. Will you take your bull-dozer out there and pull the tractor out of the canal for me?"

They agreed and I continued, determined to reach my house.

After washing up a little, I tried to determine where all the blood was coming from. I discovered most of it was coming from my nose and a large gash in my lower lip. I felt somewhat better after that discovery and phoned the office to advise Del what had happened. Then I called Jean at work. I told her that our planned Christmas shopping trip to Fort Myers that night would have to be canceled — I was hurt and heading for the hospital. She insisted that I stop and see her on my way off the island with Del.

Soon Del showed up and couldn't believe what he saw. I had only given him the basics and asked him to hurry when I tele-phoned. We stopped the car at Scotty's Pub so I could talk to Jean a moment. She was waiting anxiously, standing on the side of Periwinkle Way in front of the restaurant, as we approached. I told her we were going to Fort Myers Community Hospital (now Columbia Regional Medical Center/Southwest Florida).

Shortly after Del and I walked into the emergency room, Jean arrived and took over my care. Del headed back to Sanibel. X–rays revealed no fractures at the most painful spots: the left side, hip, and upper thigh. My nose was broken and both wrists severely strained, all injured when I was knocked to the ground by the giant tires. My neck and scalp had second-degree burns caused by the hot hydraulic fluid. Urinalysis showed no kidney damage, at least no blood in my urine, so I was treated for shock, observed by the medical staff, and told to see a plastic surgeon for my nose. In a couple of hours, I was released.

A few days later, I was back at the hospital. A second series of X–rays revealed three broken ribs, and I was told only time would heal them along with the torn muscles and ligaments. The prognosis was that I would recover. But I never have.

* * *

Ron Hight became Refuge Manager on April 6, 1983, replacing Del Pierce, who transferred to a remote refuge in North Dakota on January 8, 1983.

As the decade closed, I took advantage of early retirement. After 32 years of full-time employment with the U. S. Fish and Wildlife Service, I retired officially on April 1, 1990. I was 53 years of age on my last day of work at J. N. "Ding" Darling National Wildlife Refuge.

A week later, on the 7th, Ron and the Refuge staff threw me the "mother" of all retirement parties. Over 150 friends, coworkers, and relatives attended the fantastic affair at the Sanibel Community House. I was overwhelmed! "Ding" Darling was indeed correct when he told me so many years ago, "The Fish and Wildlife Service is a great outfit."

Jean and I continue to be permanent residents on Sanibel. Our immediate family remain close to the island. Leslie married Tim Young, and with our granddaughter Amber Young, they reside in south Fort Myers. Chuck is still a bachelor, at least at this writing, and is still an islander. He lives on Pine Island where he continues to chase fish.

Of the five original Sanibel City Council members, only three of us survive: Porter Goss, Francis Bailey, and me. Porter advanced politically to become our United States Congressman, and Francis continued to serve on the City Council until the end of 1996. I never reentered the local political arena, although I have been approached by Sanibel voters several times to do so. Zelda Butler died on February 21, 1981, and Vernon MacKenzie passed away on July 4, 1983.

Duke Williams spent his last days on Sanibel. He died at our home on July 25, 1987 — on his 84th birthday!

Tommy Wood settled in Tarpon Springs a few years after his retirement. Around Christmas 1989, I called him to check on his welfare and to bring him up to date on what was going on around Sanibel and the Refuge. I told him I would soon leave the Fish and Wildlife Service. We kept in touch through the years after his retirement, and I visited him whenever I was in the vicinity of Tarpon Springs. His last visit to Sanibel was in April 1978, when I met him in Tampa after successfully completing my Coast Guard Captain's License examination. I brought him down to the island for a few days to stay with us at the lighthouse.

Tommy was bedridden and in failing health during our last conversation, but his mind was keen and he had to be filled in on every detail about Sanibel, his old friends, and his Refuge. He always wanted to know how our duck population was doing. He passed away peacefully at his home on February 22, 1990, just days before I retired. I miss him!

Life on Sanibel Island has been — and still is — very special for me. Few people have ever enjoyed the experience, the utmost quality of a unique lifestyle, as much as my family and I have. Hopefully my children will always appreciate their roots which first flourished on a real island: Sanibel B.C.

As for me? There's one very special element missing in my everyday life: The close, constant, and faithful flash that is generated each night after dark from inside the lantern room of the Sanibel Lighthouse.

Remember, it was 1952 when that distant beacon attracted my attention. Its bright flashes above a dark horizon beckoned me to explore Sanibel Island. On Sanibel, I discovered my personal paradise. This is a paradise that has since been lost due to human progress, overcrowding, and environmental change. But today, other visions of an island paradise continue to be discovered by those people who visit and fall in love with our modern but still unique seashell islands.

Now, around every gorgeous full moon in any June, I get rest-less and pack the car. Jean and I leave our Sanibel home for a few days to enjoy our annual sea turtle pilgrimage. We travel across Florida's peninsula to the opposite coast, where on any one night on our special beach, I'll see more loggerhead turtles than I ever saw during any of the 33 complete seasons I worked with this threat-ened species on Sanibel and Captiva Islands.

But then at bedtime comes the void: The lighthouse's flash no longer illuminates the trees outside our bedroom window as I snug-gle Jean, close my eyes, and drift off to sleep — thinking to myself, "Goodnight, Sanybel Light."